CAN'T
SWIM RIDE RUN

FROM COMMON MAN TO IRONMAN

ANDY HOLGATE

KNOW
THE
SCORE

Pitch Publishing Ltd
A2 Yeoman Gate
Yeoman Way
Durrington
BN13 3QZ

Email: info@pitchpublishing.co.uk
Web: www.pitchpublishing.co.uk

Published by Know The Score Books 2011
Know the Score Books is an imprint of Pitch Publishing

4

Text © 2013 Andy Holgate

A CIP catalogue record for this book is available from the British Library.

ISBN: 9781848187436

Cover design by Olner Design
Typesetting and origination by Liz Short
Manufacturing managed by Jellyfish Print Solutions
Printed in Great Britain

CONTENTS

ACKNOWLEDGEMENTS

I have so many people to thank who have played a significant part in my story; some have been out there in all weathers with me, others have been waiting anxiously and supporting, and others have offered advice and support from afar. If I don't mention you by name here it's not meant as a slight, more simply a cock-up on my part.

Firstly I'd like to thank my editor Richard Roper for all his hard work, and everyone at Know the Score and Pitch Publishing.

I'd like to thank the online triathlon community who offered so much advice (and still do). Although I'm a Pirate and we are tongue-in-cheek enemies, the people over at Tri-Talk have been brilliant. For keeping me grounded, for indulging me in my blogging and again for their support I'd like to thank the residents of Hotel Tri Bastardos.

To all the staff at work, thank you for supporting and listening to my stories. It's a major plus on a Monday morning after a race to have so many of you asking me how it went. And especially Helen for keeping everyone informed of my adventures.

I'd like to thank Michael Dunne for showing me how to blog, without your help I would have never started writing and this book wouldn't have existed.

Thank you to everyone involved with Barrow Athletic club but most especially Les and June Middleton, Alf, Sue and the others that used to drag me round the streets every week.

To all those that have supported me: Paul Moore, Gareth, Andrew and David Holme, Annie, Suzie and Sam of Team Spartan, Lou, Jamie and Jordon of Team Viking, The Southport

Collective, Fat Face, Lou T, Dave "The Hulk" Hassall and his Princess of Power, Jacko. Thanks.

Richard Gnosill is not only one of my best friends but he's also a great motivator. When I had doubts about my ability to write this book, he gave me the bollocking I needed, and for that, and our lunchtime training runs, I'm very grateful.

Lesley English for pushing me so hard when we run together, and for not killing me when I constantly rib her. You're an amazing friend, Lesley. I'd also like to thank Richard, Jake and Charlie English for looking after my cat, Crosby, when I go away to race. Knowing he's in good hands really helps.

John Krug for helping me so much with the swimming and biking. It is no exaggeration when I say if it wasn't for you I'd never have discovered the world of Triathlon. Thanks mate for everything.

To all the Pirates, you guys are bloody awesome. Your support is amazing; racing in the yellow and black is like a performance-enhancing drug. I am so glad that I stumbled along that gangplank four years ago and joined the Ship of Fools. Thank you one and all, and "Aarrrghhhh".

To everyone involved with COLT (City of Lancaster Triathlon), if Carlsberg made Triathlon clubs it would be you guys. Training and racing with you all has been a privilege. Surrounding myself with the likes of Chris Wild, John Knapp, Richard Mason, Steve Stretch, Mark Hammond, Andrew McCracken, John Towse and Sarah Patterson, to name but a few, makes me feel very humble. You are all top class people. Stuart Foy, those long Saturday morning runs were so much fun, lets keep it up. To Sam, Louise, Amelia and the two Chris's for making me work so hard on my running at club nights. To the fastest farmer in the world, John Carr, thanks for all the motivation and belief, you deserve every success my good friend.

A big shout out to everyone that has read my blog and taken the time to comment or send me a message, your support kept me training and competing.

Lee and Pam Green, quite simply two of the best people on the planet. Thank you for always being there for me through everything. I am forever in your debt.

To my very good friends Lucy and Will. There is much I could say but none of it would do you justice. Thank you so much for everything. Here's to a lifetime of Looney moments.

To Emma "Min" Tilston, you are wonderful. Your support, honesty and friendship blow me away. We've been through so much, I'm sure there is more to come, but whatever you do and wherever you go you will always have my support and respect.

To Dave "The Ex-Spartan" Bottoms, you are a living legend. I am so glad that we went on this journey together, you've taught me so much, and the respect that I have for you can't be measured. I raise a Guinness to you, a true friend and gentleman.

To Andy "Viking" Greenhalgh, you are my partner in crime. I'm fond of saying "It's all Viking's fault", but I would do anything for you mate. You are quite simply the best. Thank you for the laughs, the pain and the friendship. It's been emotional.

Andy and Pam Holme, you guys feel like family to me. I can't thank you enough. Andy, I would never have done the things I've done without your help. We've spent countless hours together training and yet I never grow tired of your company. Your humour and enthusiasm make the cold winter rides fly by and your handiness at bike fettling has kept me on the road for years. I often say "anything is possible", but none of this would have been without you.

Finally I must thank my family, to all the Holgates, the Cubins, the Myerscoughs, the Cookes, the Joneses and the Healeys, thank you. Family means everything to me and you guys are quite simply the best.

Craig for the support only a brother can give, Mike for jumping to the dark side, Jean for always believing in me, Alan for implanting the running bug in us all. Pam and Fred who have always been there for me. Maggie for her love and support, Matt for his style tips and humour and John for his enthusiasm for all things cycling, your support is brilliant.

And to my two youngest supporters, Eloise and Georgia. "Go Pirate Go".

To my Mam and Dad, Gary and Marie. I cannot thank you enough for everything you've ever given me. I couldn't have asked for two better role models. I wouldn't be who I am today without your love and support. Thank you for everything.

Finally to Emma, quite simply my best friend, my soul mate and the person who showed me how to live again. I wouldn't be half the man I am without your love and support. Thank you, I love you.

Right, that's enough of me being soppy, let's get on with the story.

For Mam, Dad & Emma
The best supporters in the world

AN INNOCENT CONVERSATION?

Sitting here reflecting on the last few years I still find it hard to believe. I've swum the equivalent of the English Channel more times than I care to count. I've run the same amount of miles as London to Toronto. My cycling has taken me the equivalent of New York to Los Angeles and back. Yet remarkably, all of that training and this incredible story began because for just one split second I stopped. Let me explain.

It was a glorious 2006 August afternoon in Lancaster, the students had left for the summer and it was quiet at work. Being a library I suppose that was only appropriate, but this week was taking the calm to a whole new level. My boss was away on holiday and I was enjoying running the department in her absence, thriving on the extra responsibility I'd gained in the past two weeks.

Life outside of work was good as well. I'd been in the new house for six months and it was looking great. I was no longer facing a 115-mile daily commute in the car, days were suddenly less tiring and I was energised. My fiancée Emma, who lived in Liverpool, had just heard the day before that she'd got a job in Lancaster and would be moving in with me within a month. We had joked that with 12 months to our wedding day we'd be married but living and working in separate cities. So as I walked into the staff room for my coffee break I was feeling upbeat about life and had a sense that I could take on the world and win. That was my first mistake.

I sat down next to Pam Holme, the effervescent departmental officer who conducted daily proceedings with military style efficiency. Behind the "all business" facade she was all heart. Being the mother of three grown sons, she was constantly looking out for me. We'd been friendly in the seven years that we worked together, but the friendship really blossomed when I moved to Lancaster from Barrow. Pam and her husband, Andy, knew that I was alone in the city and invited me into their home for the occasional meal. I got to know Andy H really well. This softly-spoken yet cuttingly sarcastic Liverpudlian and I shared similar interests. It came up one evening that I was a lapsed runner, whilst he was a committed runner and cyclist. We talked for hours and in those moments a lasting bond formed, we just didn't know it then. Andy H invited me out to train with him, and although I declined at first I would eventually relish the times we would spend running. Football was another hotly debated topic in our conversations. Andy H had been born within spitting distance of Goodison Park, and had Everton blue coursing through his veins. I had a passion for Newcastle United, something Andy H sarcastically warned me not to mention in this book: "For God's sake Andy don't mention you're a card-carrying member of the Toon Army, it'll put people off you straight away." Please keep reading.

Back in the staff room conversation gravitated towards running. The renewed energy that I'd discovered once the lethargy-inducing commutes had stopped had seen me recently start running again. I'd survived a couple of easy-paced runs with Andy H, and although I was under no illusion that he'd been taking it easy with me, the sense of achievement I felt when I completed my first three-mile run was not diluted because of his charity. Pam and I chatted about me meeting her husband for a run that night. Andy H had entered his village's triathlon. He's finally lost all sense of reality I thought. "It's the start of his mid-life crisis, he'll be wearing leather pants and buying a motorbike next," I joked with Pam. Now most villages have fetes, the posher ones have tea parties. Cockerham just outside Lancaster didn't get the memo and has a daft swimming, biking and running race.

John Krug, a veteran of several of these daft races, joined Pam and myself. I got on well with John. A computer expert, his quiet demeanour hid an insightful, witty intelligence that you often find in almost laconic personalities. At times he seemed so laid-back he could be horizontal. He was passionate about triathlon and in particular cycling. His eyes would come alive and his whole body animated when he described his latest ride through the countryside. I'd taken an interest in his "unusual hobby" and we'd talked many times about running. Being a lapsed runner I could still talk a good race, even if my legs couldn't carry me through one. He had been goading me for the last 12 months about how running was dull and that I should try at least one triathlon. It was no surprise then that John's ears pricked up when he heard Pam mention the T word. "Are you going to do Cockerham, Andy?" He lifted his head slightly, his raised eyebrows daring me to answer.

"Well … errr." That was my second mistake.

The mischievous smile widened as he focused on my pause. Like a shark circling a struggling fish, John knew he had me and made his move.

"It's a great event, very beginner-friendly and its only short. It's the sort of thing that would give you a challenge," he continued, nonchalantly sipping his black coffee and awaiting my response. He'd laid out his bait.

There was that word: challenge. Challenge to me was like chicken to Marty McFly in the *Back to the Future* films; it wasn't a word I could walk away from.

My mind was racing; it was as if time and everything around me stood still whilst the devil on my right shoulder argued with the angel on my left:

"Andy you can't swim and it's in a lake, your bike is knackered, you don't run – you jog, and you're a bit fat," said the angel, trying to prevent me from rising to John's bait.

"Nonsense, you got some swimming certificates at school, your bike has got two wheels, what more do you need? You're running again and it's a CHALLENGE," the devil countered with a fierce jab.

I was doomed.

I was snapped back into this realm when I heard Pam say with a little too much enthusiasm, "My Andy is doing it and he could help you train." Reeling from my surrogate mother's willingness to see me sacrifice myself to the triathlon gods I stammered, "It's not my sort of thing, I can barely run, my bike doesn't work and I'm scared of swimming in a deep lake. In fact I can't really swim at all. So no I'm not going to do it but I'll come along and watch." I was hoping my offer of spectator support would get me off the hook.

My brain and mouth were obviously having communication problems because in reality what I said was, "Ah go on then, I've got three weeks to train, I'll do it." It was like an out-of-body experience watching my enthusiastic maverick self agree to something that my sensible self would have run a mile from.

That was my third mistake, and after that I lost count. There would be many more, I just didn't know it yet.

John laughed, which unnerved me a little. He came alive and never paused for breath as he began to enthusiastically explain details about the event, the distances, the course, what I'd need to race, how I'd need to train etc. ... but I never heard a word of it. All I could think of was the deep dark water and how cold it would be, what was lurking down there ready to grab a floundering victim such as myself. John stood up to leave and said something else that didn't register in my confused state. I just nodded.

"You'll enjoy it love," said Pam, "and it'll give you and Andy something to talk about tonight on your run." Too bloody right it would.

"Well at least afterwards I'll be able to look back on it and say I completed a triathlon once." I didn't sound convincing. I wasn't convinced. Could I really do this?

Little did I realise that life would never be the same again. The match was out of the box, the inferno was to come and I didn't own any flame-retardant underwear.

The word "challenge" was my Achilles' heel because I'd been facing challenges since the day I was born, almost two months prematurely. I weighed less than a bag of sugar, had two full blood transfusions and spent the first months of my life fighting in an incubator for my right to face future challenges. My parents would later joke that they decided to call me Andrew because A was the first letter of the alphabet and they didn't have much time to think about it. They had been advised to prepare for the worst.

My weight has always been a major factor in my life. I started out weighing too little and ended up as an adult weighing too much. After a battle with illness that saw me dependent on prescribed steroids my weight ballooned to over 18 stones. For someone who had once been so active, playing football and running, it was very depressing. I was the wrong side of 30, with a waist that was the wrong side of 40 inches. Not happy in my marriage, I was seeking solace in food. At work I would lock myself in the toilets and hungrily devour flapjacks and chocolate, convincing myself that if no one knew then the calories didn't count. The pattern would continue at home where I could eat my way through four or five packets of crisps without pausing for breath. I was miserable. I felt fat, undesirable and trapped. Surely I'd never find anyone else if we split up? I took it all in, died some more inside and reached for the crisps. For a few seconds I felt great, and then the horror and the disgust would kick in. I never once felt suicidal, but I avoided mirrors and stopped going out with friends, trying to hide myself away from the world. If I didn't want to see me, why would they? Laughing and joking at work, Mr Sociable would disappear as soon as I got in the car to drive home, a place that I didn't want to go to. I know I wasn't innocent in the collapse of my first marriage; I wasn't much fun to be with at times. It takes two people to make a marriage and two people to fail at one. I should have stood up for myself and tried to talk things through but I wasn't man enough. Eventually one day after being asked to leave I grew a pair and never went back, which was the correct decision for both of us. We've both since moved on and found happiness. Funnily enough the secret eating stopped that day.

Finally realising I had a problem with my weight I went to see my doctor who prescribed me a new drug that stops the body from absorbing too much fat. He explained to me that I would no longer be able to eat anything that contained more than four grams of fat in every hundred grams of food. If I did the consequences would be very unpleasant: stomach cramps, nausea and uncontrollable bowel movements. He also suggested that I started to do some exercise again. Like my weight, exercise and sport had always been a major part of my life; unfortunately though, my health let me down. At the age of nine I had major invasive surgery on both knees. This was because I would regularly wake having dislocated my kneecaps during the night. In the day my knees would lock whilst I was walking and I'd fall over in agony. The surgery at the time was clearly necessary, and it corrected the immediate problem, but it left me with a lifetime of pain. I loved playing football and rugby but for months I couldn't whilst I recovered. I'd stand in the playground watching my friends, mentally kicking every ball, torturing myself. I used to have physiotherapy twice a week at Barrow Rugby League Club, and my cries combined with the gruesome sight of my kneecap in such an unnatural position would clear out the treatment room. The team physio would joke that you could tell if a player was really injured if he stayed to witness my treatment.

My knee problems weren't helped by my young age. With plenty of growing still to do I spent most of my teenage years with one injury or another: Achilles tendonitis, cruciate ligament tears, torn hamstring, torn knee cartilage. I could have been a case study in *Lancet*. Determined to be "normal" I played football and, coming from a family of runners, I took up running. However with each growth spurt I experienced agony, my knees would give way and I'd spend months unable to exercise. Medicine in the 1980s obviously wasn't as advanced as it is now, and I was constantly being given cortisone steroid injections, which we now know can weaken the joints in the long term. Medicine in the 1970s was even less advanced and although I'm not a doctor I think the treatments that I received as a premature baby – massive amounts of iron, iodine and other drugs – led in part to my weight and knee problems. When the body produces too little iodine it can cause an underactive thyroid. As a newborn baby my blood was dead, the result of a very rare incompatibility of genes between my parents, resulting in my skin being a purple colour when I was born. In order to live I was given two full blood transfusions and massive amounts of iodine, and as a result my body never adapted to regulate iodine production, hence causing the severe underactive thyroid that wouldn't be diagnosed until adulthood. The consequences of this condition are muscle and joint weakness, lack of energy, weight gain due to inefficient metabolism and depression. I'm constantly tired, constantly battling with my weight, and have knackered joints and muscles. And although this doesn't apply now, if I'm honest, mild depression as a result of being injured and being in the wrong relationship in the past has caused me to eat for solace. Why else would I have felt so ashamed of myself that I had to lock myself away in a toilet to eat a chocolate bar? My colleagues were sat the other side of the wall eating theirs, they wouldn't have thought I was a freak for doing so. Unfortunately I did. The experiences I talk about in this book, however, have changed me forever. I don't want to come across as weak, or a moaner, I don't want your sympathy, I just wanted to share with you a part of my past that hurts but drives me forward.

At the time that my doctor prescribed the pills and the exercise I was making a 115-mile commute every day from Barrow to Lancaster, rising before 6am and not returning for at least 12 hours. Overweight and unfit and working long days, I was knackered. I started running again, only going out after dark when no one would be able to see me, conscious of the fact that I looked like the Michelin man. That first time I went out almost killed me. I managed to make it round the block, a distance of about 400 metres. Each time I went out I challenged myself to run a little further, even if it was just to the next lamppost.

Before long my confidence grew and I started to jog around campus in my lunch hour, no longer embarrassed to be seen exercising in daylight. The exercise and the drugs meant that I started to lose weight. After a couple of months I'd lost half a stone. Conscious of the damage I could be doing to myself with the drugs I stopped taking them, determined that I would triumph without them. It would be hard work but by the end of the year I'd lost a stone.

With my new life, I was up for the challenge. I was happy with Emma and we talked about our future together, so in 2005 I made a concerted effort to get fit. Unfortunately I injured my knee again and wouldn't start running again until 2006, so my weight stalled around 17 stones. But I was happy; there was a difference in my attitude. And that attitude saw me rehabilitate by gently running with Andy H, enabling the staffroom triathlon conversation to happen in the first place.

When I walked back to my desk there was a piece of paper on my keyboard staring up at me. In everyone's life pieces of paper herald life-changing events: birth certificates, marriage certificates and winning lottery tickets. Mine said: 'Cockerham Triathlon Entry Form.'

Thanks John.

That night I met up with Andy H for what had recently become our twice-weekly run along the old railway line from Glasson Dock to Lancaster. Andy H was an experienced marathon runner who had recently been dabbling in multi-events. Although he was 19 years older than me, he was quicker and fitter. At first I struggled to keep up with him but as time progressed and I lost weight and gained fitness I was no longer holding him back and was matching him stride for stride.

As we ran along admiring the blood-red sunset over the Lune estuary, Andy H told me what to expect at Cockerham and I began to wonder if I'd taken on one challenge too far. The 350m swim he explained would take place in a disused gravel pit; the 15km bike ride would be through fields and along the beach with only a small section on the road. Finally the run would be across uneven, sea-drenched marshes. Hopefully the tide would be out.

We finished our six-mile run in just over an hour and I wasn't my usual red-faced self. We'd been chatting so much that I hadn't noticed we'd gone further than before. I felt alive, energised, like I was getting back to the form that had deserted me years ago when injuries, illness and personal circumstances took their toll. Thoughts quickly turned to the triathlon and my bubble instantly burst. Elation was replaced by fear and doubt. Andy H noticed that the colour had drained from my face. He tried to reassure me: "You'll be fine, don't worry about it mate." It wasn't working. "I tell you what, let's go and have a look at the gravel pit."

My heart was racing as I climbed over the farmer's gate and we crested the brow of the field. There, staring up at me, was a sheer black hole about 300m long and 200m wide. I couldn't take my eyes off it. It both terrified and hypnotised me. "I must be bloody mad to go and swim in that," I croaked, my voice like my courage quickly disappearing. Andy H laughed at my reaction but quickly added, "It's going dark, it looks better when the sun is shining on it, and it'll be the middle of the afternoon when you get in there."

Maybe he's got a point, I thought as we dodged the curious cows that looked up from their grass mowing as we walked to the water's edge. I dipped my hand in. Cold doesn't even come close, I've felt warmer ice cubes. "Just swim quicker and you'll warm up," Andy joked. "I'll have hypothermia by the time my head hits the water," was my uneasy response disguised as humour.

We turned to walk back up the hill. To our right one of the cows that had been carefully watching these two strange creatures test the water walked towards the black expanse. I thought she was going for a drink, but I couldn't have been more wrong. She entered the edge of the water, lifted her tail, and a steady stream of fresh cow shit poured into the water. Andy H laughed and said, "Don't forget to keep your mouth closed when you swim."

2

LOSING MY VIRGINITY

I had three weeks to prepare and train. What did I know about triathlon?

Well truth be told, not a lot. I knew there was such a thing as an Ironman race, that took place in Hawaii and involved distances I couldn't comprehend. As for a 'normal' triathlon, if such a thing existed, I was clueless.

I saw my first triathlon in 1985 when I was 12 years old. I was on holiday in Nottingham with my parents, Gary and Marie, and my younger brother Craig. We were staying in our caravan near the national water sports centre at Holme Pierrepont.

It was a glorious Saturday morning; we were walking along the side of the rowing basin when we noticed a large group of people with next to nothing on. My dad asked a bloke with a clipboard what was going on. "It's the National Long Course Triathlon Championships," came the reply.

As a family we were keen on sport: my dad was a marathon runner and an international rugby league referee, Craig was a very good footballer and cross-country runner and I'd been a decent rugby player before I'd had operations on both knees three years previously. My mam was used to watching my dad referee most weekends, and she never missed watching her two sons compete in whatever sport was flavour of the month. We stood transfixed for hours.

These people seemed to be superhuman to the impressionable boy watching; I'd never seen anything like it. Why were they swimming in a cold pond, didn't they know swimming pools were much warmer? It was when they jumped on their bikes and started cycling without getting dry or dressed that I decided they were really nuts. They'd be freezing, and they'd graze their legs if they fell off. It was all very risky but at the same time really cool. They were going so fast, their legs seemed to be constantly turning like they were part of the bike. I could only imagine going that fast.

I wished I had my Peugeot Robert Millar racing bike with me. I wanted to ride it there and then. In my head my ten-speed racer would have propelled me to the front and I'd be the champion. As children, both Craig and I could never watch a sport without instantly wanting to emulate what we'd seen, and that day in Nottingham was no different. That evening we raced our bikes and ran around the campsite. Earlier that summer I'd watched my first Tour de France, and every night after seeing the Lycra gladiators scale mountains that reached as high as the moon, Craig and I would race our bikes around the block pretending to be LeMond, Millar or Delgado. We used to fight not to be Laurent Fignon because he had a girlie ponytail. Those were the innocent days when my sporting idols were heroes. They did everything right; they were successful, friendly and general good eggs. I'd never heard of steroids and doping. It would be another three years before another of my heroes, Canadian sprinter Ben Johnson, would shatter mine and most of the world's illusions.

This was better than the Tour on TV though because it was real, it wasn't in some faraway land (to a 12-year-old France is about as far away as you can get), it was happening right in front of me. I could reach out and touch them; I was part of this race. It was the coolest thing but it was about to get even better.

"It's Mark, go on Mark!" my dad shouted. His enthusiasm caught our attention.

We all whirled around to see that yes, it was indeed Mark. Mark Knagg lived across the road from us in Barrow-in-Furness. I'd seen him going out on his bike on Sunday mornings whilst I was being bundled into the back of the family Volvo to go to my rugby match, but I thought he just rode round the block like me. I was mesmerised. I knew a person in the race; not only that but he was in the lead. This was like living next door to Greg LeMond. How cool was I? I just remember screaming a lot as Mark went on to win the National Championship. This made him a superstar in my eyes. He showed me his medal and I was transfixed.

Little did I know that I'd be doing the same in 21 years' time. Only I wasn't going to win the British Championship, I would be settling for survival.

With survival on my mind I did what any respectable librarian would do: I read a couple of books. I devoured *The Lance Armstrong Performance Program* by Chris Carmichael from cover to cover. I figured if it was good enough for the seven-time Tour champ from Texas then it was good enough for me.

I didn't really understand about cadence, lactate thresholds, gear ratios, power output, maximum heart rates or the numerous other phrases contained within. The photos were good, though, and reading the book made me feel like I'd taken a step in the right direction.

Inspired by my newly-gained knowledge and confident that I was going to be a world-class rider, I got up at 7am that first Sunday morning to begin my first day of triathlon training. I went down to the cellar to unleash my speed machine, which in reality was a clunky old steel mountain bike that I'd bought some 15 years earlier for the princely sum of £99. (That was back when £99 was a lot of money.)

The previous night I had readied my steed, which had lain dormant in my parents' garage for five years. I pumped up the tyres and sprayed everything with WD40; nothing fell off when I rode it around the block so in my eyes it was road, and race, worthy.

Not a soul stirred as I pushed the bike up the alley at the side of my house. The sun was up and it was going to be a warm August day. I donned my sunglasses and my newly-purchased helmet, which I'd reluctantly spent £10 on in Tesco. I'd never worn a helmet before; they looked daft, but on the entry form for Cockerham it stated clearly that under British Triathlon Association (BTA) rules a helmet must be worn. They took it so seriously that they even penalised you if you touched your bike (assuming you'd not drowned in the swim) without a helmet perched on your head.

I rode through the deserted city centre, passing a lass doing the 'walk of shame' in the previous night's uniform of skyscraper heels and microdress. I felt positively overdressed in my baggy shorts and t-shirt. I went north towards Kendal on the busy A6 as I didn't know any routes other than the main roads. I was surprised at how fresh I felt as I passed the county border near Milnthorpe. I'd cycled over ten miles for the first time in many years and I wasn't in need of an oxygen tent. *This cycling lark is easy*, I smugly thought to myself.

A few moments later the easy part of my day disappeared. It was getting harder to pedal. Strange. I still felt fine.

Thump, thump, thump.

I looked down and observed the first of many punctures of my triathlon career. In the past I would have wheeled the bike home and asked my dad to fix it for me. Dad was 50 miles away, probably enjoying a coffee and the Sunday papers, but I wasn't going to panic. After all I was a triathlete, and a prepared one at that. I'd been to a discount store and bought a pump and a puncture repair kit for £3.99. I'd have the tyre off in a matter of seconds, the hole located and sealed, and the tyre inflated and ready to roll quicker than you could say supercalifragilisticexpialidocious. Who was I kidding?

I was covered in oil after removing my back wheel; it had not been a wise choice to wear a white t-shirt. Things then picked up as the mountain bike tyre came off quickly, I located the hole by listening for air escaping and patched it using my kit. *That was easy*, I thought to myself as I started to pump air into the tyre. After three strokes I snapped the barrel of the pump. I couldn't believe it.

The sheep in the field behind me were treated to some colourful words about my failed pump. I might as well have been holding a bloody carrot for all the good it would have done me.

There I was 12 miles from home, before 8am on a Sunday

morning with a broken bike, no mobile phone (who would I have rung? Emma hadn't moved in yet), and no money. There was only one thing I could do. It would be a long walk home, or a shorter (in terms of time at least) run home. I turned my bike training session into a running one. I must have been a strange sight running along the side of the road pushing a bike when I should have been riding it.

I arrived home, threw my bike in the cellar in frustration and collapsed in a heap, vowing never to buy a cheap, i.e. crap, bike pump again.

Bike training after that consisted of riding up to the university campus and riding laps around the perimeter road. I'd do 11 miles before work and after work. My confidence grew, and I was safe in the knowledge that if my bike broke I was only three miles from home. I'd also visited my local bike shop and bought a snazzy pump that the assistant assured me would not break.

I was also still running a couple of times a week with Andy H. I didn't change that in any way. I knew I could do the run leg of the race, so I pretty much thought if it ain't broke don't fix it, and concentrated on what was very broken.

Swimming was just alien to me. It was something I did once a year when I went on holiday. My holiday swimming consisted of swim a length, stand and chat to Emma, suck the stomach in, get out and lie by the pool. Swimming had just never felt natural. It was only 350m, though, that's not even a full lap of a running track, and how hard could it be?

I went along to the university pool in my lunch hour and ploughed headlong into my first length of the 25-metre pool. My arms and legs flailed in all directions radiating impressive waves to every inch of the pool, probably drowning a few old ladies in the process.

That first session I could only manage 40 metres before I had to stand up and gather my rapidly failing breath. I was knackered. How could it be so hard? Surely you just kicked as hard as you could (like running) and moved your arms back and forth like a windmill?

Embarrassed at my utter failure, I skulked out of the pool and back to work. That night I searched YouTube for swimming instructions and found out that apparently it's all about technique and in fact in order to go faster you have to first go slower. Weird. The man in the video talked about making yourself long, about gliding on the surface of the water, and about swimming each stroke as if you were reaching for the side of the pool. It all sounded plausible but could I apply it?

The next day I couldn't stop thinking about swimming, and when lunchtime came I was psyched up and ready to glide. Easing myself into the water, I put my goggles in place, took a deep breath and pushed off …

Instantly I was thrashing; a lifetime's bad habits would not change in an instant. I stopped and walked back to the end, talking to myself. I could sense parents moving their children away in a defensive and protective manoeuvre.

I tried again.

It wasn't perfect, and maybe it was psychological, but I felt longer. I was swimming slower but I wasn't out of breath. Before I realised it I had done four lengths (100 metres) without pausing for breath. By the end of the week after two more sessions I was swimming 400 metres, 50 metres further than the Cockerham distance. I was so pleased with myself. Maybe, just maybe, I'd get through all of this in one piece. All bets would be off though when I swapped the clear, warm water of the pool for the cold, dark abyss of the pond.

The day before the race I was really nervous. Emma had stayed in Liverpool that weekend as she had to work, and would miss my first attempt at a triathlon. I was disappointed but there would be a safety blanket of support there, ready to pick up the pieces. I rang my parents again to make sure they knew what time they needed to be there to witness the proceedings. My Auntie Jean and my cousin Mike were also making the 115-mile round trip to see if they'd still have to send me a birthday card that November or not.

At about 5pm I got an unexpected phone call from Andy; he

was full of cold and wouldn't be racing. I was on my own. My training partner would not be my racing partner. My mind was racing too. Should I still do it? Could I do it? I did what any normal man would do; I opened a beer and watched a DVD. Seeing Luke Skywalker blow up the Death Star for the hundredth time seemed to calm my nerves, or maybe it was the beer. I was the young naive rookie on a quest to conquer the dark side, and, like Luke, I'd lost my mentor. But surely I'd win in the end? Or was that just the beer talking?

Race day had arrived. I lay in bed telling myself that it was all just a bad dream and in a minute I was going to wake up. I was going to have a normal August Bank Holiday with friends; beer, a barbecue and the traditional awful weather. I closed my eyes, once, twice, three times, but each time I opened them, in the corner of the room I could see my running shoes and the word 'triathlon' screamed in my head.

I tried to sink into the pillow, seeking safety and reassurance under the duvet, but it just wasn't working. Reality had set in, I only had myself to blame. Today I would be jumping in a dark, cold, shit-infested pond and trying not to drown. I'd told all my family and friends that I would be making my triathlon debut, hell everyone at work knew and had wished me luck. I had to succeed or I'd be looking for a new job. I had all the motivation of a man walking to the gallows but there was no backing out, or I would be forever labelled as a quitter. I'd often read that fear is a great motivator. I was scared of failing, of coming last, of being laughed at, of having to explain to family and friends that "I just couldn't do it, sorry." But most of all I had a very genuine fear of not being able to complete the 350m swim without drowning. It was an irrational fear because I'd swam more than that distance in the pool in training, but it was a fear that I just couldn't shake as the day went on.

Unlike most triathlons, which take place at daft o'clock in the morning before the rest of humanity has fallen out of bed, Cockerham takes place at the rather civilised time of four in the afternoon. The traditional thinking behind the 6am and 7am starts for most races is because the organisers want to get most of the cycling over with before the roads get busy. As I paced around my empty house that day clock-watching, I realised that line of thinking was total bollocks. If more triathlons started at 4pm in the afternoon there would be more time for people like me to talk themselves out of turning up and doing it. With a 7am start, you fall out of bed and fall into some cold water dressed in rubber or lycra before you realise the stupidity of your actions and then it's just too late and you have to start swimming.

Besides clock-watching, I spent most of my day rechecking the kit that I would be taking with me to the race. I was a runner – I usually turned up for a race wearing my shorts and vest under my tracksuit, stripped off and started the race. Simple. Triathlon was a completely different creature, hell it even came with written instructions on what to wear and where to put it. Not to mention a compulsory safety briefing. Did the organisers know something I didn't? Was it really that unsafe that they had to warn us? Would there be a solicitor present checking that my will was up to date? Was triathlon secretly a government scheme to reduce the population by having those of a less than full mental capacity willingly go to their deaths in mass suicides disguised as a sporting challenge?

Re-reading the instructions for the hundredth time, I checked that I had what it said I needed: swimming shorts, goggles, bike, bike helmet, running vest and running shoes. I also had a few things that weren't mentioned but that I was taking along for comfort such as socks, cycling gloves and sunglasses. As I placed my socks back in my kit bag I just hoped I'd get chance to wear them.

My bike was actually in Andy's garage as I'd taken it down earlier in the week so that he could give it a maintenance check. I'm ashamed to admit that I had no idea how to adjust brake cables, index my gears or even adjust my handlebars in relation to the seat to get a good riding position. Andy had done an admirable job of preparing my old steel warhorse for battle, even overlooking the fact that he'd almost put his back out lifting the thing. I would soon discover that 'bike fettling' was one of Andy's favourite pastimes, so he was in his element adjusting cables with pliers and tightening bolts with Allen keys. Watching him work on my bike it became apparent that he'd drifted off to a time in his youth, to an age when Meccano was more interesting than girls.

"It's solid and it'll get you round in one piece," Andy said, patting the saddle. That assessment was good enough for me. We closed the garage door and left my trusty steed in peace for a couple of days, until it would be unleashed on the triathlon world.

There was a knock on the door. My heart skipped a beat and I sucked in air; I knew what that hollow sound meant. It was time to put on my game face. I couldn't let on how nervous I actually felt. My parents, Auntie Jean and cousin Mike had arrived. Mike was a very keen runner, something he'd inherited from his late father, Alan. He and Jean had a passion for anything remotely related to athletics, and as such they'd joined my parents in making the long trip to see my triathlon debut. I picked up my carrier bag of gear and headed to the car for the 15-minute drive to Cockerham. It was the quickest car journey of my life. Sitting there in comfort I secretly hoped that we'd get stuck in traffic, or better still be turned back because there had been a major international incident on the quiet Lancashire roads. No such luck.

The field by the gravel pit where the swim would take place had been turned into a temporary car park. As we pulled up Mike surveyed the scene. His incredulous laughter showed his thoughts were mirroring my own as we stared at the turbulent surface of the water. "You're swimming in that? Rather you than me Andy."

"I'll just have to swim faster," I joked, a comment that was borne more out of male bravado than genuine belief.

There was still an hour to go until the race got underway. I left my support crew in the car as I walked across the cowpat-covered field to the registration tent. My instructions had informed me that I needed to be there at least 30 minutes before the start so that I could get registered. This was a new concept to me because I'd already filled in a form and paid my entry fee. Yes, you did read that correctly. Not only was I possibly about to die, I was paying 20 quid for the privilege of doing so.

As I joined the queue of fellow competitors I soon discovered that, unlike running races where you pay your money, turn up and run, triathlon registration is an ordered ballet of precise timings and processes. I got to the front of the queue and was met with the barked command of a harassed volunteer. "Name?" I stood to attention and gave my name.

"Number 78." She handed me a bright yellow swimming cap. I stood staring at the latex object in my hands. I must have looked like a village idiot because she looked up from her list and sighed. "Check the boards at the back of the tent to see which wave you are in, join that queue there for number marking. You must show your race number to enter transition and make sure you are outside the tent ten minutes before the race for the race briefing. Next?"

I shuffled over to the next queue where a less stressed volunteer was brandishing a magic marker with intent. "I need to write your number on your right arm and your left calf." I lifted my shirt and then flashed a bit of leg and was rewarded with temporary tattoos. I was no longer Andy Holgate, I was number 78. I instantly knew what Patrick McGoohan felt like in *The Prisoner*. The reason for the body marking is that it acts as another form of identification for race referees. I was further reminded, "You need to go and find out which wave you are in. Check the boards at the back of the tent there."

Like a sheep I was shepherded over to the boards. Maybe I was now really just a number, as I was mindlessly following orders. It was efficiency in its highest guise, like being in an IKEA one-way system. I was scared that if I turned round I would be trampled to death by a herd of fellow triathletes or ridiculed for rebelling against the system.

I quickly learned that I would be in the fourth wave. A wave is the term in triathlon given to different starting groups. In some races the groups are split by ages. For example, wave one would be 30-35-year-olds, wave two would be 35-40-year-olds and so on. At Cockerham they were split by ability, with the fastest swimmers in the first wave. In total there were five waves. To my utter disbelief and amazement, there was another wave after mine, which meant that on paper at least I wasn't the slowest swimmer present. A certain relief flooded over me; there were people here that were slower than me, I wasn't going to be last. It was like a weight had been lifted off my shoulders. Okay, so it was still entirely possible that people had underestimated their swimming ability and I would indeed finish last, but I now knew as I looked around me at the toned, slim, muscular gods and goddesses that underneath their perfect exteriors some of them were more nervous than me. I actually grinned.

"Oi Andy!" I turned around to see Andy H strolling through the field pushing my bike.

I was actually pleased to see it, and him.

He handed it over and then walked me down the hill to transition, discussing how I was feeling. "I'm terrified," I replied, which he neutralised with a paternal pat on the back. "Just stay focused, stay calm and you'll be fine." My mentor looked me directly in the eyes and in that instant I believed him. My smile indicated to him I'd got the message and he patted my back again in silence.

I had to show my race number to gain entry into transition. Transition was a small corner of the field where three rows of scaffolding poles had been erected about ten metres from the water's edge. It was a hive of activity as people buzzed around inflating tyres, filling water bottles, laying out towels, pouring talcum powder into their running shoes and other alien activities. It really was another world to me.

I racked my bike, letting it hang from a scaffolding pole by its saddle. I'd found a small space about halfway along the row furthest away from the water. On the grass next to my bike I placed my helmet, sunglasses, cycle gloves, running vest and running shoes with a sock tucked into each one. I looked around and took stock; there were about one hundred bikes there and mine must have been the oldest, heaviest and least expensive. It no longer worried me, though, because Andy H had told me that my bike would get me round in one piece, and I had every confidence in his misguided faith in both my bike and its rider.

We walked back up the hill and I introduced my family to Andy H and Pam just as the heavens opened and the traditional bank holiday downpour started. *This has to be an omen*, I thought to myself.

Andy H and Mike accompanied me to the safety briefing whilst the others kept warm and dry in the car. The race referee, the man in charge of the madness, jumped onto the back of a tractor trailer and announced that the safety briefing was about to begin. A silence fell over the crowd as a long list of dos and don'ts was read out:

"If you get into trouble roll on to your back and raise your hand; the safety canoe will be with you quickly. Don't grab the canoe, you may capsize it."

I thought, if I get into trouble, sod the comfort of the canoeist, he's wearing a life jacket and will be able to swim. There'll be a hostile takeover and I'll be paddling to the shore.

"Wetsuits are not compulsory, however the water is freezing, and it's your own personal choice. Oh and the farmer said he's fed the fish so don't worry."

Oh shit, now if I was lucky enough not to freeze to death I was going to get eaten alive by the Cockerham piranhas.

"Make sure you put your helmet on before you touch your bike, you may be disqualified or penalised if you ignore this rule."

I'd been warned about this one. Triathlon as a sport takes safety very seriously. Although the government will let you ride through Piccadilly Circus dodging black cabs and WAGs in Chelsea taxis without any protection other than your wits, the British Triathlon Association won't let you ride your bike across a Lancashire field without your head being encased in a protective plastic and foam shell. You have to take your hats off to them for being so safety conscious. On second thoughts scrap that idea or you'll be disqualified.

After more instructions the referee ended the briefing, wished everyone present a good race, and added that the first wave would start in five minutes. People started heading towards the water, while I quickly ran in the other direction to the one Portaloo. I couldn't believe my luck, there was no queue. Any running veterans reading this will know all about the length of toilet queues at major events. I've often considered taking the Harrods sale approach and camping out with my sleeping bag two days beforehand just so I'm at the front of the queue come race day.

I opened the green plastic door and stepped in. CRASH. My triathlon career was almost over before it had started. My sandals slipped on the drenched plastic floor and I went sliding violently to my side. I put my hand out to brace myself and in doing so almost pushed the whole cubicle over. I swear the bloody thing left the ground. It must have been an amusing sight for anyone stood outside. I regained my composure, not to mention my balance. Exiting the foul-smelling capsule, I wished the next occupant "good luck" as I held the door open for them.

The leaders of the first wave had turned past the first buoy and were heading along the longest part of the course. They looked so graceful, almost like they were floating just below the surface of the water, a sea of yellow-capped heads with metronomic black-clad elbows breaching the surface in a display of rhythm and speed. As the battle for race supremacy was unfolding before me, the second wave of athletes made their way to the water's edge. All but one of them, like those already in the water, was dressed in black rubber. Wetsuits are compulsory at a lot of events in the United Kingdom because the water temperatures are so cold that prolonged exposure can lead to hypothermia. With the swim being so short at Cockerham, hypothermia was very unlikely, and therefore wetsuits were optional. It was apparent, though, that most of those who were wearing them were serious about their sport, and pretty quick to boot.

Looking around, the majority of those waiting to race in the final two waves stood in the rain, wrapped in jackets but bare legged without a hint of rubber. Maybe like me they were new to the sport and hadn't decided to invest in a wetsuit yet.

There was an exception to the wetsuit rule in wave two who did own one, he just chose not to wear it. He later told me it was because he thought he'd lose time in transition taking it off. As the referee blew the whistle to start the second wave, John Krug, bare-chested, sprinted into the water and dived under the surface without flinching. Two powerful kicks of his legs and pulls with his arms and John was half a body-length ahead of everyone else. Gone was the laid-back aura that defined him at work. Powerful and smooth were the words that sprung to mind, watching my colleague glide across the dark surface of the water. He made it look effortless. I stood transfixed watching in awe. I could only dream of being able to swim like that.

Moments later the third wave entered the water and started swimming away. The moment of truth had arrived. The rain had stopped but the dark clouds hung ominously above my head as I removed my fleece and handed it to my dad. Wearing only lycra tri-shorts, my latex swimming cap and a pair of goggles, the cold hit me like a hammer. Surrounded by my family and friends, their good wishes ringing in my ears, I said goodbye. I don't know who looked more nervous, me or my mam.

Several people in my wave were in the water warming up, swimming a few strokes, getting acclimatised. Deciding against this option, preferring to keep warm for as long as possible, several of us stayed on the bank. The referee called, "Wave four, one minute to go." Those that were swimming hurriedly emerged from the water, and ran up the bank to join the less adventurous, still dry but not warm, on the start line.

"Twenty seconds, I'll count you down from ten," the referee announced. Cold and nervous, heart racing, standing at the back out of the way of the serious-looking athletes, I took one last look at the nervous faces of my supporters and made sure my goggles were secure.

"Ten, nine ..." The world stopped, I was lost in my own nervous yet positive thoughts. The training had been done. I was consciously convincing myself that I could do this. It was time to raise my game and become a triathlete.

The shrill sound of the referee's whistle signalled a flurry of activity as we surged forward. Four or five strides and I was knee-deep in the water. Jostling bodies moved on my right but there was nothing to the left other than the bank, and plenty of cheering spectators. The leaders of the wave were already into their swimming a few metres ahead of the pack. This played into my hands as it meant there was a gap immediately ahead of me, so there would be space for me to swim without being kicked by the legs of those in front of me.

Taking a deep breath, I leaned forward and dived ungracefully into the water to start my life-altering journey.

OH SHIT.

The freezing cold water enveloped me, stabbing at my exposed body like a hundred knives. My testicles took their self-preservation seriously and retracted towards internal safety somewhere in the vicinity of my gasping lungs. Adrenaline flooded every inch of my body and I started thrashing wildly, forgetting all that I had learnt about swimming technique. Not surprisingly I winded myself.

Knackered, only about fifty metres from the start, I ground to a halt. I gasped for breath, treading water, as I took a few seconds to dispel the panic. I told myself to get a grip, quitting was not an option and besides the hardest part was over with. I'd jumped blindly into the cold, dark water and wasn't dead.

I plunged forward, reaching out with my right hand, throwing my left arm above me. Having learnt my lesson, I counted out a rhythm with my arms. One, two, three, breathe ... One, two, three, breathe. The panic subsided. As I moved through the water my lungs didn't seem to be working so hard any more. I took this to be a good sign and, encouraged, I pressed on.

Passing the first buoy, I noticed that one of the swimmers ahead of me was quitting. He had his goggles and swim cap in his hand and was being wrapped in a towel by a concerned-looking woman at the water's edge. It was survival of the fittest. I took a somewhat perverse and selfish joy in realising that I could no longer be last because someone had quit. This spurred me on. However, swimming the 200 metres to the next buoy was hard work, especially as the wind had whipped up and was blowing directly into my face.

Wave upon wave of water slammed into my tired, exposed body. I become disorientated and rather than swimming the shortest point from buoy to buoy, I blindly zigzagged my way along the course. As I weakly turned my head to breathe, a torrent of foul-tasting water entered my mouth and flooded my windpipe. Gagging and coughing, it took all of my self-control to stop myself from being sick. For a few seconds, I had no idea what I was doing or where I was.

As I rounded the final buoy I smiled; there was only 50 metres to go. I would soon be on dry land, an altogether more appealing prospect than where I currently was. Within a few minutes the water had become too shallow to swim in, and with each stroke my hand was dredging up what I hoped was silt.

Planning to surge out of the water with speed and power, I stood up. The world started spinning. Feeling drunk, I splashed embarrassingly backwards into the water. Instinctively I jumped back to my feet only to suffer the same fate, plunging forward this time. Taking stock, I slowly and methodically unfolded my crumpled body until I could stand up straight. Feeling like a toddler taking his first step, I gingerly tried to move my legs. Thankfully the blood that had deserted them, causing my clumsy ballet, had returned, and I finally scrambled out of the water.

I tore off my goggles and swimming cap as I stumbled into transition. The swim had been as bad, if not worse, than I'd imagined because of the elements and my own mistakes, but it was behind me. I'd done it. That feeling of relief was immense, I'd survived the worst part. I could enjoy it now.

Conscious of the rules I placed my helmet on my head, determined that there would be no disqualification for me. As I reached down to pull on my trainers my balance deserted me and I fell on my arse. Laughing out loud, not caring, high on the emotion that the bike and run would be easy after that swim, I savoured every moment. This is actually fun, I thought. I took my bike from the rack and ran pushing it towards the mount line. My family were there, and I couldn't help but grin at their cheers of encouragement and responded with a reassuring wave before cycling away.

Once underway I took a long, satisfying drink from the bike bottle containing orange squash. The taste of the foul water was soon masked by the sweetly satisfying citrus taste. I placed the bottle back in its holder and looked into the distance, focusing on three riders ahead of me.

I was surprised that my legs didn't feel tired after their cold water exposure. In no time at all I had crossed the field and was heading out across the airfield. The other riders were closer now, no longer just objects. I could see legs turning. Feeling strong, elated, invincible even, I chased them down like a man on a mission. Working a big gear, I mashed the pedals and surged forward. As I came out of the airfield, a tight right turn almost caught me out. I braked hard and steered sharply to the left. Relief washed over me as I somehow managed to turn the corner and miss the wall. I regained my speed and composure, making a mental note to thank Andy later for tightening my brakes.

The bike course was very flat, and with long straight sections it allowed me to survey what and who was ahead of me. As a chaser I used this to my advantage, soon passing the three competitors that had been in my sights since transition. Feeling great, I could see a larger group ahead and focused on chasing them down. Breaking the race into smaller battles made it go by so much quicker. That particular contest was won with a rather reckless move on my part. The course crossed through a wheat field, following a narrow path along a central drainage ditch. The narrow path created a bottleneck, and a group of six riders were riding wheel to wheel in single file. Patience, according to my mother, has never been a virtue of mine, and it wasn't about to materialise then. Swinging wildly to the right I ploughed blindly off the path and into the crops. It was a risky move because I couldn't see what lay in my path. The presence of any ditch, rock or hare and my race probably would have ended in a spectacular crash. A combination of luck, momentum and determination carried me ahead of the group. The gamble had paid off, swinging back onto the path and safely through the gate out of the field. I now had clear road ahead of me. From that point the roles were reversed. I was being hunted; those that I'd just passed would now have me in their sights. I was motivated by that thought. Ploughing on, I was determined that they would not catch me.

The rain had made the roads quite slick. Riding through fields had dredged up mud and made conditions quite treacherous in places. I'd got away with some reckless riding on parts of the course but my luck was about to run out as I swung the bike through the gate into the field leading to transition. Taking the corner too sharply and then braking hard in a panic caused my back wheel to lock at the unfortunate moment that it was passing through a slurry of manure. Slipping on the rancid stuff, my bike slipped from under me and I was thrown unceremoniously into the hedge. Luckily I somehow managed to land on my feet and was completely unscathed.

I shook my head in disbelief as I hurriedly picked up my bike, which in a split second I had examined. Apart from being covered in shit it seemed fine. Remounting, I swore under my breath as a rider passed me. How dare he? However, transition was only about 300 metres away. *Oh well, it'll give me someone to chase on the run*, I thought as I resumed pedalling for all I was worth.

The five kilometre run course at Cockerham was a mixture of both cross-country and road running. After racking my bike I set off to run through the first field, wary of where I was planting my feet in the ankle-length grass. Having weak ankles and knees I'd given up cross-country running in my youth as I kept twisting them on the uneven surfaces, so I was being very cautious. This, coupled with the fact that the bike and the swim had taken more out of my legs than I'd planned for, meant that the guy I was chasing was slowly getting away from me.

Come on Holgate, keep chasing him, I thought, trying to spur myself on as I crossed the deserted field and emerged into the sodden salt marshes. Glaring at the man in front, I forgot to look where I was going; my right foot slipped, my ankle turning at a funny angle. Warm, sharp pain shot up my leg. Grimacing, I limped forward, trying to keep my momentum going, trying to shake it off. Thankfully it worked and in a few seconds I relaxed back into my running rhythm. A quick glance over my shoulder as I emerged onto the road with a mile to go told me that no one was going to catch me. I sighed, however, as the man I was chasing was out of sight. Leaving the marshes for the road I knew I was almost done. With firm ground under my feet I increased my speed, no longer content with just finishing; I wanted to be as quick as I could.

Triumphantly cresting the final hill and turning into the village, I gave it everything. This was now a 400m race everything before was forgotten as I urged my body to find some long-lost speed. Seconds later I turned onto the village football pitch to see the finish banner hanging from the goal posts. Have I ever run faster I wonder? I burst over the line in 1:16:10 with clapping ringing in my ears. I slumped forward, hands on knees, feeling like I was gasping my last breath. I was red-faced and grinning like a fool. WOW. I'd done it.

My family and friends were soon by my side congratulating me, telling me how well I'd done, how proud they were. Physically I was done in but emotionally I was soaring. My dad handed me a much needed bottle of water, which I drank greedily.

A beaming John Krug, sickeningly looking as fresh as a daisy, came over and shook my hand. Asking how I enjoyed it, I replied that I'd loved it. He laughed and said, "Yep, just plain running will seem boring after that."

Standing there covered in mud and shit, legs screaming, lungs burning, I thought: he's right, how am I going to top that?

3

IT'S ALL HOLGS'S FAULT

Lying in a warm bath reflecting on the day that I'd just had, I still had to pinch myself that I was now a triathlete. The buzz in the car on the way back from the race was uplifting. Mike said that once he had recovered from the Achilles injury that he'd been suffering with for a while, he was going to have a go at a triathlon because he'd loved watching it. My mam proudly said, "If someone had said to me a couple of years ago your Andrew will do a triathlon, I'd have thought they were having me on."

Now that comment may have seemed a little harsh but I knew exactly what she meant. My life had changed radically within the last couple of years, and completing my first triathlon was proof of that.

As I've mentioned I'd had a traumatic birth and first few weeks of my life, which, along with some unwise lifestyle choices, had made me an unhappy fat person. In my old life I wouldn't have even contemplated entering a triathlon. I was worthless, fat and I wouldn't have been allowed the time to train. The moment I crossed the line at Cockerham that person was dead. Everything in my life now seemed to be positive. I had a loving relationship, a great job, and now I had the start of a new addiction: triathlon.

When on doctor's orders I started running again in 2003 I would be criticised at home for spending too long at it; I would worry about the consequences if I spent more than an hour away from the home. Thankfully I could relax at the weekend when shopping trips meant I could run relaxed without clock-watching. I was experiencing freedom for the first time since I was 17, and I was loving it. I entered a few running races and surprised myself with how well I was doing, moving from 10Ks to half-marathons. My running became my therapy as my marriage dissolved. I started going along to Barrow athletic club again and training in a group allowed me to progress, testing myself against other runners a couple of nights a week.

Devouring anything running related I started reading *Runner's World* magazine, and contributing to discussions on their online forums. After testing myself at the gruelling Haweswater half-marathon I was posting the next morning about my experience and about how everything ached that day. In the days building up to the race a guy using the online name of Fat Face and I got into a discussion about the race. We were chatting online that Monday morning and discovered that we'd actually finished together. I'd just about managed to hang on as he finished the stronger of the two of us. We'd shaken hands oblivious to the fact that we'd been talking to each other in cyberspace for days.

I built up an online friendship with Fat Face and he emailed me a photo that had shown us both finishing. I looked awful, like a beached whale. I used that photo as motivation. Keeping it in my desk drawer at work, I would look at it every morning to remind myself that I was now a runner and runners didn't get faster by sneaking into the toilets with a Mars bar or three.

Talking with my new girlfriend Emma one night, she made a very astute assumption about me. We were at the 'getting to know each other phase', and unlike a lot of women she wasn't put off by my animated talk of collecting action figures. She listened intently as I described the difference between a vinyl- and cloth-caped Jawa. Most women would have glazed over or bolted for the door. Analysing these new facts with what she already knew about my passion for running she said, "You have a pretty addictive personality." For the next few hours we sat there in the flat overlooking Sefton Park, the bright lights of Liverpool city centre glowing in the distance, discussing what made me tick. Em listened as I told her of my body issues and she offered some great advice. I'd never thought that I was an addict, but she was right, I had been a food addict. They say once you admit to the problem you've almost beaten it, and that night I realised that to be true. I decided to channel my addictive energies into my running, and vowed that I wasn't going to let this wonderfully kind and intelligent woman slip through my fingers.

Back in the virtual world Fat Face was arranging a social gathering of *Runner's World* forumites in Liverpool of all places. So one wet September's night in 2005, Emma and I jumped into a taxi heading for a city centre pub. Looking at me quizzically she said, "So we're off to the pub to meet a load of people you've never met before, you have no idea what they look like, and you don't know their names? This could be an interesting night."

Technically she was mostly correct, however I did know Fat Face, well I'd met him for a few seconds at the end of a race about six months earlier. And I knew Cougie, Dave the ex-Spartan, Monique, Wolfy, Jakesy, and several others by their forum names. But Christ knows what they'd look like.

Luckily they were instantly recognisable, as strange-accented heavy drinkers wearing running shoes stood out a mile in the traditional ale pub in a heaving Liverpool city centre. The ale flowed and relationships formed. I discovered that Dave the ex-Spartan, a bear of a man, was originally from Morecambe, and that his mother had been a librarian. We hit it off with tales of running and would become good friends.

The night was a great success and a couple of months later, towards the end of 2005, the scene would be repeated. Given the fact I was spending every weekend visiting Emma in Liverpool I had joined the *Runner's World* Merseyside thread. Online banter led me to befriend those who posted there, including Dave and Fat Face. Other people found their way to the thread and I was looking forward to finally meeting Viking, Cath, Loon and Min. We sat in the pub discussing all things running-related.

Viking (Andy), although a couple of years younger than me, was a veteran of several marathons. He instantly earned my respect. Min (Emma) could have been the poster girl for a sportswear company; slim, toned and fit, she looked like the perfect runner. Cath had been struck by an aggressive form of cancer, but she was a determined fighter and had thankfully kicked its arse. She was full of life.

Loon (Lucy) was softly spoken, with an air of intelligence and an infectious laugh. As the alcohol flowed she became louder and started discussing the rights and wrongs of thongs with Dave. Fat Face kept us amused with his jokes and tales of growing up in Blackpool. I went by the nickname of Holgs, something that had stuck with me since school. By the end of the night we were all a bit worse for wear and dancing to cheesy eighties songs in a crowded Irish bar.

Although we wouldn't see each other for months at a time, it was nights like that one that cemented the friendships and we all became pretty close, talking to each other daily in cyberspace, often about nothing but more often than not offering each other support and advice on life. Some would fall by the wayside but others would become great friends. Strangely, I guess, to this day we never call each other by our first names; we always use our forum names. Viking isn't Andy, he's Viking. Calling him Andy just seems weird. Min has never been Emma to me. The exception to the rule is Dave the ex-Spartan, as the first part is his real name; he's just Dave. In all honesty if any of them called me Andy instead of Holgs I'd get worried.

Unfortunately just after we all met I became injured, with knee problems that saw a surgeon tell me that I had to face the possibility of a permanent leg brace if I didn't give up playing five-a-side football. Naturally I took the advice and worked hard with the physio at the hospital. It was a major blow, but I'd been here before, I just had to get on with it. The support of my new friends kept me sane throughout 2005 and 2006. They'd all been there and could relate to the frustration I was feeling. Almost nine months would pass before I began running again with Andy H in the months preceding Cockerham. It was like starting all over again, but I'm glad I did.

They say mothers know their sons, and mine certainly did. I was a different person completely; I was happy, had a great new relationship, a slimmer figure, a renewed passion for running, and some great new friends. Completing the Cockerham triathlon was confirmation that my new life was on track.

Lying there soaking my aching muscles, reflecting on my triathlon debut, my thoughts turned to one of those friends.

Viking listened intently as I gushed away about how great the race had been. We were bouncing off one another's enthusiasm, me high on the adrenaline of my achievement and him contemplating the buzz of a challenge. I honestly think it's the longest I've spent on the phone to another bloke.

"I want to do a proper one, one with road bikes."

Viking pointed out that I didn't own a road bike. "I'll cross that bridge when I come to it," I said, nonchalantly dismissing his truthful observation. Drowning in a cocktail of excitement and bravado, practical thinking had gone out of the window. Eventually we said our goodbyes and Viking must have thought I'd finally lost the plot. I'd talked at him for over an hour. He would have reached for a glass of medicinal red that night as I hung up with the comment, "When I find a race we could do it together."

My enthusiasm for my new-found sport was fuelled further the next day when my work colleagues congratulated me on my achievement. Comments were also forthcoming on the forum where Dave, Min, Viking and I were discussing what I'd said in the race report I'd posted. As the day wore on, momentum built and I felt invincible. I knew how Rocky Balboa felt when he crested the steps of the Philadelphia Museum of Art. I was Holgs the underdog challenger, and I was ready to take on the world.

At home that night hours were spent scouring the Internet. I trawled through websites looking for my next race. I lost myself in threads on the *Runner's World* forum and discovered that there was a wealth of experience, knowledge and opinion about all things triathlon. There was quite a bit of comment about a group calling themselves Pirates. The more I read the more vague memories came back from the first social night in Liverpool. Monique and Cougie had talked to me about triathlon; most of it went straight over my head or was absorbed by the Guinness. They had talked about how they raced as Pirates, a group of forumites who shared a common interest in long-distance triathlons. At the time I'd listened politely but just dismissed them all as nutters. But the more I read, the more the Pirate ethos appealed to me. The Pirates had formed in 2004 after a guy called Candy Ollier and Monique had competed at Ironman Austria.

Reading their race reports I was totally hooked; they didn't take themselves too seriously, something that I could relate to. As a newcomer to the sport it appeared that triathlon could be expensive and cliquey, almost elitist. Of course any new hobby can feel like that at first when you don't know how it works. These Pirates offered a beginner like me a friendly alternative, offering advice and support on training and not breaking the bank, something I was very keen to avoid. In an online article about the unorthodox triathlete band there was a quote from their founder, Candy:

"I think it's largely down to the fact that rising to the Ironman challenge in the first place needs a positive, can-do attitude, so negative people don't even bother to register an interest. And then, when people join in, it quickly becomes apparent from the forums that a strong sense of humour is required; mutual piss-taking is the order of the day. So people who take themselves too seriously or demand respect because they reckon they are 'great triathletes' soon lose interest. So we are left with a great bunch of people, with a huge can-do attitude who aren't afraid to laugh at themselves and each other in the process. That's what the Pirates are all about."

I found myself inside that description and it inspired me. In my head I declared an unspoken allegiance to the Pirate Ship of Fools. There was only one problem: the Pirates raced at Ironman distance, which was about a thousand times longer and harder than what I had achieved.

The first Ironman race came about as a result of some leg-pulling between friends. US Naval commander John Collins got involved in a discussion about who were the greater athletes, swimmers or runners. The Hawaii-based Collins listened intently and then argued the case for cyclists, making it a three-way competition. Of course the discussion never reached a conclusive answer because all three athletes believed that their sport was the toughest test of endurance. After all Mark Spitz would beat Eddie Merckx and Bill Rodgers in the pool, Merckx would be the quickest to circumnavigate France on a bike and Rodgers would be the fastest around the Boston Marathon. So to solve the seemingly unwinnable argument Collins suggested a challenge based on three local events, one from each sport, giving all the athletes an equal chance to succeed and claim their sport as the toughest. The events were the 2.4-mile Waikiki Rough Water Swim, the 112-mile Around-Oahu Bike Race, and the 26.2-mile Honolulu Marathon.

Fifteen people signed up for the 1978 inaugural event, which was described as "lunatic" by the only press reporter present. There would be no rest periods between events, and each athlete had to have their own support crew. Twelve people would finish, being led home by Gordon Haller. Haller, a taxi driver and fitness fanatic, beat the pre-race favourite, Navy SEAL John Dunbar, in the final stages of the marathon. Dunbar's support crew ran out of water, and in desperation gave him beer. The heady mix of dehydration, exhaustion and alcohol saw Dunbar stagger wildly about the course, allowing Haller to pass him and claim the victory in 11:46:40. The man behind the event, John Collins, came home in 9th position in a time of seventeen hours, a number that would eventually be used as the time limit imposed on those seeking to complete the gruelling event.

Over thirty years later and with over 30,000 finishers at the Hawaii Ironman, the original question still hasn't been answered. The competitors are no longer allied to one sport, they are Ironmen. The event captured the public's imagination after it was first televised in 1980. It epitomised the strength of the human spirit and the individual's journey to reach further inside themselves to succeed. This spirit was at the forefront of the 1982 race when a young woman by the name of Julie Moss changed the Ironman forever. Moss, who had been leading the women's race, collapsed within 15 feet of the finishing line suffering from severe dehydration and exhaustion. She tried to stand but collapsed again, allowing Kathy McCartney to claim the victory. The world watched on as a determined Moss crawled along the road on her stomach, lifted her left hand, and placed it over the line before drifting into unconsciousness. Every sport needs its defining moment in the thoughts of the viewing public. Football has "They think it's all over, it is now"; cricket has the Bodyline series; the Grand National horse race has Red Rum and Ironman has Julie Moss.

Due to the growing popularity of the sport, more events were added globally, allowing more people to achieve their endurance dream. Events now take place in Germany, Japan, Canada, Australia, Brazil, France and the United Kingdom, amongst others, and it is a billion-dollar business. Ironman is actually a registered trademark of the World Triathlon Corporation, and the only races allowed to be called Ironman races are those sanctioned by the WTC. Success breeds imitation and Ironman is no exception. All around the world, 'Iron-distance' triathlons have appeared that offer the same 140.6 mile challenge but without the brand and all that goes with it. These low-key events such as Embrunman in France, Norseman in Norway and Challenge Wanaka in New Zealand are no less of a challenge, and as branded Ironman races often sell out within minutes, these can be easier to gain entry into.

After several hours and gallons of strong coffee it was one of these unbranded races that caught my eye. Having trawled through lots of race websites, and dismissing them because of cost, geography, unavailability of entries and clashes with other commitments, I had a shortlist of one.

The Big Woody was a completely new event, the brainchild of Trevor Kingdon, a triathlon coach and a veteran of several Ironman races. The iron-distance event would take place in the

Forest of Dean, a picturesque corner of south-west England. Reading the information on the website and the positive reviews of Trevor's other events, I was drawn in. Sod it, I thought, no one will expect me to attempt an Ironman, hell, hours ago I wouldn't have expected it of myself. I was hooked on triathlon after one small hit; it was time for me to let it take over my life, it was time for me to show the world what I could really do. No one had expected me to survive my first day on this Earth. I'd proved the doctors wrong and now I was about to embark on a journey to prove the world wrong and complete one of its toughest challenges.

Whilst waiting for the entry form to print out, I reached for my chequebook and scribbled my signature authorising the entry fee of £150. Glancing at my watch, it was gone midnight, and with a full day of work on the horizon a normal person would have headed to bed. I grabbed my coat. I was so excited, my fingers and toes were tingling as I walked down the hill to the post box. Pausing for a brief second in the moonlight I looked down at the sealed envelope in my hands, and a huge grin formed as I remembered a quote from the Ironman website: "Anything is Possible." With that thought I posted the envelope and practically floated back up the hill. The positive energy kept me awake all night as I imagined what it would feel like to turn the final corner in the marathon, to see the finish and realise my new-found dream of becoming an Ironman.

Sitting at my desk at work the next day I was still high on what I'd done; the practicalities of what lay ahead of me in the next 11 months had not yet kicked in; the lack of sleep had not dampened my blissfully ignorant and glowing mood.

I was about to receive a serious wake up call.

An email arrived from my fiancée, Emma (luckily she hadn't run for the hills after discovering my habit of meeting strangers in pubs to discuss lycra, and had accepted my proposal of marriage with a smile rather than a look of fear). Emma said that she'd arranged for a wedding dress fitting that weekend in Liverpool and would I be okay to take her and her mother, Maggie, in the car. Typing a positive response to Em's request I then told her that I'd entered the Big Woody. I explained about the event and typed that it would take place on 1 Septem… My heart almost stopped; the word September remained unfinished on my screen, the cursor blinking, almost taunting me.

Emma is going to kill me. I'm a dead man walking. How could I miss the fact that the race that I'd just entered, a race that could see me potentially crippled, would take place on 1 September? Emma would probably think I was insane for wanting to attempt something so mind-bogglingly tough but she'd be more concerned that I wasn't taking our relationship seriously, because a mere seven days later, on 8 September, we were due to get married. Everything was booked, and we were both looking forward to our big day. Had I just jeopardised the biggest day of my fiancée's life with a rash, unthinking, selfish moment of madness? My mood quickly dampened. Deleting the part of the email relating to the Woody, I told her I'd call her that night.

After work I gathered my thoughts as I ran home along the canal, eventually covering eight miles instead of the usual four. It gave me plenty of time to rehearse my responses to the points I believed Emma would be making. To say I was a little apprehensive when she answered the phone would be an understatement. We chatted about our days, dealing with overdue books and demanding students – library talk, the sort of topics only two librarians would find remotely interesting. Asking about my evening's run and if my legs had recovered after their triathlon adventure, I took the plunge and said, "Funny you should mention triathlon, I've got a confession." Already used to my running exploits, Emma listened intently as I told her all about the Woody, explaining the distances involved and the reasons I had for wanting to do it. She was very supportive. Her only concern was for my physical well-being, as she was well aware of my weak knees. I explained about the training I would have to do and put her mind at rest when she raised the issue of if we'd actually manage to see each other. It was going much better than I could have imagined, however I hadn't mentioned the proximity of the wedding to the race.

"You know I'll support you in anything you do, just promise me you'll be careful and that you'll be at the wedding in one piece." I paused in response to Emma's statement and she picked up on it immediately.

"Okay Andy, when is it? Don't tell me it's a couple of weeks beforehand?"

"Seven days," came my nervous reply.

Silence, and then laughter. Was I about to get the bollocking I was expecting? It certainly felt like it as I waited for Emma to say something.

Calmly and softly spoken, she said, "So, let me get this straight. Seven days before our wedding you are going to attempt some insane challenge that could quite possibly cripple you?"

"Yes—" I didn't get to finish the sentence.

"I always knew you were daft but this is insane. I don't doubt for a second that you'll do it, you're the most determined and stubborn person I know. And I wouldn't want to stop you from doing something you really wanted to do. Just promise me that we'll be able to have our first dance together at the wedding because right now I have visions of you struggling to walk let alone dance."

Making that promise was easy, how could I not? A woman's wedding day is the biggest day of her life, they dream about it since being little girls, and I had just told the woman that I was about to marry that I was potentially threatening her big day. The fact that she'd taken it all in her stride proved to me that Emma was special and that I would be an idiot to jeopardise her faith and trust in me. I couldn't let her down. In the months to follow, when I was faced with the prospect of long lonesome bike rides in icy wind and rain, it was that thought that saw me take the first step out the front door. Training would be the insurance policy that would get me through to 8 September in one piece.

Somewhat relieved about how well Emma had taken things I next told my parents, who had always been supportive of any venture either of their boys undertook. This would be no exception; both of them said they knew I'd succeed if I trained hard enough. My mam expressed concern for Emma and the wedding on hearing the date, something which would be echoed by every single person that found out about the race in the days, weeks and months to come. Most believed I was nuts; at times I thought they were probably right.

The phone rang. I was in the kitchen making a coffee. Figuring it would be Emma or my mam with a question they'd forgotten to ask, I picked it up.

"Holgs, it's all your fault." The serious, stern words from Viking caused my mind to race as it searched for a memory of something I could have done to upset my running buddy.

"I'm in. The cheque is in the post. Couldn't let you kill yourself on your own you daft bugger. I know I'm going to bloody regret it." I'd sent him an email telling him of my plans, expecting him to be the voice of reason. Deep down I knew he wouldn't be. By the time I'd gotten off the phone the water in the kettle was stone cold.

The next day I posted on the Merseyside *Runner's World* forum declaring mine and Viking's intentions to attempt an Iron-distance race. It was Viking's idea to sell it to our friends as my alternative stag weekend. I'd agreed to this on the condition that he would not be dressing me up in drag or expecting me to swim in handcuffs. Again expecting to be shouted down about the insanity of it all, there was a response from Dave within minutes expressing an interest, although he did say he'd prefer a stag weekend in Amsterdam with strippers and copious amounts of alcohol. Min was soon on board, making a merry band of four. Loon and Fat Face considered joining us but after much soul-searching took the sensible decision that their present circumstances wouldn't allow for the training commitment involved. Andy H also declared himself out as we discussed the matter on a mid week run. I tried to convince him that he'd easily meet the challenge; after all he was an exceptionally strong cyclist and a decent runner. The problem was he couldn't swim confidently and had no real desire to start learning now, and was increasingly spending most of his working week in Scotland. He promised to support me fully and to help me with the biking side of things. I'd get the same response and offer of support from John Krug, who, whilst admitting the thought of doing an Ironman appealed to his adventurous side, couldn't commit to it as he had a young family.

So, I'd come out of the Ironman closet and was not alone. I had the backing of friends and family and a very strong motive in wanting to succeed. It was at this point that the enormity of what I had set out to do, and how far away I was from succeeding, struck me. I couldn't swim properly, certainly not for 2.4 miles, the equivalent of swimming 152 lengths of a standard 25-metre pool. I knew very little about cycling; I didn't own a bike let alone know what I should be looking for. Although I was confident in my running ability I'd only ever finished a half-marathon, and when I had, my legs were shot. Now I would be running double that distance with a body that had already been pushed way out of its comfort zone just to make it to the start line of the marathon. With a wedding to finance, trying to do it all on a shoestring budget could be the biggest test of all.

Reflecting on a busy few days, I thought to myself, *Yep, it really is all your fault Holgs.*

4

LIKE A BEAR WITH A SORE ARSE

My Big Woody training got off to the worst possible start as my weak left knee kept giving way on me every time I tried to run. Not again, I thought. I'd already come back once from a long lay-off. Like a typical runner at first I tried to ignore the pain, kidding myself that it would go way. When it got too much I rested for a week or two. My knee would feel better but then as soon as I foolishly started to run again the searing lightning bolt of pain would strike and I would have to limp home dejected. I reluctantly pulled out of my main race for the year, the 2006 Great North Run. Emma described me as being "like a bear with a sore arse". She had just recently moved in having secured a job at a local university, and was the recipient of most of my dark moods. Thankfully she didn't kill me and suggested that I should concentrate on my weaknesses rather than my strengths. Her argument was that provided I wasn't injured my running would take care of itself, yet I could hardly swim and didn't own a road bike. So I had three things to correct: the injury, the swimming and the lack of a bike. Not much work to do then.

I wasn't alone, however. Once their initial excitement had died down, Viking, Dave and Min were faced with the cold reality of the monumental task that lay ahead of us all. The three of them had finished multiple marathons, so barring injury they knew that they could complete the running portion of the Woody. Dave was perhaps the most experienced of us all having been riding a road bike for a while, and he'd even recently finished a small triathlon. Viking, Min and I were all clueless when it came to bikes. I'd had a racer in my teens but that was ancient history. A rumour surfaced on the Internet that Viking's bike still had the stabilisers on it, which he vehemently denied, although he did admit to the one about the Spokey Dokeys.

The four of us really fell apart, however, when it came to swimming. Yes I'd survived at Cockerham and managed to swim 350 metres but I was slow and uncoordinated. Viking, Dave and Min could only swim breaststroke. Dave had actually swum breaststroke in his triathlon but now realised its limitations and began to learn the crawl. We'd all really need to work hard or we'd fail. This was quickly becoming the stark reality.

In an attempt to improve my swimming I started going along to the university pool in my lunch hour. Thinking like a runner, I perceived my improvement to be in direct proportion to the amount of lengths I was swimming. As a runner I gauged my fitness and strength on the distance I'd covered: the greater the mileage, the greater the reward. I was swimming a lot further, almost a mile now, but I was totally knackered and feeling sick by the end of each session. This feeling, coupled with the fact that I was having to rest at the end of each length for a couple of seconds to get my breath back, dampened my enthusiasm for swimming. Whilst the other three had been taking lessons and telling stories of great improvement I had been too tight to invest in a teacher, and I was now beginning to find any excuse to miss a planned trip to the pool.

Fear of failure once again got me back on the right path. If I didn't get my arse back to the pool there was a real danger that I wouldn't complete the swim at the Woody. Whilst struggling one lunchtime a fishlike John Krug passed me. I watched underwater through my goggles as he quickly went away from me and I couldn't help but admire how effortless he made it all look. He was soon lapping me. He appeared to be 12 feet long in the water and hardly moving, whilst I was splashing around like a toddler in a paddling pool. Feeling utterly useless, I dragged my sorry frame out of the pool and into the changing rooms. John entered a few moments later. Enquiring as to how my training was going I replied, "It isn't really." He listened as I whinged and asked how he did it. He explained that I was probably just employing bad technique and a few minor changes could make huge improvements to my swimming. When he offered to look at my technique the next day I almost hugged him.

John watched carefully and then hit me with his analysis. "You're making loads of mistakes but they are easily correctable. The problem you've got is you've conditioned yourself to swim badly, employing a lazy style." I wasn't holding my body correctly in the water, my head position was too high, I was kicking from the knee and not the hip... I could continue but this book would end up longer than *War and Peace*. Changing my head position so most of it was underwater and concentrating on not lifting my head out of the water completely to breathe made it much easier. This, combined with John's advice on making my body as long as possible, rolling from side to side with each arm stroke as if pulling myself along an invisible tightrope, worked wonders. Over the next few days my confidence grew. I was no longer breathless and was actually starting to enjoy this swimming lark.

A couple of weeks later I noticed a sign in the university sports centre advertising "Adult Improver Swimming Lessons". Enquiring at reception, I learned that they had availability for the lessons starting in the new term after the Christmas vacation. I met the requirement of being able to swim four lengths of the pool and best of all I qualified for a staff discount. It would only cost me £3 for the weekly session, meaning swimming lessons were no longer a luxury I couldn't afford.

I'd also been doing my homework when it came to cycling. Not owning a road bike yet meant it was a theory
-based learning curve rather than a practical one. However I was lucky enough to be surrounded by cyclists who were very knowledgeable and didn't mind me looking at their bikes.

Emma's dad, John, was about as fanatical a cyclist as you could meet. The man ate, breathed and slept cycling. In the form of books, magazines, videos and DVDs he had more information on the sport than the British Library. He referred to it all lovingly as his "Bike Porn". He combined this with an annual pilgrimage to the Alps to watch and then ride around the stages of the Tour de France. His son Matt was equally immersed in the world of lycra, carbon and bidons. Both of them answered my basic questions and didn't laugh at my lack of knowledge. They both rode Italian-designed Bianchi bicycles, well known for their distinctive celeste-green colour. They let me try their bikes and it quickly became apparent that John's bike was way too big for me. However Matt, being only slightly taller than me, had a bike that I could ride along the road without dangerously overbalancing. I didn't have the specialist shoes that attached to the pedals but luckily I could still balance my running shoe-clad feet and take the bike for a spin. At first I couldn't find any gear levers. I was looking on the frame and didn't realise they were attached to the brake levers on modern bikes, making them easier to ride without losing precious seconds or power by having to reach down in an unnatural riding position. It would be my first taste of the new generation of racing bikes and I loved it.

Andy H had been cycling for years and had a very nice Ribble racing bike. He spent many hours talking about the technical specifics of the bike I should be looking for, and given the area we lived in is very hilly, he suggested I went for either a triple or a compact. Both terms refer to the chain ring, the circular bit near the pedals that the actual chain turns around. Traditional racing bikes, the types favoured by 'purists', have double chain rings. The advantage given by a triple or a compact is that they make it easier to go uphill by giving you a greater range of gears. I didn't really understand Andy's talk of gear ratios (this would be a recurring pattern over the year) but I understood that anything that made going uphill easier was good for me. John Krug, who explained that using a triple would put less strain on my knees, further enforced its advantages. Given the fact my knee was injured, I decided I wouldn't consider anything else. John rode a bike made by Giant, a slick black machine that was way above my price range. Between the Ribble, the Bianchi and the Giant I had a serious case of bike envy. I was lucky enough to try all the bikes for size and decided that a medium 52-inch frame would be the correct one for me. I was constantly reading that getting a bike that fits your body is the most crucial part of selecting one. The wrong size could put too much strain on your body, causing the vital loss of power and speed and the risk of serious injury, not to mention making the rider an unsafe liability on the public roads.

Combining my experience of trying my friends' bikes with information gained from the Internet and bike porn, I decided that I needed a good quality bike with a sound reputation and it had to have a triple chain ring. I soon discovered from visiting the area's bike shops and from the many online suppliers that what I wanted could not be had for less than five hundred pounds. That amount would only buy me a very basic road racing bike. Triathlon-specific racing bikes retailed for several thousand pounds. Add specialist aerodynamic wheels and the bike would be worth more than a decent small hatchback car. None of this was money I had or could afford with a wedding on the horizon. Discussing it with Emma and doing our sums we concluded that I could afford to spend three hundred pounds at the most. That left one conceivable avenue open to me: a second-hand one from eBay. It was a risky move but I was confident I could get a bargain and not get ripped off.

After several weeks of searching and sadly observing the bikes I was interested in rising out of my price range, I discovered a gem. The Giant OCR2, listed by a shop that specialised in selling goods on behalf of other people, was described as being 'like new'. No technical details were given about the bike but I could see from the photographs that it had three varying-size chain rings, so it was a triple. It also had a visible sticker declaring it to be a medium, a size I knew would fit me from trying John Krug's almost identical bike. There was also a photograph of the original purchase receipt to prove that the bike had not been stolen. The price stayed low, probably as a consequence of the unwillingness of the seller to post the bike; it had to be collected from Liverpool. This of course was not a problem for me. For the next three days I nervously watched the progress of the auction. I would hold my nerve and not bid until there was less than a minute to go in an attempt to surprise the other bidders. Sitting there with half an hour to go the price, which had stayed the same for days, began to rise. Within 25 minutes the bidding had doubled the previous price but it was still within my range. As I constantly clicked the refresh button, a bead of sweat trickled down my temple. The screen flashed 30 seconds to go. Typing like my life depended on it, I entered my maximum bid and clicked submit. With 20 seconds to go eBay informed me I was the current highest bidder. One click of the refresh button later I punched the air in victory. I was now the proud owner of my dream bike. And the best thing was it came in under budget at £260. The phone rang and it was my mam congratulating me on finally getting my bike. My parents had been watching the proceedings nervously on their computer. I now had a bike to go with the clipless pedals they had just bought me for my birthday. I'd been buying essentials as I'd been finding them on offer or going cheaply on my favourite auction site. I had cycling shoes and a cycling computer that would tell me my speed and distances ridden – all I needed was a helmet.

I picked the bike up a couple of days later and was pleasantly surprised that it came with some accessories that weren't mentioned in the auction description. There was a brand new Giro helmet, a carbon pump and padded gel gloves, all of which made my pristine-looking bike more of a bargain. It was the start of a beautiful relationship.

The plan was to get used to riding the bike in the cellar for a few weeks. Now I don't have the world's biggest cellar, but what I did have was a turbo trainer. I had been lucky enough to have been given one free by Julie at work, as her husband needed the space in his garage for motorcycle spares. A turbo trainer attaches to the frame of the bike and holds it firm, whilst a revolving drum creates friction on the rear tyre which simulates travelling on a road. So layering up in the sub-zero November temperatures, I spent an hour a night pedalling away. I got used to changing gears (although I didn't really understand them still), my backside became one with the razor's edge saddle and most importantly of all I spent at least ten minutes at the end of each session unclipping my feet from the pedals. I had heard so many horror stories about cyclists coming to a stop at a junction or traffic lights and crashing to the floor as they had forgotten they were clipped into the pedals. I laughed hard as Andy H told me how he'd tumbled for the first time one summer's evening outside a crowded pub, and how embarrassed he was by it. Telling him that I'd been practising and that it wouldn't happen to me, he chuckled, gave me a knowing look and quipped, "Yeah right".

With wedding and family commitments, and the icy, dangerous weather, it would be early December before my bike and I ventured out onto the roads. I was to meet Andy early on a Sunday morning and he'd take me on a magical mystery tour of south Cumbria and north Lancashire. Before these outings I didn't know of the beauty of little villages and hamlets such as Wrea Green, Hambleton, Silverdale, Chipping and Arnside. Andy was a great tour guide and there wasn't a cyclist's café in the whole of the North West that he hadn't been to. He could quite easily write the *Michelin Guide to Toasted Teacakes*, and we joked that he could sniff a warming currant from 12 miles away. Later when we increased the mileage, Andy employed self-control and decided we weren't allowed to stop until we'd ridden for three hours. But for now we were riding for an hour or two, enjoying a coffee and generally socialising. It was nothing too serious and was just the gentle introduction I needed. I fell in love with my bike and the freedom to explore that it gave me. Cycling became the new running.

Although we consciously made time to see each other, I was training and Emma was embarking on her second Masters degree. The endless research and essay writing was wearing her down and to make matters worse she'd been missing her cats, which had stayed with her mother Maggie in Liverpool. As a result she was making noises about us getting one. I've always been a dog person, and was a little apprehensive so said no initially. She eventually won, as women have a habit of doing, with a comment she knew I had no response to. "It would stop me from getting lonely when you start your proper training after Christmas," she said, and with a wicked laugh added, "And besides, I let you get a bike." Just over a week later a chunky, battered, one-toothed tabby cat, which had been rescued from the streets, joined our happy household from the local animal shelter. Life would never be the same again. There was a new sheriff in town and his name was Crosby.

With Emma suitably distracted I began to spend longer in the cellar, moving an old TV and DVD player down there, and the boredom of stationary cycling subsided. My nightly sessions had increased to roughly ninety minutes or two episodes of *Angel*. The do-gooder vampire would get me through a harsh winter's cycle training. After a period of swimming three times a week for 30 minutes and cycling for 8 hours, I began to notice that my clothes were feeling looser and my legs were feeling stronger. Talking to Andy on one of our bike rides I raised the topic of running again. He'd already suggested that I seek the help of a specialist, so I asked him to email me the details of the guy that 'fixed' him. A few days later I sat in the office of a sports podiatrist who specialised in lower limb injuries. After an examination and several tests I was filmed walking and running on a treadmill, both with my running shoes on and off. The results were shocking. Played back at normal speed there was no apparent fault in the way my legs moved. However, when the same footage was played in super slow motion even I could see that my left leg, the injured one, had a problem. I had what is known as biomechanical dysfunction. People had been telling me for years I was dysfunctional, but that was nothing to do with my running. The video showed that at the point where my left foot pushed off from the floor the lower leg twisted violently, causing the crippling pain in my knee. My cause wasn't helped by the fact that I was also landing on the ball of my foot and rolling backwards to push off the heel, the complete opposite of a natural gait. Two things would cure me. Firstly he recommended some off-the-shelf orthotics for my shoes that I was to wear at all times. These would stop the twisting motion by altering how my feet lay in the shoes. The second solution sounded implausible; he wanted me to learn how to run again.

I was given a programme to follow and I began by walking and really concentrating on placing my heels firmly into the ground and consciously rolling forward onto the balls of my feet. My calves and Achilles ached as they were working differently than they had all their lives. A week later I tentatively left the house for my first run in three months. I ran once around the park as slowly as I've ever ran in my life. I had to concentrate on heel, roll, push ... heel, roll, push, for 20 minutes. My mind was more exhausted than my body, but my knee felt strong. I couldn't have wished for a better Christmas present; I was running again. Within two weeks I was running six miles pain free, and as happy as a pig in ... Well you can guess the rest.

As Jools Holland counted in the New Year we celebrated with friends and toasted the passing of time. "To our wedding year," said Em. "And Ironman," I added with a wicked grin. Nine months until the two biggest days of our lives. I had a feeling it was going to be an eventful year. I wouldn't be wrong.

5

"SO ANDY, EXPLAIN GEARS TO ME AGAIN."

The year 2007 started with a bang, literally, as my balance and luck deserted me. As I decelerated to meet Andy H outside the hospital early on a crisp Saturday morning my brain was apparently still in bed. Totally forgetting that my feet were clipped into my pedals, I had one of those slow motion moments where you can see what's about to happen but are powerless to prevent it. Timberrr ... thud. My right elbow hit the floor first. "Bollocks," was my less than eloquent reaction as I writhed around on the floor like a fish out of water, struggling to unclip my still-attached feet from the prone bike. Reaching down to offer me a much-needed hand up, Andy pulled me to my feet. "I told you you'd fall off at some point." His voice grew more concerned as he pointed out that my elbow was bleeding. I did the macho thing of shrugging it off and saying it was just a graze, wiping away the blood with the back of my glove. Eventually we set off and only when Andy was ahead of me did I allow a grimace to appear on my face; my elbow hurt.

We dropped down through the town centre and out towards Silverdale, taking in a couple of nasty little climbs on mostly deserted roads. We arrived in Silverdale and approached a crossroads. As we slowed down Andy said, "We'll go left. I think I know where we're going." We descended round a bend and straight into a sign reading, "WARNING QUICKSAND".

We both skidded to a halt as the road ended abruptly in front of us and was replaced by a ramp down on to the notorious sands of Morecambe Bay. My brain was awake by now and it sent the message to my feet to unclip, allowing me to use both legs as anchors. We couldn't help but laugh about our lucky escape. "You and your bloody directions, no wonder you have a sat nav in your car," I quipped. "I was just testing you to see if you could unclip yet." The instant response from Andy was typical. I should have known that I'd never get the last word with a Scouser.

The views across Morecambe Bay that morning were simply stunning, the peaks of the Lake District bathed in crisp winter sunshine. This is what cycling should be like. We cycled round a secluded bay and up another winding hill. Andy told me to look back; the view was breathtaking. With the steep cliffs and crashing waves, we could have quite easily been riding along the famed Californian coast. It's moments like these that make me feel privileged to live in such a beautiful part of the world, something I think I take for granted most of the time. Since I started cycling and training with Andy and John I've witnessed beautiful countryside and stunning sunsets, on roads I never knew existed. Get out on your bikes folks and just ride; get off the main roads and explore. Trust me, the world around you will suddenly feel a much better place. That spectacular view raised our spirits and we didn't seem to notice the steep hills as much after that. As we approached the village of Milnthorpe and the main crossroads with the A6, the lights turned red. Obediently we stopped at the side of the road waiting for them to change. I unclipped my left foot and put it on the kerb to rest but my foot slipped and I over-adjusted my balance in the saddle. "Bollocks not again," I cried as I fell to my right, sprawling in the middle of the road. Luckily the car behind us was a few yards away and stopped. If one had been closer it would have been extremely dangerous. I must be jinxed at that junction. Five years previously a woman failed to stop at the lights and ploughed into my car causing me neck injuries. As I rose sheepishly to my feet there was no time for a dust down as the traffic lights changed to green. We stopped when we got clear of the junction and I surveyed the damage. I'd managed to fall and bang my arm in the same place, resulting in two very tender swellings less than a centimetre apart. Added to this there was blood trickling down my knee. They say things come in threes but thankfully we completed the rest of our 50-mile ride without incident. The third fall would come two days later.

It was a glorious morning; cold, crisp, a slight frost, but also the sort of day that would require sunglasses. Keen to get out on my bike again, I set off for work. I'm lucky enough to live at the top of a very steep hill so most of my rides either begin or end with a hill climb. The route to work takes me over a couple of short yet steep rises, but this usually isn't a problem.

As I approached the first junction, I started the process of stopping – left leg twist, unclip, foot down whilst the car passes. I'm getting the hang of these clipless pedals, I thought, smugly. I continued with the process – look left, look right, look left again and push to set off. As I tried to clip my foot back in I slipped. In a compensatory move I tried to put my right foot down to steady myself. "Oh shit, not again," was my panicked response as I realised my foot was still clipped in. Result ... TIMBERRRRRR (again).

Yep, I hit the floor quicker than Viking at a Spice Girls appreciation night.

As soon as I hit the ground my foot unclipped. "Bloody typical," I cursed as I quickly jumped up and looked around. None of the curtains were twitching; I don't think anyone noticed. I jumped on my bike and cycled away with my pride intact. Well, almost.

However my last fall was my worst, not in the sense of physical damage, rather cringing embarrassment. Coming back into Lancaster at lunchtime on a Saturday after completing my first ride of over 100 miles, I was totally drained. As I came over a sharp rise into the main city square the lights in front suddenly turned red. I don't know if dehydration had affected my brain but it forgot to talk to my feet. Forward momentum had gone, and as my hands gripped the brakes I remember relaxing. This lasted a second before being replaced by a startled flurry of activity. It was too late. Although I managed to unclip my right foot I couldn't save myself. Landing unceremoniously amongst the shoppers crossing the road, I stared up at the sky in disbelief.

Two shadows came into focus; wrinkled, rouge-painted

concerned faces clad in headscarves. "Oh young man, are you okay? Grace, ring an ambulance." Seeing a mobile phone emerge from a handbag and weathered, wrinkled fingers move to operate it, I jumped to my feet. "No I'm fine thanks, there's no need for an ambulance." The panic and embarrassment was apparent in my voice. I cut a sorry sight limping to the side of the road, blood trickling down my leg with Grace escorting me by the arm and her friend, Doris, wheeling my bike. It was certainly amusing the teenagers sat on the bus. At that moment I wanted the ground to swallow me up as I stood there blushing. After convincing both of my rescuers that I wasn't injured or the victim of a car getting too close, they let me go. I thanked them both and rode home. The embarrassment of that fall has kept me from repeating the incident, although many would argue that I'm still unbalanced.

So that was it for falls for several months. Much like when driving a car, I taught myself to watch ahead and to try and anticipate junctions and other road users. Using this technique, when approaching a junction I would unclip my foot so that I would be able to place it on the floor quickly if the situation required it. I also realised that part of my balance problem came from the fact that my left foot was the one I would try to unclip. This was asking for trouble, as my left leg is the weak one. Physiotherapists over the years soon discovered that I could not stand on that leg without falling over. It's a good job I don't live in the United States where traffic police, as part of their sobriety test, ask you to stand on one leg and touch your nose. I'd be charged with drunk driving and locked up. So I hit the turbo trainer in the cellar on the dark wet nights after work and practised and practised until my brain was retrained to instinctively unclip the right leg. I employed this technique for months without incident, and still do now. At a recent 'Numpty Cyclists Anonymous' meeting I was able to stand up and say with pride, "My name is Andy and I've been fall-free for two years."

Falls weren't the only problem I faced on the bike in those first few months of intense training. I seemed to get a puncture on almost every other ride, yet Andy H never once suffered the same fate. One very wet and cold February morning I punctured four times, twice with each wheel. Having used up my two spare inner tubes, Andy H gave me the two spares that he had. By the third puncture my hands were so cold I could no longer grip the tyre levers. Andy stepped in and changed the tubes for me, and that was the beginning of his role as my domestique. A domestique is a bike rider who looks after his team leader, fetches water and food, shelters them against the elements and whose sole purpose in a race is to protect their leader. Given the amount of punctures Andy would help me with in these months, 11 in total, his role of protecting me became our joke. Soaked to the skin, hypothermic and really pissed off, we abandoned our planned ride that morning, having only covered 25 miles in three hours.

Frustrated at having to abandon training, I spent the rest of the day hidden away in the cellar checking my tyres for weaknesses. Not finding any I decided I just needed to buy replacement inner tubes, and new tyres could wait. After a quick cup of coffee I browsed the Internet and discovered that you could buy tubes that contained sealant. The premise was that if air got out of the tube through a puncture, the sealant would activate and instantly mend it. This sounded like the answer to all my problems. Not wanting to wait for an online order to arrive I rushed to the local bike store and bought four of these miracle cure tubes, and replacement traditional ones for Andy. They were a lot heavier than normal tubes, which was something the triathlon purists on the *Tri-Talk* forums had warned me about, but I figured that, being two stones overweight anyway, a few extra pounds on my wheels wouldn't make that much difference. Keen to make amends for the lost training miles, I rang Andy and explained my bike was roadworthy again and ready to be tested. We agreed to ride again the next morning.

The day started well, cold but dry. We'd been cycling for 46 miles when the heavens opened and once again our mood turned from "What a great day to be out cycling" to "Brrrr this is hard work, let's just get home". We had less than ten miles to go when my bike started to feel bouncy, no longer rolling along smoothly. Looking down I could see my rear wheel was in trouble, deflating and haemorrhaging neon-green slime. I shouted down the road at Andy who had opened up a gap whilst I'd been losing forward momentum. I pulled off the single track lane into the gateway of a field. "It's another sodding puncture," I said. "But it'll be okay, it should seal itself. I'll just put some more air in and we'll be on our way." As I removed the valve there was a hissing noise, and a volcano-style eruption of green slime covered my hands – it was just leaking out everywhere. The valve was faulty. Just my luck. I was stood there soaked and angry, using words that were not appropriate for a Sunday morning. Lightening the mood, Andy pointed at my feet, which were slowly being enveloped in a puddle of green goo. "It looks like we've conducted an alien autopsy."

I couldn't help but laugh, as I pictured someone chancing on the scene after our departure and their look of bewilderment. Thankfully the spare tube wasn't faulty and we got home in one piece. However I'd had enough of punctures and invested in 'bomb proof' tyres, the Continental Gator Skins. They were expensive but worth every penny as that was the last of my puncture problems, although it wasn't the last I heard about it. Running with Andy a few days later, I should have expected him to have the last word on the matter. "I've contacted the tourist board and they have agreed that when you're a famous Ironman they'll attach little blue plaques to all these farm gates saying: 'Holgs punctured here'."

The topic of conversation on our early rides nearly always came around to gears. I'd talked extensively to both John Krug and Andy H about the mechanics of bikes when I was looking to purchase one, and as a result I'd opted for a triple chainset. The discussions would come about usually after we'd been up a steep hill. I'd hit the hill at the bottom in the wrong gear and pretty soon I'd be hardly moving. My legs would feel like they were turning pedals in quick-drying cement. Andy, however, would be riding away from me with a smooth action. Apparently it was all to do with selecting the right gear for the task at hand. We would have the same conversation on each ride, and I'd nod in the appropriate places, but it just wouldn't sink in.

After running one evening I once again asked Andy a gear-related question, and I could sense the frustration in his voice as we'd been over the same thing a hundred times. To be honest with you, even now the physics and mechanics of it all still passes me by, so rather than explain it myself here's Andy H's take on my mental mechanical block.

I remember us talking about gears and discussing the relative merits of double/triple chainsets. I explained that it didn't really matter how many 'gears' a bike had, be it 18 or 27, it was the range and ratio of the gears that really mattered. I also pointed out that not all the chainrings and sprockets on each bike you see are the same. I then tried to explain that gears were one time referred to in inches, and the smaller the inch, the lower the gear. This seemed to puzzle Holgs.

It was apparent from the look on his face that I might just as well have been trying to explain astrophysics to our dog. However I think I did try again but this received a similar blank look followed by a shake of the head. "No sorry Andy, I don't get it, me dad's tried to explain it to me and I didn't understand it then either."

It was then that I realised how 'Father Ted' Crilly felt on that rainy day in the caravan, when he tried to explain 'perspective' to Father Dougal Maguire. Holding a small plastic cow up he says, "OK, one last time. These are small, but the ones out there are far, far away. Small ... far away ..." Dougal looks at him blankly before shaking his head.

And on that note I'm off to join the priesthood.

6

REAL MEN WEAR YELLOW

At around the same time that I was flinging myself to the ground in dramatic fashion at every opportunity I was also undertaking a couple of new endeavours that would have a profound effect on my triathlon career.

Firstly I began my swimming lessons. That first Tuesday night, stood on the poolside with four female classmates, I felt totally out of my depth. Oh well, at least I'd have some male support from Peter the swimming coach, I thought. I was worried that I was about to show myself up and sink whilst they swam like dolphins. A blonde emerged from the water where she had been teaching a group of kids, grabbed a towel and introduced herself as Peta, our coach. I would be the token male then.

The first session was used to gauge what we wanted to get from our coaching. The rest of the class wanted to get fitter and toned. They looked fine to me, and between them they had less body fat than a supermodel. As all eyes turned to me I explained, "I'm a triathlete, and in eight months I need to be able to swim 2.4 miles without drowning. I need to improve my technique."

"Great, I can have some real fun with you," was Peta's hearty response. As a former competitive swimmer she thrived on an enthused and regimented training ethic, which she passed on to her students. Over the coming months I would often say to her after an intense session, "Is this your idea of fun?" She'd laugh and admonish me for having the energy to moan at her when I should have been using it on my swimming.

After the first session, which was just used to see how fit we were, things really took off. There would be a general warm-up followed by individual training. The warm-up was always the worst part for me because it included breaststroke. I couldn't swim breaststroke. I would just sink due to a severe lack of co-ordination in my arms and legs. The frog-like kicking also hurt my dodgy knees. I would complete one length of the pool whilst my classmates would complete four – yes I was, and still am, that bad. However, Peta insisted it would increase my stamina in the water, so through gritted teeth I persevered with it.

It would then be technique drills, distance swimming and timed front crawl laps for the rest of the session. Peta was pleased with my progress, as was I after a few weeks. But my kick was still weak. Apparently this is a common thing amongst triathletes. I was set homework each week. I had to swim 100 metres without using my arms after each of my scheduled swimming sessions. Holding on to a float and kicking my legs from the hip soon improved my kick. I kept hearing Peta's advice: "Imagine you are sat on the sofa kicking a pair of socks off your feet. Legs straight, toes pointing flat and kick, kick, kick!"

In one particular session I was feeling knackered because I'd run eight miles before work and my legs were sore. I explained this to Peta and she said, "Okay, we'll have an easy session tonight." I should have known better.

The session went as follows:

Warm-up: 2 x crawl, 2 x backstroke, 2 x breaststroke (which I managed without drowning).

8 x 25m lengths using just legs, pushing a float (I ached at the end).

4 x 25m lengths crawl holding my breath, with 30 seconds' recovery between each (designed to help my stamina).

2 x 25m lengths concentrating solely on breathing.

2 x 25m lengths of arm technique, concentrating on reaching forward.

Peta then asked what was the shortest distance I'd be expected to swim in a race. Thinking of my upcoming race at Skipton I informed her it would be 400m. Her response floored me. "Right we've got about 10 minutes left, I want you to swim 16 lengths [400m] in under ten minutes." So much for an easy session for my aching legs. Determined, though, I set off through the water like a rocket, trying to remember everything I'd learned and applying it. My mental mantra went something like this: Long body, strong reach, long toes, kick from the hip, don't forget to breathe. Exhausted, my hand touched the end of the pool at the final lap in 9:44. Like a child telling a parent they got an A grade for their homework I announced my time. "Well done. Next week I want you ten seconds quicker. Work hard this week." Peta was either going to kill me or cure me when it came to swimming. She brought the best out of me and although I'm never going to be one of the first out of the water, she gave me the confidence to survive and compete in triathlon.

The second significant endeavour was that I started to write an online blog recounting my day-to-day training and thoughts as I prepared to face the biggest challenge of my life. John Krug had been keeping one detailing his cycling escapades, which I was an avid reader of. I'd never thought that I would have the technical skills to develop my own presence on the Internet until a colleague at work explained how blogs could be set up. Michael Dunne, our information systems librarian, had just set up a blog reporting on library news and events. Sharing an interest in I.T. we got talking about the opportunities blogging offered, he showed me where to download the software and gave me a few lessons on using it. A few days later I set up my blog entitled 'Ironholgs: The Musings of a wannabe Ironman' (http://ironholgs.wordpress.com), and I've been sharing my thoughts ever since.

The blog was a great way of keeping me motivated. I'd post what sessions I'd done and people would comment. There would be the usual banter from my friends experiencing the same training highs and lows. I would use my blog when I was feeling down or injured to look back at how far I'd come in the previous months. It was a visible timeline of my progress as a triathlete and a person.

I couldn't believe how popular it was getting. If I didn't post for a couple of days I would receive emails from the hardcore readership telling me they needed their fix. I also received 'fan mail' from across the globe. An Australian who was training for his first Olympic triathlon described me as inspirational. Similar comments followed from Germany, the United States and from home-grown triathletes all aspiring to the same thing as I was, to complete their first Ironman. I can't begin to tell you how much of a motivation that was. Here I was, your average bloke, just writing about myself, inspiring others to athletic success. I'd never won anything, I wasn't a household personality, I was just trying to prove to myself that I could push my body to the limit and succeed. Knowing that people would be reading about my progress pushed me to train harder. I not only had myself to answer to, I had a whole host of online critics waiting to see how I was progressing. Dave and Viking followed suit and began charting their progress via blogs, and I found inspiration from reading their accounts. My competitive nature kicked in when I read one morning how Dave was making great progress with his swimming, and I forced myself to the pool. If I hadn't have read his blog I wouldn't have bothered because it was cold and wet outside. Knowing how hard Dave was working shamed me into getting off my lazy backside and going swimming. My friends were working hard because of my grand idea, I'd better not slack off.

If you're reading this and thinking you could write your own blog, then go for it. It really is a great way of charting your progress even if no one reads it but you. There are plenty of blogging sites out there. The one I use is Wordpress. It's simple and easy to use (it would have to be, wouldn't it).

My running was progressing like my writing – getting stronger and longer on a weekly basis. Using my blog I could chart my progress as I built up my mileage with my new running technique. I was running pain-free and happy, and my confidence was growing with each session. I would meet Andy two or three times a week in the evenings, and we would run a six-mile loop along the Lune coastal path. Dark night-time skies and a lack of street lights didn't hold us back, as we both ran with head torches. It took a little getting used to with the constant bobbing on the top of my head, but it was much more pleasant than pounding dark streets being blinded by car headlights. The traffic-free path also meant we were not at risk of being knocked down, which is always a bonus.

We both entered half-marathons that were to take place on the same day. Andy's was in Bath and mine was in Liverpool. This encouraged us to increase the mileage each week and by the time our races loomed on the horizon we were ready.

Em had another dress fitting the day before my race so we headed down to Liverpool early. I picked up my rucksack and a carrier bag containing my racing gear. We were running a little late, and bundled them into the boot of the car. After the fitting and an afternoon shopping in the city we were sat around the kitchen table discussing wedding invitations. Excusing myself from the table I left Em and her mum and went to get my race gear ready. Peering into the carrier bag, to my horror I discovered a cat blanket. In my rush to leave that morning I'd picked up the wrong bag. There I was, 60 miles from home, and no running gear. My watch beeped, indicating it was ten at night. An hour home, grab the bag, an hour back, was the thought that came into my head. Unrealistic, considering I would be up at seven ready to run the longest race of my life.

I then remembered that my sweaty gym kit that I'd worn that Friday was in the boot of the car, along with my brand new running shoes that had arrived at work for me that very day. I didn't care that my gear smelt, I'd be amongst several thousand other sweaty bodies. The new running shoes were a factor, though, as usually I'd wear them for a week or two to 'break them in' before running in them. Now I was going to wear them for the first time in an actual race. "Desperate times call for desperate measures," I told my female companions.

The next morning I got to Sefton Park in plenty of time. Walking towards the rendezvous spot that myself, Viking and Min had arranged to meet at, my phone beeped. It was a text from Viking. His travelling companion Min had slept through her alarm and they were running half an hour late. I killed time by people watching. The slim, long-limbed 'proper' runners mingled with the very obvious Scouse fun runners, decked out in their freshly ironed Stevie G shirts and those well known running shoes, the Adidas Samba, more suited to the football field than a half-marathon course.

Eventually my mates turned up and we wandered over to the start area. At 9.15am we stripped off and handed our bags in ready for the 9.30am start. When you're standing on frozen ground wearing a t-shirt and shorts you really don't want to hear the race director announce over the PA that, "The start has been delayed for at least 15 minutes. Try and stay warm people!" Oh bollocks. Trying to keep muscles warm, whilst wearing only shorts and a t-shirt in early March in northern England, is not an easy or pleasant experience I can tell you.

Eventually we were told the start was imminent. I wished Viking and Min well and went to line up in between the 1:30 and 1:45 markers. Why races have these indictors of finishing times is beyond me because the 'fun' runners ignore them. I lost count of how many large and old people I passed in the first mile, walking along red-faced in their various charity t-shirts. It's great that they were doing their bit, but if you know you are going to walk stay at the back out of the way. After avoiding the obstacles I got into my running quite early on and felt comfortable. My times were looking good through eight and nine miles when the new shoes took their toll. My legs ached. They were not used to the way they were being held by the new shoes, and my orthotics were back at home. There was a burning sensation on the ball of my right foot, which experience told me was a blister. A few years ago I had a verruca removed from that exact spot by my doctor with a soldering iron device. The resulting crater acts like a magnet for blisters. After finishing the race in a very pleasing 1:44:33 I limped to the kerb-side and removed my shoe. The blood-stained sock underneath told me everything I needed to know. A blister had formed as the new shoe rubbed my foot; it then burst, removing the raw skin. I wouldn't be able to run for a few days whilst the antiseptic blister plaster I applied worked its magic. Viking and Min finished together in just under two hours whilst my training partner, Andy, finished the Bath half in 1:45:07.

I was really pleased with my progress as I'd only really been running again for about three months. I had just less than six months to go until September 2007 and the Big Woody. Things were slowly but surely falling into place.

A *Runner's World* article that I was reading a few days later informed me that to get fitter, faster and build more endurance you have to constantly challenge your muscles. This fatigue-induced muscle fibre breakdown combined with rest and recovery helps you to grow. Given the amount of muscle fatigue I'd felt over the last two days, I expected to have bloody big leg muscles by the end of the week. I analysed the last few days:

Stage 1: The breakdown. Well that came on Sunday, with a physical jolt. Some would argue that the mental breakdown happened years ago, but my therapist says I'm cured.

Stage 2: The rest. That was Monday, and I wasn't in any condition to do anything other than wince every time I sat down or went up stairs.

Stage 3: The recovery. Tuesday night. Andy and I, both fresh (yeah right) from our weekend races, decided to go out for a very gentle recovery run along the Lune estuary. My hamstrings and quads were protesting but by the end of the run they felt fine and the cycle that I'd read about was complete.

Recovering quickly was what was needed because both Andy and I had entered our first 'proper' road bike triathlon at Skipton in Yorkshire. This took place a couple of weeks after our half-marathon endeavours and marked the opening of the triathlon season. Triathlon season tends to run from late April until late September in this country because of the severe winter weather. It would also be Andy H's birthday that day. Doing a triathlon wouldn't be your average bloke's idea of celebrating, so it's a good job he's not average I suppose.

In the weeks building up to the event we altered our training. Brick sessions, where we would run immediately after getting off the bike, were introduced and played a major part in our preparation. Andy H mapped out a bike course on his computer that was the same length as the race and had almost the same elevation. We would ride this course, enter transition (Andy's garage to be precise) and then run five kilometres along the lane that his house was on. It would turn out to be just the preparation that we needed for race day.

We'd scheduled our final pre-race ride for four days before Skipton. Having an hour to kill after work, I leisurely cycled around the lanes on my way to Andy H's. It was a fairly uneventful ride apart from two ducks playing chicken with me (they must have had an identity crisis). I could see them in the middle of the road as I was descending towards them at about 25mph and they weren't moving. I couldn't slam on the brakes because of the slick wet surface. I gently squeezed the brake levers, stood up on the pedals and pressed my weight down into the bike to try and increase the friction on the road. I then had to shout "Wooaaaahhhh!" at them as loud as I could. What a sight that would have been if anyone was about: a big guy clad in lycra screaming like a banshee at some ducks. Anyway, thankfully with much quacking the two pancake-dodgers flew in opposite directions. It just goes to show that although you may cycle on quiet country roads you have to be prepared for obstacles appearing at any time.

Arriving home after my ride with Andy H, a big bowl of pasta was waiting for me (Em was having one of her unusual domestic goddess days). As I sat down to eat she handed me a parcel. I'd been expecting it and couldn't hide my excitement. "I can tell from the sender's address this is my Pirate racing kit. Dave got his today as well, he emailed me. I'll be racing as a Pirate on Sunday." Em nodded, smiled and wrapped some spaghetti around her fork. She was getting used to my reactions as parcels arrived. They tended to contain triathlon gear and I'd act like a kid at Christmas. Putting the empty plate by the sink I said, "I'll do the pots later, I'm off for a quick shower and then I'll try my kit on." I rushed upstairs clutching the padded envelope tightly.

As I ripped open the envelope my first reaction was *It's very yellow*, as I stared down at the unmistakable tri-top of a Pirate. The empty eyes of the black skull stared back at me, the sockets burning a canary yellow. I examined the lycra top and shorts and felt absurdly proud that I was about to wear the infamous kit for the first time. Pirates were triathletes with a sense of humour, but proper triathletes all the same. Was I good enough to join them? Only time would tell. I pulled on the black shorts. Bloody hell they were short. Next the tri-top was pulled down over my head and shoulders. It was probably the tightest item of clothing I'd ever worn. Standing in front of the full-length mirror in the bedroom in this kit was all the motivation I would ever need to lose weight. It was unforgiving for a bloke of my build. Sucking the gut in, the image looking back at me looked a lot better. *Maybe I could pull this off*, I thought. I'll go see what Em thinks. "Oh my God, you look like Daffyd from *Little Britain*. Andy you are the only gay in the village." This wasn't quite the reaction I was looking for. "Sod off you, I've seen you wearing worse," I said, sticking my tongue out. "Anyway I don't care because real men wear yellow." As I flounced out like a drama queen a mocking shout came through the door: "Nice hot pants gorgeous." Once again I'd not got the last word.

Four days later, my fiancée wasn't in the mood for wise-cracking. Em sat on the edge of the bed. Her eyes were not yet open and she clung to a mug of tea like her life depended on it.

"Why am I up at 5.15am on a Sunday? This just goes to show what a great girlfriend I am." Kissing her forehead I replied, "You're the best girlfriend in the world. Now come on, get a move on. We need to be away by half past." I'd just finished my coffee and porridge, a breakfast that would become a race day staple for me, when my future wife staggered past me into the car with a grunt. "Why can't you find a hobby that allows me to have a lie-in?" By the time we'd reached the end of the street she was, to use the female terminology, "resting her eyes and breathing". To me it looked like she was sleeping and snoring like a motorbike. The motorbike ground to a halt when we pulled into the race venue car park at 7am. "I wasn't asleep," I was indignantly informed.

I'd just closed my car door when I was greeted with a firm handshake from a grinning Dave. His enthusiasm for the coming event was evident in his vice-like grip. Or maybe he was just trying to dislocate my arm? We'd been winding each other up over the last few days as we'd discovered that by pure chance we'd be setting off together in the swim. When we'd entered we'd had to put an estimated swim time. Based on these estimates the organisers then assigned you a starting time. It was the biggest showdown since Foreman faced Ali at the Rumble in the Jungle. Moments later an apprehensive Andy appeared and the usual question was asked: "Why are we doing this?" Guess who got the blame?

I racked the bike, put talc in my socks, laid everything out that I would need and double checked my tyres. Em and Pam were doing their best to calm mine and Andy's nerves. My fears were stupid really. My swimming had been going well and as long as I didn't fall off the bike I'd be alright. Andy just hated swimming with a passion, something that isn't unusual in triathlon. Dave was his usual jovial self. I've always been amazed at how nothing seems to faze the guy. He's one of the most positive people I know (must be all the Guinness he drinks).

The tension built as we queued on the poolside awaiting our numbers to be called. It was a really nice pool, brand new and modern. However I did notice a used floating plaster in my lane. I think there is an ancient law stating that pools can't open unless a manky old Elastoplast is present. I was in the same wave as Dave. He was in the next lane to me and Andy would start 16 minutes later. The water felt nice and warm as I got in with 20 seconds to go. I just had time to check my goggles and we were underway. I started my watch and began swimming...

I have never felt so tight-chested during any exercise. As I approached my third length of 16 I was seriously considering just getting out of the pool. I felt like I was being crushed, as I struggled to breathe.

What the hell is wrong with me? I can't breathe, I can't breathe. Shit. I must be having a panic attack. Where has this come from? Come on Andy you can do this. Concentrate. No, I've got to stop I'm going to die. Concentrate. Just swim and you won't die. Concentrate.

Somehow I managed to keep it together. By the time I'd swum six lengths Dave was onto his eighth. The bilateral breathing had gone and I was just concentrating on breathing every other stroke and getting to the end in one piece. Em and Pam would tell me later that they could see the panic on my face as I thrashed wildly. What a relief it was as I pulled myself out of the pool. Dave, who had miscounted and done 18 lengths, was long gone, as was most of my wave.

I grabbed a pair of old shoes that I'd placed poolside as I didn't fancy doing the 300m run along the concrete path from the pool to transition in bare feet. Out of the water my chest and throat felt fine again. *Weird, had I just had a panic attack?*

I reached my bike, pulled on the yellow Pirate jersey for the first time, and ran the 100m to the bike mounting line. Mounting the bike, I took a left turn up the hill heading out of Skipton towards Clitheroe. I got into the big gears as quickly as I could and just powered along. My breathing seemed to recover and I just went for it. I passed lots of people, and finally caught Dave at the top of one of the hills. He seemed to be going well. We exchanged greetings and then I didn't look back. At the halfway point we turned around and into a headwind for the final five miles. My quads were working overtime, legs turning as fast as I could, edging up the gradual incline all the way back to transition. The road surfaces were some of the worst I've ever ridden on and I had to keep double checking that I hadn't punctured as everything was shaking. I think I must have overtaken about 20 people, and no one came past me. My hard work on the bike in the build-up to the race had paid off.

Returning to transition, I dismounted carefully and ran along to return the bike to its designated place on the rack. I discarded my cycling shoes in favour of my running shoes, removed the mandatory helmet and entered the run course. It was mostly cross-country and consisted of running to the top of a long hill and back down. This would be repeated three times. It wasn't the most inspiring run course but I was pleased that my legs felt okay and I think I had a decent run. I saw both Dave and Andy and shouted encouragement as we passed one another. It was great finishing; no one else was around me and the announcer shouted out my name for the modest crowd to cheer. I punched the air in delight. I'd completed my first 'proper' triathlon. When I'd managed to get my breath back I grabbed a quick drink of water and a banana and walked back out on the course to support Dave and Andy. Posing for photos afterwards we all looked knackered but each of us was glowing with a real sense of achievement. I'd finished in a time of 1:22:02 and received my first ever triathlon medal. It didn't come off my neck all day. I even wore it to the pub later when Andy, Pam, Em and I went for a well earned meal to celebrate Andy's birthday. Dave and I had taken our first racing step on the road to the Big Woody. Andy had just enjoyed his most unusual birthday ever.

I knew as soon as I started swimming that Sunday in Skipton that something was wrong, I just couldn't get my breath. For the rest of the day I think I was high on an intoxicating mix of adrenaline and success. I had been aware of feeling exhausted but I just put it down to my exertions. The exhaustion got steadily worse the next day. As I helped my dad move a fridge I was wheezing and coughing like an 80-year-old with a 30-a-day habit.

I must have been worried as I rang the doctor without any nagging from Em. She would be the first to tell you that like most blokes I have to be almost at death's door before I seek medical help. Luckily my doc is a runner and took things seriously when I told him what had happened. He listened to my chest and hooked me up to a machine that graphed my lung capacity. The results would show that my lungs were working at just under two-thirds capacity. Looking down my throat he discovered that I had a swollen trachea which was restricting my breathing. Apparently this can be made a lot worse with chlorine contact, a possible reason for my panic swimming at Skipton. He prescribed a very strong steroid inhaler to take for two weeks. Never having had one before, I struggled with it. Em, who is asthmatic, had to show me repeatedly how to use it. It frustrated me, and I was not in the best of moods anyway as I wasn't getting my exercise fix. *It's a good job one of us in this relationship has patience*, I thought to myself. The doctor said that hopefully I would be able to train again by the end of the week, but to just see how I felt. I was gutted about missing my swimming lesson and the bright sunshine that week taunted my lack of cycling. For the next couple of days I was shuffling around, wheezing like an old bloke. I couldn't make any phone calls because the heavy breathing would have seen me arrested. If you'd seen me you would never have believed that I'd just completed a triathlon. I was a shadow of my former self, looking grey and worn out. Then the steroid inhaler seemed to help open my windpipe and allowed my lungs to work again. Things started to look up. For once my sensible head was on and I just stayed away from anything to do with training with the view that, long term, it was better to sit this week out rather than sneak back and bugger myself up.

The following Tuesday I managed a 12 minute swim and a seven-mile cycle to work and back. My glorious comeback hadn't gone quite how I'd planned. I had hoped I would be back to normal as I had a series of races coming up including a triathlon in Rossendale and the brutally hilly White Rose Classic cycle race around the Yorkshire moors. All thoughts of racing had been abandoned as I took myself to bed before 6pm. I felt awful, and my inhaler wasn't helping much. I started to worry. *I'm a fit, healthy bloke. This shouldn't be happening to me. What the hell is wrong with me? I can't afford to be ill, I can't afford to miss training. It's got to be a bug. Where's the flu capsules? I'll take them, use the inhaler and get an early night. Yeah I'll just sleep this off and wake up as normal feeling great.*

I'd taken a turn for the worse by Wednesday night. Em wanted me to go to casualty but I rather stubbornly refused on the basis that I was seeing the doc on Friday. I continued getting worse and my doctor immediately sent me to hospital. This was a bit of a shock, as I thought I'd get some antibiotics and be sent on my way. I was admitted and put on oxygen and had what felt like a gallon of blood taken out of me. I then had the full MOT, including an ECG (a test to check my heart was working correctly) and a chest X-ray. I baffled the doctor treating me so she called in a consultant. They scared the shit out of me when they said they were considering a blood clot on my lung (no flying, there goes my honeymoon), but thankfully it wasn't that. They then informed me that my breathing test results were at the opposite end of the scale to asthma and actually mirrored asbestos poisoning. Talk about out of the frying pan and into the fire. That diagnosis was ruled out when I explained that I worked in a fairly modern building. So they still had no ideas and said they'd monitor me over the weekend. Although I wanted to go home I wasn't strong enough to argue.

It was entertaining on the first ward I was placed on. They admitted an alcoholic who kept screaming that she was getting attacked by spiders and white snakes. Apparently she was a regular and the nurses treating her were obviously used to her antics. Witnessing the effect it was having on her was enough to put me off alcohol for quite a while. It was scary.

Once a bed was free I was moved upstairs. The ward I was put on could have passed for an asylum or God's waiting room. I was the youngest on the ward by about fifty years, and the only one that could hold a conversation, albeit a raspy one. The poor guy in the bed next to me was 91, and not of sound mind. He remained wide awake all night having conversations with his mother. His mumblings kept me awake all night too, and the sympathy I'd felt for him earlier faded away rapidly. I'm not a good person when I'm ill and deprived of my sleep as Em and my parents would find out the following day. To say I was irritable would be a gross understatement. It was a shame as I'd been clock-watching until they turned up, longing for some intelligent and friendly conversation. Unfortunately my frustration got the better of me and whilst they sat at my bedside all I did was moan and bitch. "There's nothing wrong with me, this is stupid, as soon as you go I'm going to discharge myself. I'm fine I could go for a run now and I'd be alright." All three of them told me in no uncertain terms that I was not to discharge myself. Em actually called me Andrew. I only ever get my Sunday name when I'm in trouble and it caused me to shut up quickly. I guess it was just the situation of feeling helpless. I wasn't in control and I hated it. I was also worried.

With no conversation from my fellow inmates I managed to read four magazines (*220 Triathlon*, *Cycling Plus*, *Empire* and *Nintendo Magazine*) and *Fatal Voyage* by Kathy Reichs (a very good forensic murder mystery). I was so bored that I also read *Today's Golfer*, despite having no interest in golf. It didn't help my mood, however I did learn that the new Nike driver is the one to buy if you have £300 to spare. I even read all the labels and instructions on my drugs. The one for my inhaler was the funniest thing I've read: "Taking this medicine may cause you to collapse, if you do please contact your doctor."

I was just drifting off to sleep at about one in the morning when all hell broke loose. I was snapped into consciousness and my heart rate soared as the room echoed to the sound of, "For fuck's sake Arthur shoot the fucking German, we've already lost 26 men." I sat bolt upright in bed and there, wild-eyed, staring back at me was the 94-year-old bloke from the bed opposite, his wrinkled bony arse hanging out of his gown, shouting orders to nonexistent soldiers. "Shoot the Nazi fucker!"

Three nurses came running and helped him back to bed and within minutes he was sleeping like a baby. Unfortunately the rest of the ward was wide awake and the man in the bed next to me was crying for his mother, who must have been dead for a good twenty years. *How the hell am I ever going to get better in this place?* I thought to myself.

"Can I go in the TV room for a while whilst he calms down?" I pleaded rather than asked. I was granted a leave of absence by the nurse on grounds of diminished responsibility. I'd had enough. The same nurse woke me some two hours later, and I returned to the now silent ward and a few restful hours' sleep.

After seeing four more doctors on Monday morning they were still none the wiser. The ENT (ear, nose and throat) consultant was trying to figure me out along with the respiratory consultant. They sent me on my way with some more inhalers, and I had to record my lung performance twice a day. On the Friday when I was admitted it had been a lowly 300 but by Tuesday morning it was 680. It was a significant and reassuring improvement, and it gave me hope that I was actually on the mend. My voice continued to fade and recover, and it continued to feel like someone was gripping my throat tightly for a day or two (I'm sure there's plenty out there who would volunteer for that job).

I would be recalled to the hospital six weeks later for full tests on my heart and lungs, and to have my throat investigated. Those tests would prove inconclusive and the doctor decided that I was most likely allergic to chlorine. The chemical had been used in both the Lancaster and Skipton pools in the days before I swam there. Although I'd never had a reaction before he explained, "You may be exposed to the same chemical for thirty years without reaction but the body can develop an allergy at any time. The concentrated level of chlorine may have triggered the initial reaction and then you had a further one when you swam again. Your symptoms do match some recently-published research into this subject." From that moment on, before I even think about swimming in a pool, I have to ask if they use chlorine. Thankfully most pools tend not to use the chemical these days for precisely the reason I need to know. Who'd have thought that open water swimming would turn out to be the safer option for me?

On returning home from hospital I had quite a few get well cards waiting for me. The one from my cousin Mike made me laugh. Inside he'd scrawled "From Ironman to Iron Lung, keep on tri-ing." I wouldn't have expected anything less from the sarcastic sod.

I was signed off work and not allowed to do any training for two weeks. I'd made the mistake of joking to Em one night that whilst she was out at work I'd sneak down to the cellar for a turbo session on the bike. I didn't get the chance to follow through on my joke as Emma confiscated the cellar door keys for my own protection.

The consultant suggested that I should not do anything at full speed until the results from the tests (that would be done in six weeks' time) were known. Unfortunately this ruled out my participation in the White Rose and Rossendale triathlons. As I spent my time convalescing, reading and watching DVDs, reality dawned on me. I'd had the time to do a lot of soul-searching and over dinner one night with Em I said quietly, "I have to consider that if the results aren't good then I'll only be looking at one major event this September and it won't involve yellow lycra."

7

COSTING THE CAT ONE OF HIS LIVES

Unable to train, my thoughts turned to shopping and more specifically rubber outfits. Now before you write to the *Daily Mail* in disgust ("University Employs Rubber-Wearing Weirdo"), I'm talking about a wetsuit.

Much like when I'd chosen a bike I scoured the Internet, reading reviews, forum opinions and looking for a good offer. We'd just paid out for our wedding reception and therefore I needed to find a really good offer. Luckily I found one: a brand new Orca Speedsuit, which was going cheap because there had been two updates to its design. As with running shoes, where a change in colour can mean you can pick up a brand new pair of the old style for a fraction of the price, the same can be applied to wetsuits. Again much like my bike I'd measured myself up so I knew what size I'd need, and if I got it wrong I could always return it in the post. So a couple of clicks later I'd bought my big rubber outfit.

A few days later I was awoken by a loud knock at the front door after I'd unusually slept in until after 11. My wetsuit had arrived, but unlike when my Pirate gear had been delivered I had no one to share the moment with. Em was at work, and the cat was next door keeping our elderly neighbour company. The fact that she supplied him with tuna, a roaring fire and a comfortable armchair had nothing to do with his willingness to pay her a visit. Eager to try the wetsuit on, I unpacked it carefully, then paused and looked at my fingernails. Dave and Min, who already had their wetsuits, had warned me that I'd need to make sure that my fingernails were blunt and short, and therefore unlikely to rip the neoprene rubber. Whilst convalescing I'd received an email from each of them.

Dave's showed him dressed from head to toe in rubber, striking quite the pose (how the hell it got past our good-taste email filters still baffles me). Min had sent two photos in an email entitled, "I don't know which outfit I prefer." In the first photo she was resplendent in tight rubber, in the next she looked stunning in a white cocktail dress that she planned to wear to a friend's wedding. I did what any bloke would do and told her the wetsuit suited her better. Surprisingly she's still speaking to me.

Five minutes later with freshly cut and smoothed nails I was putting my wetsuit on for the first time. There wasn't much give in the rubber and it was a real fight to stretch it into position. Finally both legs were encased in neoprene and I pulled the suit up over my shoulders. As my arms went into the sleeves I realised I'd made a schoolboy error. Looking down at my groin I noticed that there was a zip. Now in any other outfit that would be fine; however I knew that wetsuits zipped up at the back. Thankfully no one was there to witness my mistake. Later that year I witnessed a guy with his on back to front, and I had to tell him as he clearly hadn't realised. A few moments later I was stood correctly dressed in front of the mirror. *You look like Shamu*, I thought, comparing myself to the performing killer whale. As I stood there encased in black with a swirling thigh-length white motif, I could see why the company was called Orca. I didn't really care about aesthetics, though, as this suit would keep me warm and help me stay afloat in open water. It could have been fluorescent pink with yellow daisies on it for all I cared.

Later that evening Em was in the kitchen making tea when I came downstairs wearing my wetsuit and a bright red swimming cap. She was just about to make a comment, probably featuring sarcasm, when Crosby, our cat, waltzed through the back door after an 'all you can eat tuna fest' next door. He took one look at me; his fur stood on end, his ears pinned back and a primeval growl came from his throat. He bolted for the door, leaving one of his nine lives on the kitchen floor in shock. I took that to mean that he didn't approve of my outfit. If cats could type I'm sure he would have been in touch with the *Daily Mail*.

He'd get his revenge a few weeks later. I'd only been training again for a week when my planned bike ride was ruined by our lovable feline. I dragged myself out of bed at 6.15 with plans to do a very easy 20 miles before work. As I got my bike out, Crosby tried to escape onto the front street. Ever fearful for his safety on the busy road, I managed to shoe him back into the yard and quickly closed him in. Seconds later I was stood outside the front of the house putting my helmet on. I stopped dead in my tracks at the sight of the bloody cat waltzing down the street towards me, looking ever so pleased with himself. He must have legged it up the back wall and emerged about three doors up. It's a busy road and he knows he's not allowed out the front. Cats, however, are not big on following rules, especially not human-made ones. I attempted to catch him and get him back in. I wasn't going to let my naughty cat be the boss of me. I should have known better as he spent the next twenty minutes playing a great game of hide and seek with me. I of course couldn't fit under the parked cars, which were his preferred refuge. One of the neighbours must have thought I'd finally lost it as I was sprawled on the floor, dressed in figure-hugging lycra playing good cop, "Come on then sunshine, who's a good boy then?"

"Morning Andy," she said as she got in her car, not batting an eyelid.

Admitting defeat, I retreated into the house and woke Em up. Annoyed and frustrated, I instructed her to come and get *her* cat. We looked out the front door just in time to glimpse the fugitive making his bid for freedom at the top of the street. Em went back inside the house and reappeared with a can of tuna and a fork. I looked on in complete bemusement as she walked up the street tapping the tin. She got Crosby's attention and he stopped dead. The little bugger walked obediently next to her all the way back down the street and straight into the house. By this time almost forty minutes had passed and I only had time to ride to work. I emailed Em later that day and said, "If the cat thinks he's getting any knee time from me tonight, he's sadly mistaken." Of course, being the sucker I am, I resisted for about a minute and the pair of us were best of friends again, cuddled up on the sofa that night, my aborted ride forgiven. They say never work with animals or children. Well I don't have any kids yet but they're certainly right with the first one.

Three weeks after coming out of hospital I finally plucked up the courage to do some exercise. I had been following the doctor's instructions religiously: I wasn't getting out of breath, I took both inhalers twice a day and recorded my peak flow (another name for lung capacity) immediately after getting out of bed and last thing at night. When I was admitted to hospital my readings had been extremely low for a man of my age, regardless of fitness. Two weeks after coming home my readings were higher than average, which is what I would have expected. Aerobic training such as running or cycling increases a person's lung capacity. Although the improved readings helped, I was still worried that I might become breathless again. So when I stepped out of the door at my future mother-in-law, Maggie's, it was with trepidation.

I needn't have worried. Although my legs felt stiff as I ran along Crosby Beach, near Liverpool, watching the tide envelop Antony Gormley's Iron Men sculptures, my lungs felt strong. I was so relieved. The wind was powerful, lashing the waves against the sculptures in the sand, but I loved every minute I was there. Having grown up on an island I've always found something almost mystical about running to the sound of crashing waves, matching my footfalls to the rhythm of the advancing sea. I felt good and ran further than I'd intended, covering five miles instead of three. On my return a worried Em glanced up from her breakfast. "Everything okay? You were longer than I thought you would be." I beamed at her, and the relief was obvious in my voice and in my smile. "Yep, I just felt alive again. I had to rein myself in. I could have kept going and going." My aching legs reminded me the next morning that I'd done more than enough.

I rested on the Monday, to give my legs time to recover, and

I'd also promised Em that we'd finish off making our wedding invitations. So we spent the evening playing with card, stencils and glitter. I should have been a *Blue Peter* presenter. As I slaved over a hot lightbox (used to emboss card) Em sat at the other side of the kitchen table writing out envelopes. There were over one hundred invitations to write and send. We fell into bed just after one in the morning. I was knackered. Turning to kiss my fiancée good night I remarked honestly, "You know what, planning a wedding is as tiring as training for an Ironman."

The following morning I was out of the door at 6.30am for a 20-mile comeback ride before work. Completing the first five miles took me past a significant milestone. The evidence was there in front of my eyes on my bike computer screen. I had ridden one thousand miles since buying my bike. It felt so good, momentous even. It was the motivational shot in the arm that I needed to fuel my comeback, and I wondered if I could reach the second thousand in less time. Feeling energised and really happy to be out again, the time seemed to fly by; they say it does when you're having fun. It certainly didn't feel like I'd lost what limited cycling ability I had whilst enduring the forced layoff. My legs were spinning beautifully, the sun was coming up over the fells, and, best of all, my chest was moving up and down in perfect rhythmic fashion. Having worked my way along the back roads I descended into Galgate, the little village at the southern approach to Lancaster. I slowed down as I approached the traffic lights at the junction with the A6, intending to turn right before the lights. Doing so would take me down a side street that would lead up the quiet way onto the university campus. Having just double checked that nothing was coming from the A6, I was turning right when THUMP. Out of nowhere a car came from behind me. It cut across me into the turn, catching my leg and wheel and flipping me over onto my left side. As I hit the floor elbow first I just caught a glimpse of a large maroon-coloured car as it sped off leaving me lying in the middle of the road. I picked myself up gingerly. I was more in shock than I was physically injured. As the day wore on the stiffness set in and the bruising came out, especially on my elbow and hip. It was hard work cycling home that night. A good soak in the bath eased the aches. Em was livid and wanted to call the police, but there was nothing they could have done as I wouldn't have been able to tell them the make or registration of the car. Even now it amazes me how the car didn't see me. I had a fluorescent yellow jacket on, I'd been signalling with my arm, and, alarmingly, it had come on the inside of me. The driver may not have felt the car clip me but I would have thought he would have noticed a six foot bloke sprawled on the floor lying in his wake. Bastard!

I believe the phrase is, "If you fall off the horse you have to get straight back on." The swimming pool was my horse and I needed to saddle up. Although I wasn't feeling entirely fit after my hit-and-run incident the day before, I'd been psyching myself up all week to get back in the pool. Plain and simple I was shitting myself.

What if the breathlessness comes back? The last thing I want to do is end up back in hospital, but I need to do this. I have no choice. I have to train in order to give myself a chance at completing a 2.4-mile swim in less than three months. Come on, you asked at reception and they said there was no chlorine in the pool. Oh hell, what if a chlorine allergy isn't my Achilles heel? Could there be another chemical lurking, waiting to destroy me?

I was sweating as I got changed. The fear almost got the better of me. Half naked, I took a moment, went to the sink and splashed cold water on my face. I looked at the worried face staring back at me from the mirror above the basin and I mouthed silently, "Just bloody do it."

Moments later I was waist deep in the pool, staring towards the other end; it seemed to go on forever. I pulled the goggles down over my eyes, inhaled deeply, and pushed off into the unknown. Six hundred metres later I stopped. Not because I was ill, or struggling, just simply because I'd finished. I was so relieved. My relief was communicated by email to everyone I could think of when I got back to work. There had been talk on the forum from the gang about it not being the end of the world if I had to miss the Big

Woody, and that there would be other opportunities. Now Min, Dave and Lucy were telling me it was brilliant I was back. Viking added, "Dodgy breathing, throwing yourself under cars; as things come in threes, apparently, make sure you wrap yourself in cotton wool. If you can't make it to the Woody because you're dead I'm coming round with a voodoo priest to bring you back to life. Then I'll kill you myself!" With friends like Viking, who needs enemies?

A couple more lunchtime sessions at the end of that week gave me the confidence to go to a different session. This was no ordinary swimming, it was open-water swimming. Every other Monday, Preston Tri Club meet up at the lake near Carnforth for an hour's training session. I'd found out about this on the *Tri-Talk* forum after I had posted asking if there was anywhere close to home that offered this kind of swimming. Viking had yet to dip his toe in open water but both Dave and Min were becoming quite the aficionados. Dave was swimming in Salford Quays at an organised session and Min was a regular in the River Dee. As keen as I was, I didn't fancy a 100-mile round trip for an hour's swim at the most. So I was delighted when, as a consequence of my posting, the organiser of the session, Andrew McCracken, sent me an email inviting me to come along.

The evening didn't get off to the best of starts as I'd gone to the wrong lake. I'd gone to Pine Lake when the session was actually happening next door in the lake at the leisure village. As I got out of the car I knew I was in the right place, this time. I was greeted by the sight of thirty-odd rubber-clad, serious-looking athletes. I've seen more body fat on Posh Spice after a detox.

I was totally intimidated by the beefcakes on display. There were six pack abdominals as far as the eye could see. Peter Andre in his prime would have put a shirt on. Sucking my stomach in whilst I put on my Orca, I double checked that I had it on the correct way round. The guy getting changed next to me pulled his wetsuit out of an Ironman Lanzarote rucksack. *Wow, this guy is the real deal,* I thought. The bag had caught my attention, causing me to glance sideways, my eyes lingering longer than a red-blooded male should when standing next to another in swim trunks. Freud would have a field day analysing that scene. Standing six foot tall, his goateed face complemented the blue tinted Oakley's that hid his eyes, his Iron Maiden-length hair falling over chiselled shoulders. He looked like the archetypal metal god, a primeval Ironman. And that was before I spotted the M-dot tattoo. This is the badge of honour that some Ironmen have inked on to their bodies to remind them of the pain and the glory. "Alright, I'm Chris. Not seen you here before." Christ on a bike, the Norse god of thunder was talking to me, the pretend triathlete. We got chatting, and that was how I met Chris Wild, multiple Ironman veteran. There followed a quick safety briefing. Andrew McCracken, the organiser, looked the polar opposite of Chris Wild. He was equally impressively muscled, yet he modelled sensible hair and a clean-shaven face. He could have been straight out of a Calvin Klein advert. Sounding very much like a schoolteacher instructing a class, Andrew explained the triangular course, water quality, temperature and how to signal the safety canoes. And then we were off.

It was bitterly cold to start with, and my body took a few minutes to adjust. I was grateful for my natural insulation and that of the wetsuit. It felt weird and claustrophobic being in a pack of people. I had never really experienced that before because my only other open-water experience had been at Cockerham, where I started at the back and stayed there. The fast swimmers just went away from me like they were on jet skis. I couldn't help but be impressed. There was a group of four of us all swimming together and it felt really good. Water visibility was poor but I did see a couple of big fish when I looked underwater; thankfully they didn't bite.

I struggled a bit on my third and final lap, having zigzagged my way around most of the course. That first evening I was the last one out of the water by a good fifty metres. When I eventually emerged I felt great. There was no dizziness or sickness, however my neck was killing me. It was then that I realised that I'd been a plonker. I had forgotten to put lubricant on my neck; consequently the rubber and the Velcro fastener had been constantly chafing my skin. Whilst swimming, the cold had stopped me from feeling it, but on dry land it felt like I was on fire.

For my first open-water swim I managed 1,700m without any rest in 41:43. I thought to myself, *It's slow but if I can keep that up or improve slightly with a straighter swim then come the Woody I'll be getting out of the water in a) one piece and b) hopefully under 1 hour and 45 minutes, thus setting me up for a good crack at the bike.*

Most of the swimmers were stood on the bank fully dressed, dry and having a brew when I emerged. Chris and a guy called Richard said well done which made me feel great. Richard Mason, although visibly older, made Chris look like a stick insect; the veins on his arm muscles looked like the London Underground map. He was also a veteran of Ironman, and a bloody quick one at that. He wasn't as chatty as Chris but he was still friendly. Andrew McCracken came over to introduce himself and asked about what I was doing in triathlon. He too, like Richard, was at the top of his game having just returned from the half-Ironman World Championships in Florida. The three of them were in a different league yet that night they talked to me like I belonged. I didn't know it then but the three of them would play a significant part in my development as a triathlete.

I arrived home happy with my achievement and banging on about how great everyone had been. Em listened faithfully. She was alarmed, however, when I showed her my wounds. The fact that my neck looked like someone had tried to decapitate me did not sit lightly. "That looks really painful. Will it happen every time you wear your wetsuit?" she said, and then before I had time to respond, "Will you be able to get a shirt and tie on for the wedding?" Laughing, I assured her that I would and explained that if I put lubricant on my neck it shouldn't happen again. She seemed to buy it but insisted I treat the wounds. Covering my neck in very strong antibiotic cream, I winced as my skin stung. My male capacity for pain amused Em. The next morning I had to travel to work in the car and abandon my scheduled ride because there was no way I could put my rucksack on without aggravating my neck. But the worst thing was that it looked like my neck was covered in love bites. That kind of thing looks awful when you are 15, and positively degrading when you are in your thirties. In a pre-emptive strike I showed my colleagues my neck and explained the circumstances of acquiring the unsightly wounds.

"Typical bloke, always jumping in without proper lubrication," was the response from Julie that had us all laughing. Thinking that I'd got away lightly, I discovered a money off coupon for KY Jelly sitting on my keyboard the next morning.

8

A TALE OF TWO TRIATHLONS

This sport of triathlon really gives you the full emotional spectrum; from frustration (punctures) and pain (high levels of training), to sheer elation (when it all goes well and you perform much better than you expected). Thankfully I was at the elation end of the scale at the Chester Deva Olympic Triathlon.

The race wasn't until Sunday but I had been unbearable since the Thursday, which probably explains why Em flew to France for a week (actually it was a pre-arranged trip with her mum). I didn't mean to be miserable but I was just withdrawing and trying to psyche myself up for the race. June 2007 had arrived and that meant one thing: the Chester Deva Olympic Triathlon. This would be a big step up from my previous effort at Skipton. In Cheshire I would face a 1,500m river swim, a 40km bike ride and a 10km run. The thought of 1,500m in the River Dee terrified me. It was irrational really, as I had proved that I could swim that distance the week before in my open water training session in the lake. I think my nerves stemmed from the talk on some of the triathlon websites about how fast the river was flowing after all the rain that week in the neighbouring Welsh mountains of Snowdonia. Other influencing factors were the cold, and plainly just the fact that I'm not the strongest swimmer in the world and here I was planning on getting into a fast-flowing, grimy river. My mood, however, was positively tranquil compared to poor Viking. This would be our first and only race before the Woody as a foursome. Viking, Min and Dave had agreed to meet on the Saturday afternoon before the race so that they could register. Because of geographical reasons I would register early on the morning of the race. Sat there on the riverside eating ice cream, debris from up river came shooting past them like powerboats. The usual banter from Viking dried up. "I'll never forget the look on his face. I thought he was going to cry," Dave would later tell me. To fully understand what was going through Viking's mind we need to go back seven days to when he tried open-water swimming for the first time:

"To say it didn't go well doesn't really do the situation justice. Utter shite, complete bollocks, complete nightmare: that comes close to describing my first open-water swim. It was very cold, I couldn't see anything, and I struggled to breathe. I hated every minute of it and didn't stay in for very long before giving up. As a result I was very pissed off with it all that night. I couldn't sleep until 2am as I tried to suss out where I went wrong, what I could have done better, and what to do next. I racked my brain cell and tried to see where I would go from here."

We had spent all week emailing and texting one another. The three of us had been trying to convince Viking that he could do it. We all recognised his fear, we'd all been there. Swimming in open water is not normal. Your body's fight or flight mechanism kicks in, and when it does, trust me, you have to fight the urge to take flight. We were a team, the four musketeers, one for all and all for one. For once no one took the piss, which as you will have gathered from my ramblings was a rarity. This whole adventure needed Viking on board, and he had to overcome his fear or he wouldn't even be at the Woody. Having just come out of hospital and overcome the possibility that I'd miss the Woody myself, I couldn't bear to think that one of my friends would now suffer that fate.

What would a triathlon be without an alarm call at stupid o'clock? On this occasion it was 5.30am. A bowl of porridge later I was on my way. I psyched myself up in the car listening to Bon Jovi. 'Living on a Prayer' before 6am would be enough to wake anyone up and get them ready for anything. By the time the CD had finished I'd convinced myself that I could do it. After all it was the same as Skipton, only longer and with a fast-flowing river.

I met Dave at his place and followed him in to Chester. Without his help I would have got lost, and you'd probably still be able to find me driving round the confusing traffic system of the ancient walled city. Dave was already registered, so he showed me where to go. He guarded my bike and gear whilst I got marked up and collected my numbers. I spent the next ten minutes sorting out transition, carefully laying out gear in the order that I would need it: bike gear was laid out near the front wheel of the bike and running gear at the rear wheel. My helmet, gloves and sunglasses rested on my tri-bars. Satisfied that I was prepared, I just had time to wish Min and Dave luck, as they were both in waves before me. Viking appeared and I chatted to him whilst he set his gear up in transition. He was still scared but his attitude was now: "I'm just going to do it. If I have to stop I will but at least I'll know I tried." We were interrupted by an announcement giving a warning that my wave was to set off in ten minutes. I shook hands with Viking and we wished each other luck. He'd be setting off in the wave after me. "Don't you bloody overtake me," I warned him. That seemed to bring some colour back to his grey face. I returned his smile and turned away, leaving my mate to contemplate the challenge ahead.

The walk down to the river from transition was awful. The coarse gravel made every step uncomfortable on my bare feet, and the thought of running back up it after exiting the river didn't fill me with joy. Rather amusingly, right by the start was a sign proclaiming "Dangerous River. No swimming!" The irony of several hundred people ignoring it and doing the exact opposite within its shadow was not lost on me. I smiled to myself. With five minutes till the off I plunged into the dark muddy water. Shit it was bloody cold. After a couple of minutes of swimming and treading water I'd warmed up a little. I started at the back of my wave and was a good five or ten metres behind the start line when the gun went off. The river suddenly became a maelstrom of churning foam; this was the infamous washing machine effect, as hundreds of arms swirl the water around. Mass start swims in triathlons have long since been described in this way. Witnessing it for the first time,

I was glad I'd hung back, it looked savage. The time I would lose letting the bulk of the swimmers go was worth it in my mind. I didn't have the confidence yet to put myself in the spin cycle, and besides Em would kill me if I lost my front teeth before the wedding.

So I had a smooth swim and didn't get hit or kicked at all. I had decided to just swim relaxed and not look at my watch until I got out of the water. This was me racing me; for once I wasn't bothered that people were swimming away from me. I was just content to be competing again. It worked, I never once felt out of breath and was so relaxed; I loved it. Although I'd never swam against a strong current before it didn't seem too bad. As I rounded the halfway buoy I turned to swim back downstream. The current was with me and it felt great. I sped through the last 800m. It actually felt like I was a natural swimmer and I caught people and passed them all the way along the course.

Remembering to kick hard in the last 100m to wake the legs up, I covered the remaining distance in a heartbeat. Suddenly hands appeared to pull me up onto the pontoon and my swim was over. Every step back up to transition hurt more than it did on the way down. Having spent over half an hour in the water, the soles of my feet had softened and now I was paying the price. The wet grass of the transition field felt like crushed velvet in comparison. Running up the hill, I tore my goggles off and stripped my wetsuit to my waist. I reached my bike, peeled the wet rubber from my legs and put my helmet on. My cycling shoes and number belt quickly followed. I was out of transition in less than 40 minutes on my watch. Elation washed over me. *Wow this is superb!* Before the race I had expected be looking at about 45 minutes for the swim alone.

Feeling confident, I mounted my bike. A few sharp turns later and I got into my rhythm as the course straightened out before me. Thankfully, the cold water hadn't deadened my leg muscles too much. I changed into the big ring and worked my legs, passing loads of people as I powered along. I couldn't help but laugh to myself as I overtook people on state-of-the-art carbon dream machines from Planet X, Quintana Roo and Cervelo. I knew from reading the magazines that these bikes cost upwards of two grand. I actually laughed out loud at the next thought that entered my head as I looked at them: *£260 quid from eBay and it's going faster than yours.*

In fairness some speed merchants came past me later on. They were obviously the faster athletes from the next wave; thankfully not Viking though. I saw fellow Pirate, Wicket, a couple of times as the course doubled back on itself and a mutual nod of respect passed between us. I was also serenaded by plenty of shouts of "Go Pirate" from spectators and officials alike. Racing in the yellow does have its advantages.

As I reached 20 miles the heavens opened in spectacular fashion. The road became very slippery and as I rounded the final corner I could feel my back wheel sliding; thankfully I remained upright. Hitting the dismount line, I ran back to rack my bike. It was like monsoon season had started in Cheshire. I had to pour water out of my running shoes before I could put them on. I slid my feet in and felt them squelch as I started my plod around the 10k run course.

There were a couple of nasty, sharp hills on the run and because of the rain, water was cascading down them like a waterfall. There was a gravel trail section in the park alongside the river, which quickly became transformed into a swamp. At one stage I was ankle-deep in water. I thought to myself, *Isn't there only supposed to be one open-water swim in this race?* I saw Dave and Min who were both on their second laps and high fived both of them. They were running really well and despite the awful conditions I could tell from their gleeful faces that the pair of them were loving every minute of it. Coming off the bike my legs had felt heavy, especially my left hamstring, so I deliberately ran conservatively on the first lap just to be safe. Convinced that my leg would hold up, I picked up the pace a bit on the second lap and was running quite strongly. With about 2km to go I looked at my watch and realised that if I put my foot down I'd break 2 hours 40 minutes. With this new goal I really sped up and passed about a dozen people on the final stretch. I even managed to sprint across the finish line to finish my first Olympic Triathlon in 2:39:39.

Once I found the energy to crack a smile, I couldn't stop for the rest of the day. I was over the moon with my performance. I thought beforehand that given my swimming weaknesses I might just dip under three hours if I was lucky, but realistically I believed my time would be 3:15. I had smashed that and I'd never been so proud of any athletic performance in my life. Four weeks earlier I had been lying in a hospital bed struggling to breathe. I'd missed two vital weeks of training, and only lightly trained in the build-up to this race. It was nothing short of a miraculous recovery. In my transition bag I had both of my inhalers. After this day I never had cause to use them again. In my mind I'd drawn a line under the whole sorry episode and had moved past the obstacle in the way of my athletic goal. I'd just completed the distance that was deemed the standard to compete in the Olympic Games. This, therefore, was the point at which I began to seriously consider myself a triathlete and not just a runner with tendencies.

Dave and Min were waiting for me when I crossed the line. Both had raced superbly, like me completing the distance for the first time. The satisfaction and pride radiated from them in a warm glow. Min had just completed her first triathlon. She would share that achievement with Viking. As he crossed the line the PA system was booming out the Stone Roses; he was more excited about that than he was finishing. He would later reveal that he'd panicked in the swim and decided he wouldn't be finishing the race. He had been cold and terrified when a light bulb went on in his head. He realised that he only had about 400m to go, and that he was over the worst of it. He felt jubilant getting out of the swim, almost invincible. He would soon be brought back down to earth in transition. As he stripped his wetsuit off it got stuck on his left arm. No amount of tugging would shift it. It was at that point that he remembered he'd put his watch on over the sleeve and that was pinning his suit to his skin. He had to put the wetsuit back on to get the watch off. Of course I didn't laugh when I found out.

After hot coffee, the source of the warmth slowly creeping back into our aching limbs, the four of us stood, spent, reflecting on the race. In a rare moment of sentimentality, Viking said, "I can't thank you all enough for your support, especially this last six days, without which I would never have finished today. You're all stars. If I hadn't completed it today then the Big Woody was history. It means a lot to have your support and for me to live to fight another day." As she put a proud arm around her mate, Min summed the day up perfectly: "I think we found who we really were out there today; when it got hard we dug in, when the monsoon came, we ignored it. We all overcame fear today in our own way and the best thing is guys, we are one step closer." She was right, as women usually are. The three of them had successfully completed the longest race they would face before the Woody. I on the other hand would be facing a much longer challenge in 13 days. They called it The Steelman.

With my eye on my next race I eased back in to training two days later with a gentle four-mile run around campus in 30 minutes. There were no negative effects from my weekend's exertions. I could have kept going but I was conscious not to do too much as I had swim training that night.

When I turned up for swimming I made the mistake of thanking my swimming coach for all her help and explained how I'd improved enough to have a great swim at Chester. Peta's response was, "Brilliant, but if you can swim that fast in the river you should be able to swim a lot faster in the pool. I reckon you can do it in 30 minutes."

I laughed and protested that I was knackered, that there'd been a current et cetera … Her response was to go and get a stopwatch. My protests falling on deaf ears, off I set, powering through the water with Peta running up and down the poolside shouting at me: "Kick", "Keep your head up", "Arms higher", "Come on pick the pace up".

Bloody hell I felt vitalised, but at the same time quite knackered. In the last couple of lengths I dispensed with bilateral breathing and just powered as hard as I could with my arms, breathing on every left stroke. Reaching desperately for the side I couldn't speak and I could hardly lift my head. I felt dizzy and my heart was beating like a drum. I'd gone through my aerobic threshold and then kept going. I collapsed under the water, floating like a jellyfish *There is no way I can swim that flat out in a triathlon*, I thought. I wouldn't be able to lift myself onto the bike, let alone turn my legs. Resurfacing, I glanced at my watch and smashed the water in triumph. 29:46. I had done it. Peta was extremely pleased with me and told me to keep up the good work over the summer. This would be the last session until October and the new university term. "You've come a long way Andy. You've got the tools, and hopefully the confidence you need. Good luck for Ironman." Turning to the others she said, "Let's finish with some fun." We then got out the inflatable rafts and played at being pirates, not the yellow-clad variety but five adults trying to knock each other into the water. It was great fun and the best triathlon training I'd ever done.

A few days after Chester I was in my cellar doing some routine maintenance on the bike when I realised I hadn't looked at the data on my bike computer. Usually I'm a stickler for statistics on my training rides and runs. Before jumping in the shower I analyse what my various recording devices are telling me. After driving home from the race I was still frozen. The bike had been put in the cellar and I only had thoughts of a warm bath. Statistics didn't matter, as I already knew my overall time. What my computer was telling me shocked me. My average speed over the 40km course had been 20.01mph. That was the fastest average speed I'd ever recorded whilst on the bike. That statistic was a hell of a boost. It made it feel like all those early morning winter rides when I'd forced myself to get out of bed had been worth it. With about two months to go until the Woody, everything was coming together, and I was seeing visible results.

On the Friday night after Chester I met Lesley to go out for a run. Lesley was one of Em's bridesmaids who we had both known for several years. A fellow librarian, Lesley used to share a desk with me. However, working with me was understandably too much to take for the quiet mother of two and she left to take up a post at the University of Cumbria where she ended up sharing an office with Em. Lesley had begun running several years earlier and I'd offered her advice and shown her new routes as she slowly fell in love with running. Busy family lives meant we were only occasional training partners. I'd always get a tough run when we went out, owing to the fact that Lesley was (and still is) the most competitive person I've ever met. She has to win. When training together if I'm a stride ahead, she'll work that much harder to make sure she quickly matches me or inches in front. I'm convinced that if she'd discovered running at an early age rather than in her thirties, when her time is devoted to her family, she could have been a world-class runner. She has the perfect distance runner's build: tall, slim and graceful on her feet. Combine this with her will to win and stubbornness and she's the complete package. Her one flaw is her lack of confidence. She doesn't quite believe that she is capable of running as fast as I know she can. Once Lesley finally gets that belief, she'll have to give me a head start on our runs because she'll leave me for dead.

That Friday the monsoon weather had moved up the coast from Chester and during the hour that we were out it felt like we were running along with a fire hose pointing in our faces from close range. We talked about Chester, the wedding, and the fact that Em's other bridesmaid, Sarah, was also a runner. "You should get Lee to take up running then the whole wedding party would be made up of runners," she said, knowing fine well there was no chance of my best man joining us at any point. "I'll text him later and suggest it." If I shared Lee's later response with you this book would be banned or have the equivalent of an eighteen certificate. To paraphrase, he said: "Thank you so much for your kind suggestion but I'll have to regrettably decline your invitation."

When I rose at 5am the next morning, the weather had taken a turn for the worse. Rain was hammering down and gale force winds were bending trees. This was the last week of June for Christ's sake! The reason for my being up so early was a little complicated and involved a family city break in Cologne. The normal person's solution would have been for the four of us (me, Em and my parents) to travel in one car; however my solution meant that I could have fun on my bike.

If you've read this far you'll know that normal is not a word that applies to my way of thinking. I decided that I'd drive to Liverpool, leave the car and the keys at Maggie's house and then cycle back to Lancaster as a good training ride and pick the car up on the way home from Germany. The early morning start was designed to get me on the bike and out of the city before the roads got busy.

I set off in the rain and headed up from Liverpool through Formby to Southport. I was making decent time despite the driving wind and rain. My progress slowed considerably when I arrived on Southport seafront. The best way to describe it is 'challenging'. My knuckles froze up in the glacial rain as they gripped the handlebars, trying to steady the bike. For once I was grateful of my extra bodyweight as it acted as an anchor, keeping me upright as the Irish Sea winds tried to sweep me away. If you've ever seen the film *Twister*, there is a scene where a helpless mooing cow goes flying across the road in front of Bill Paxton and Helen Hunt. I fully expected to see livestock whizzing past my head at any moment. Funnily enough I didn't see another living soul as I cycled along the seafront. I guess it wasn't the place to be at 7am in a tornado.

I turned inland and found some shelter, which was a huge relief. There is something raw and masochistic about cycling in bad weather. Wind reminds you that however fit and strong you are, it's nothing in comparison to the power of Mother Nature. And quite frankly at that point I'd had enough of planet Earth's matriarch kicking my arse. I just wanted to get home. The roads were deserted as I headed north towards Preston; my early morning gamble had paid off. I cycled most of the way on the cycle paths. The route forms part of the national cycling network, a series of connecting cycle paths that cover the whole country. These are not always traffic-free but nevertheless they offer some great training routes.

I arrived in Preston at about 9am and lost all my speed as I went straight through the city centre past the sleeping university halls of residence and up towards the A6. This part of the ride was spoiled by just too many junctions and traffic lights, which all seemed to take great delight in turning red as I approached. It gave me plenty of practice at unclipping, I suppose. Leaving the city, I was once again alone on the country lanes. The hill just on the way into Garstang has to have the worst road surface I've ever cycled on. My body trembled from the road vibration. It felt like my bike saddle had come from Ann Summers.

I turned my legs a little faster as I passed the university, just in case a colleague saw me. I had to be seen to be making an effort didn't I? I was almost home and I'd found my second wind. I came through the door, cold and dripping wet. I wrung my overshoes out and poured water out of my cycling shoes. It had been a fun ride and I loved every rain-soaked and windswept minute of it. More importantly it had served its purpose as a pace ride for the following week's Steelman. I'd covered 55 miles in three hours at an average speed of 17.4mph. It was slower than Chester but I would have expected that; after all it hadn't been a race, more a lesson in survival.

The break in Germany was just what I needed. Feeling relaxed and renewed, it was just what the doctor ordered after the physical exertion I'd been through recently. It also stopped me from worrying about the Steelman. The half-Ironman race would take place near Catterick in the North East, and it would be the longest and hardest race I'd ever attempted. A 2,000m swim would be followed by a 56-mile bike ride and the whole thing would be finished off with an off-road half-marathon run. In Germany I switched off, and even on the Friday night at home before the race I felt totally at ease. I would be on my own; no other Pirates or family would be there to cheer me on. It would be a lesson in solitary confinement, a valuable exercise in keeping going when there is no one there to offer a confidence boost.

I was on the road at 6am for the drive across the country to Ellerton near Catterick. Crossing the top of the A66 near Stainmore, I was greeted by persistent rain and thick fog. Was this a sign of things to come? The roads had been quiet, resulting in me arriving at the race venue before registration actually opened. Eventually I got my number, swim cap and race t-shirt. This was a new concept, t-shirts before the race? At road races you only received these after you'd successfully crossed the finish line. I remember standing there thinking, *Well I've got the t-shirt, I could just go home now and pretend I did the race. No one would know any different*. I spent the next hour people-watching. I'd set up transition and was now sat in the car looking at all the bikes on display. Much like Chester there were some real dream machines there. I had serious bike envy. Some people were changing their disc wheels for HED or ZIPP deep rims given the severe wind conditions. They were replacing wheels that cost over a thousand pounds with another set of wheels that cost the same amount again. The wheels they were discarding cost four times as much as my complete bike. I remember thinking it must be nice to have that sort of money, and if I did would I spend it on wheels? I concluded I probably would. However, as Andy H is so fond of telling me, "A bike will only go as fast as you pedal it."

As I peeled myself into my wetsuit we were given a ten minute warning. Transition was less than ten metres from the water's edge so thankfully, unlike Chester, there was no razor-sharp gravel path to negotiate. The lake, we had been informed, was 14 degrees. I think the organiser had exaggerated. Treading water, my feet felt like ice. It was a deep-water start and there were about 115 heads bobbing up and down on the surface. Mindful of what I'd witnessed at Chester, I started at the back as I didn't want to get battered. A claxon pierced the tranquillity of the lake, causing a flock of ducks to take flight. Mirroring the birds, several hundred triathletes took flight, surging forward on the first of two laps of the lake. I had just settled into my stroke when some big bloke swam right across the front of me in the first 100m. BANG – he kicked me on my left hand and I was in agony. The force of the impact had been so great that I really thought he'd broken my fingers, as every time I placed my hand into the water pain shot through my arm. This lasted into the second lap and then thankfully it eased off. I had been swimming along wondering how the hell I'd get my wetsuit off or grip the handlebars of my bike. Talking to my dad later on the phone he wondered how I would have driven home. I'd clearly been focused, only worried about my race and nothing else.

The strong winds whipped up the water, resulting in big waves. Trying to swim through them made it the toughest swim I'd ever done. Somehow I managed to lose my left earplug, a consequence of an ill-fitting swim cap, and water was sloshing around inside my head. I made a mental note to wear my own cap underneath the official one at the Woody. Mine was made of thicker latex and as such didn't ride up over my ears. Wearing two caps would also keep me warmer. The lost earplug meant that as I exited the water my sense of balance deserted me. As at Cockerham I fell backwards into the water and then couldn't straighten up. I wobbled all the way to my bike, and then fell over. A member of the emergency medical team ran over to check if I was okay. I assured him that it was purely a balance problem and that I'd be alright in a few minutes. Looking around I noticed that my bike was one of only about a dozen left in transition. I hoped that I would make up some ground on the bike and the run. I had to sit down to take off my wetsuit and felt really dizzy as I got on my bike. Thankfully that soon wore off. I was away on my bike in a total time of 52 minutes.

The bike course consisted of two laps along fairly quiet roads; no real testing hills, but the course was undulating. The wind was monstrously fierce and I just couldn't get into my riding at all. Thankfully my hand had recovered because I was hanging on to my bike for dear life. Halfway round the first lap it started raining again. I'd just about dried out from the swim but in seconds I was wetter than when I'd emerged from the lake. I picked a couple of people off as I started my second lap and managed to get a few more as tired legs started to take their toll on my fellow competitors. As I passed the 40-mile marker the hailstones started. It felt like someone was sticking needles into my bare legs and arms as the relentless wind drove them almost horizontally into me. Upon finishing the race I would discover cuts on the exposed parts of my body that I could only attribute to these icy missiles. Ah, the good old British summer weather.

I was also using the race to practise my Woody nutrition plan. On the bike I consumed energy drink for the first 20 miles, and then alternated between malt loaf and gel every 10 miles until the end. It worked well, and my stomach coped with it. I'd read horror stories of dodgy stomachs and explosive diarrhoea resulting from a nutrition plan going wrong. This test alleviated my fears. Hopefully it was a sign that come the Woody my body would be able to cope with the fuel intake. I completed the taxing bike ride in 3:21:55. All that was left for me to do was complete the equal-longest running race I'd ever done in the past. However, on this occasion I had to contend with the added fatigue of over four hours of racing in my legs.

I was quickly out of transition, putting on my bottle belt as I took my first running strides of the day. Surprisingly I didn't suffer from 'Jelly Legs' and was into my rhythm quite quickly. The route was a tough one, mostly off road, combining ankle-deep rough grass and sections containing pot-holed flooded dirt tracks. Added to this were pebbled lanes that disrupted my strides and a flooded meadow where my shoes disappeared completely below the muddy water. This, combined with several stiles to climb over, and a gate to open and go through, meant it wasn't really a fast run course. I just concentrated on putting one foot in front of the other as I plodded my way round the two laps. Nature called and I had to stop to water the plants on the first lap. As I emerged from behind a bush I'd lost a bit of time but I felt much more comfortable. I sped up on the second lap. It took me an hour for the first lap and about fifty minutes for the second. Bizarrely, given the earlier inclement conditions, the sun was beating down on me throughout the run. I'd not applied any sun block and as a result I would suffer for the next couple of days with badly burnt arms and shoulders.

I managed to run the half-marathon in about 1:50 to finish in 6:04:48. This was a pleasing shock as I'd hoped for about 6:30. I had a great sense of achievement as I crossed the line, more so than when I'd finished Chester a few weeks before. This had been a much tougher challenge.

Travelling home across the moors, I reflected proudly on what I had achieved. In August 2006 I'd completed my first sprint triathlon. Now less than a year later I had a half-Ironman under my belt. What a journey I'd made and surprisingly I didn't feel as knackered as I had when I finished the Chester Olympic. That had to be a good sign.

It had been an unyielding day because of the weather, and the loneliness of the bike had messed with my head. I'd kept going when it got grim and lonely, and I would need to save that experience and draw on it when the inevitable bad patch struck on 1 September. The experience of the Steelman left me in no doubt that I could complete the Woody. Physically, and more importantly mentally, I was halfway there.

9

HENS, STAGS AND HEARTACHE

Racing in unmerciful conditions had taken its toll on my body: I was suffering with man flu. The green stuff that I was coughing up from my lungs reminded me of apple-flavoured energy gel. It was the same colour and texture, but unfortunately it didn't taste as good. Being cautious and with a little persuasion from Em, I didn't train all week. However my evenings were put to good use preparing for the big day in September. No not that one, I mean the wedding.

Choosing the music for our big day was more stressful than training. There was no floor space in the front room; we were surrounded by a carpet of CDs as we searched for background music for the ceremony. Thankfully we'd already chosen the music for our first dance, and I had chosen the song we would walk out of the ceremony to. This would be a surprise for Em. She was being very trustworthy as I'd already suggested 'Smack my Bitch Up' by the Prodigy.

Em was also preparing for her hen weekend. The contents of her wardrobe were strewn on the bed and of course despite the hundreds of outfits on display, "I've got nothing to wear" was her conclusion. I lay there with my Lemsip, hoping that I was nodding in the correct places as the fashion show unfolded before my watering eyes. She was off to Edinburgh on the 6am train on Saturday. For once it would be me getting up at daft o'clock without a reason: running her to the station would be the least I could do, repaying her early-morning sacrifices for my hobby. Sarah, her enthusiastic bridesmaid, greeted Em on the platform with a bottle of champagne and a big pink glittery sash that screamed, "I'm the Hen". It was going to be carnage. I hoped somebody had rung Scotland to warn them.

So there I was, free for the weekend. Did I plan on going to the pub? Nope. I gave Andy H a ring and arranged to go for a run. No wonder my mates didn't consider me normal. The personal rain cloud that seemed to be following me that July didn't disappoint when I met Andy H for our usual 10k run along the coastal path. Neither of us were looking forward to it. Andy H had experienced a busy week both in terms of training and work, whilst I was just feeling lethargic. We hadn't seen each other for about a month with holidays and so on, so it was good to catch up. We'd agreed on just a slow steady run so when my Garmin beeped after the first mile to indicate 7:03 we thought we'd better slow down or we'd be crawling back. We ran steadily through the puddles, chatting away about how technology affected our training. It was a really good run, the kind where you are glad to be out. We got back to the car having completed the course in 49:30. Man flu hadn't quite finished me off.

The subject of technology had come up because I'd been reading my colleague Michael's blog about how technology influences our everyday lives. From searching the Internet through to driving a car or making a cup of tea with a cordless kettle, it all involves technical developments that weren't around when I was young. And that just makes me sound old. Great.

So taking Michael's ramblings, I wondered how much the use of technology affected my journey towards the Woody. And was I better off because of it? There was only one conclusion, I was. And so was every other weekend warrior. Let me explain.

When I first started running as a child over 25 years ago the hobby was unrecognisable to what it is today. There was one running magazine, *Athletics Weekly*. This was the runner's bible. Inside you'd find adverts for all the races that you could enter. Also it was the place to buy your running shoes, as there were very few specialist running shops and certainly none in Barrow. You had to pick your shoes from the adverts for Bourne Sports or Sweatshop. Most of mine came from Bourne as they tended to have the better offers. You, or in my case my parents, had to ring up and order them. If you were lucky they would arrive in about three weeks. There wasn't much choice other than Nike or New Balance. Walsh made shoes that looked like football boots if you were nutty enough to do fell races. And then there was a limited choice of models such as the Waffle Trainer or Pegasus. Air was my weapon of choice. There was no Gel, Torsion, Wave, Abzorb or Grid – these technologies hadn't been dreamt up yet.

Today if I want to enter a race I can search for them online and enter at the touch of a button. I can order running shoes from anywhere in the world without so much as picking up a magazine. You can get training schedules, advice on injuries, talk to fellow runners, listen to the wonderful podcasts from IM Talk and wade your way through more advice on nutrition, physiology and fitness than any library can hold. Triathletes can even sign up to get coached online by the legendary Mark Allen, multiple Ironman world champion.

These days virtual athletic clubs exist. You need never meet your fellow clubmates but you can belong to the same group. As a member of an actual triathlon club you may think that I would think that's sad but I don't. Although there are many advantages to belonging to a 'real' club, a virtual one still brings people together with a common interest. If it wasn't for the Internet I'd have never met my fellow Pirates through the *Runner's World* website. There is still a place for local clubs and most of us belong to one. At the time of writing I am heavily involved with my local triathlon club, COLT, City of Lancaster Triathlon. More on that subject later.

The Internet has also widened where we run. It was almost unheard of 25 years ago when my Uncle Alan ran the New York marathon and then later the Paris marathon. Nowadays both events would seem passé to most. The Internet has opened up the world, and as a result we can enter races in some of the remotest places on earth. The Amazon, the Sahara and Antarctica are only a click away. Flights, hotels, car hire, bike hire and race entries have all been organised from this very laptop that I type at now. Running and the relatively new sport of triathlon have boomed worldwide because of the Internet. Greater numbers of people can enter races anywhere, the classic example of this being any branded Ironman race. You have to enter online and they sell out in minutes. Years ago only a few knew they existed. Ironman was just a comic book character. Now it's a phenomenon.

Injuries are being treated through technology. Ten minutes of video analysis with a computer and a treadmill and my running problem was diagnosed. Until that point I couldn't run. As a result of the technical analysis I was given the correct insoles to wear and my problem has been cured. Years ago such a problem would have been missed.

I could also mention heart rate monitors, GPS systems, bike computers and MP3 players – all technological advances that have made our training more informed and comfortable. We can now download and analyse our training runs and rides and get just about any data we want. Gone are the days of running a route and then driving round it in the car to see how far you went. Now you just look at your wrist, or in the case of the Nike iPod+, Lance Armstrong or Paula Radcliffe's voice comes through your earphones to tell you. No need to go home and get maps out to work it all out on the kitchen table, just bring your online maps up and it'll also give you profiles and elevations. This is the age of geeky running and I unashamedly love it. I'm a self-confessed gadget freak. Does it make me run faster? I think it does. I love seeing my mile splits and then trying to beat it in the next mile, watching the speed on my bike and trying to maintain it. Data can be a great motivator.

So Technology gets my vote. I think it's made our hobby more convenient and accessible. There will not be one person that reads this that hasn't benefitted from it, whether that be online shopping and race entry or training data being recorded. Even blogs can help keep people motivated, and writing mine continues to be one of my biggest motivators. I have to keep training in order to have something to write about.

Purists will say you should just get out there and run, leave all the crap behind, and yes that's great sometimes, but you can't escape technology. See that wicking t-shirt you're wearing or those Asics Kayanos on your feet? They're all designed on computer and probably bought on one as well. And don't get me started on our bikes. It was the stuff of science fiction when I was a kid. I wonder what we'll see in the next 20 years.

No amount of technology could keep Em awake that Sunday night. She was asleep within an hour of getting home. The good news was that Edinburgh survived, apparently a bit better than the girls judging by the photos taken the morning after the night before. I hoped I wouldn't suffer the hangover from hell when I had my alternate stag do that coming weekend.

It would turn out to be a select gathering. Viking couldn't make it because of family commitments, which I was quite relieved about as I had visions of him chaining me up naked to a bike. Dave had travelled up from Cheshire and my best man Lee had come down from Barrow. They would be staying at mine so they could have a drink. Lee and I had our wedding suit fittings the next day. Lee had already informed me he would be "as rough as a badger's arse". He's always had an interesting vocabulary. We sank a few beers before heading to the pub where we were be joined by Andy H and Richard G, my best mate in Lancaster. The evening started off pleasantly with some good food and then got interesting when the alcohol kicked in. Poor Richard and Lee were being educated about triathlon whether they wanted to or not. Both of them thought Dave and I were insane for attempting to complete the Woody; they also thought Andy was as bad for aiding and abetting me. The tone took a downward spiral when Lee said, "So you're riding along and you need a piss, do you stop and go behind a hedge?"

"Give over, you just pee whilst you cycle along," said Dave, grinning over his Guinness. "Just make sure you don't do what my mate did and piss on your energy bars and malt loaf." Half of us were in raptures and the other half went green. The night would get worse for them as they were informed that Dave used Durex lubricant to help get in and out of his wetsuit. Later that night, back at mine, he demonstrated this to a perplexed Lee. I was glad Em was in bed as I'm sure the wedding would have been off if she walked in to our living room at 2am to find her husband and two grown men passing round a bottle of Durex lube.

Back in the pub an informed discussion then took place on just why the hell men have nipples. This led to Richard asking if I'd be shaving my chest for the race, as he knew that I'd done it in the past as I wore plasters to protect my nipples from chafing. I'd ruined many t-shirts with bloodstains in the past. "Yeah I've witnessed it, and he looks like he's been shot twice by a sniper," Andy informed the others.

The night was over too quickly. Andy and Richard headed home. Before he left Richard informed us that he'd be dreaming about nipples and lubricant. He added that unfortunately for him the faces that he'd see would be mine and Dave's. Through a drunken haze I felt sorry for my mate.

The next morning Dave was up, bright and breezy, and full of life. He'd drunk a sea of Guinness yet he wasn't suffering for it. I was impressed. He left just as Lee was emerging. He looked the complete opposite of Dave, as he'd predicted, rough. I myself was a little fuzzy but I'd gotten away quite lightly for a stag night. Hopefully the real stag weekend would be as much fun, although I doubted that either Dave or I would be as lively afterwards.

Lee and I got measured and fitted for our suits under the watchful eyes of Em and Lee's wife Pam. Lee had returned to his wise-cracking self, the hangover was wearing thin. The tailor informed us, "You'll need to pick your suits up on the Saturday before the wedding." Before I had a chance to answer, Lee chipped in. "No can do. Dickhead here is doing a triathlon that day; hopefully he'll be finished in time for the actual wedding though." After some further, more sensible discussion, it was agreed that I could pick the suits up on the Monday evening after work.

It was a busy weekend in terms of wedding preparation as the following day we had to go to Liverpool to pick up Em's dress. I of course did not see the dress. I waited in the shop, out of the way whilst Em, Maggie and an assistant took the precious cargo and loaded it into the boot of the car. I'd been sat there reading *220 Triathlon* magazine and drinking coffee whilst a final fitting had taken place in the back room. I was engrossed in an article about improving your running coming off the bike, when I heard: "Are you looking forward to your big day in September?" I was vaguely aware that my reading was being interrupted by the manageress. "I'm a little nervous still but if I have a good smooth start I think I'll make good progress on the bike, and follow it up with some steady paced runn ..." It then dawned on me where I was. The poor woman was staring at me like I'd lost my mind. She just smiled sheepishly and found something interesting to do on the shop counter, whilst I dived back into the safety of my magazine. Thankfully almost immediately Em and Maggie came back into the front of the shop to rescue me.

A consequence of the pub discussion was that Richard G decided that he wanted to get out running. I thought I knew everything (including plenty of drunken confessions I could have done without) about my friend. However in a sober state he surprised me when he confessed that he used to run when he was a student but he hadn't done so for 14 years. "I'll accompany you on your easy runs when you begin to ease down ahead of the Woody. Just to keep you company. Nothing serious, just social you understand. And I'm not running if it's raining, that's just stupid." I ignored his last comment. So the next day we decided to go for a gentle run to gauge his fitness. I received an email from his girlfriend, Louise, asking me to take it easy with him. Em rang me and said the same thing, and a couple of our work colleagues expressed concerns for his health. Did people think I was going to kill him?

He ran really well. We managed a couple of miles in just over twenty minutes in the bright August sunshine. I extended my run for another six miles whilst Richard went home for a well earned rest. Towards the end of the run he informed me that he was feeling sick and had a stitch that was creasing him up. "When did you last eat?" I asked him. "I had a bottle of Orangina, a bag of cinder toffee and two Mars bars about an hour ago," came the gasping reply. I was gobsmacked. His sugar binge was an ill-conceived plan to make sure he had enough energy to keep up with me. He wouldn't make that mistake again.

Richard became a valuable training partner, escorting me as planned on my easy lunchtime runs around campus that August.

Taper madness was setting in. I'd been warned about this psychological consequence of easing off before the race. With three weeks to go until the Woody I'd drastically cut my training hours and distances. The 12- to 16-hour weeks were behind me and I was down to about nine, at low intensity. This consisted of a mixture of two short runs of no more than an hour, one two-hour session on the bike and a couple of one-hour rides. I was also trying to swim for one or two hours a week. Two weeks before the Woody this would be reduced to five hours, and in the week before I would only swim, cycle and run once. The madness stems from the fact that during this time you think every twinge, ache or sniffle is potentially fatal. We were sat in Starbucks enjoying a coffee one night after work when Em had to kick me under the table. The woman at the next table had sneezed violently and not covered her nose. I swear I could see the germs swimming through the air in my direction. Without realising, I had tutted loudly and was glaring at her like she'd just insulted my manhood. Em had noticed and had done her best to stop me from getting barred from my favourite coffee shop. The only problem then was I thought she'd broken my leg where she kicked me. I moaned about it for the rest of the night. I told you it was madness.

Em was going shopping for wedding accessories to the Trafford Centre with her bridesmaids Lesley and Sarah one evening after work. I used the opportunity to go for a long swim in that first week of tapering. I knew I'd have to concentrate on my technique and that would be a welcome distraction from my delusional hypochondria.

The pool was fairly quiet and I had a lane mostly to myself, although I was joined for a while by a lass who was unbelievably fast. I apologised for going slow when I stopped to adjust my goggles but she said it was fine and that she would just swim around me. Moments later the lane next to us became free, and I was swimming on my own again. I just had the intention of swimming a mile or 2,000m but I felt strong and just kept going. I concentrated on pushing my chest down, rotating from the hip and gliding the stroke through the water, trying to be as 'slippery and long' as possible, just as Peta had taught me. A mile went by, 2,000m soon passed, and I thought, *Sod it, just go the Ironman distance.* I finished strongly and felt perfectly fine – no dizziness or sickness despite losing one of my ear plugs early on.

I had finished the 2.4 miles (152 lengths) in 1:42:16. I was so relieved and proud of myself that I was now fit enough to swim that monster distance. All those hours spent going back and forth, all the pain and frustration, had given me the strength to succeed at my weakest discipline. I finished by swimming a couple of laps of breaststroke as a warm-down. I soon realised that was a mistake. I jumped out of the pool with crippling cramp in my right calf. This most definitely was not in my mind. I tried to stand but couldn't. Within seconds I was laying poolside on my back with the burly lifeguard stretching out my leg. Thankfully it did the trick. I rested the next day as a precaution, and wasn't troubled with cramp when I resumed training.

However, never one to pass up an opportunity to wind Viking up, I sent him a text.

"I don't know how to put this mate. I've just torn my calf muscle swimming. It's going to be six weeks until I can compete. I'm heartbroken. I'm out of the Woody."

Ten seconds later my mobile rang. "Ha ha very funny, you're not winding me up," was Viking's dismissive response.

"No joke mate, I thought I'd tell you first before I told Min and Dave. I'm devastated." I then explained the nature of my fictitious injury in my saddest, most pain-racked voice. The sucker bought it. "Oh Holgs I'm feckin' gutted for you mate."

I couldn't keep up the façade, and started to giggle.

"You bastard! I'm coming round to slap the shit out of you." I was pleased I lived 60 miles away.

My final run took place on the Tuesday before the race. Andy and I ran a very gentle five miles along our usual route. It was more an opportunity for me to thank my domestique, guru and most importantly, friend. Without his help I wouldn't have been within a country mile of where I was now in terms of fitness and preparation. Although he wouldn't be there physically with me on Saturday at the Woody, he'd be in my head giving me advice. He'd be the Obi Wan Kenobi to my Luke Skywalker telling me to use the Force. Or in my case it would be, "Use the gears Andy. Trust in the gears."

That day Min had emailed the rest of the gang her list of things to take. Being the ultra-organised person that she was, and a woman prepared for all eventualities, the list seemed endless. I stared at it in disbelief. I hadn't thought about making a list but it made perfect sense. After my run with Andy that night I made my own list. I intended to pack lightly so it wasn't as long as Min's, after all I wasn't taking my teddy bear.

I set out four large carrier bags on the bed, and filled them with items from my list:

Swim: Wetsuit, goggles, ear plugs, swim hat, nose clip, swim trunks, body glide, heart rate monitor.

T1 & Bike: Cycling shoes, helmet, computer, gloves, bib shorts, Pirate vest, arm warmers, socks, talc, Vaseline, towel, 2 x water bottle (one energy drink, one water), bento box with six energy gels, sliced and cling-filmed malt loaf, pump, saddle bag with 2 x inner tube, puncture repair kit and tools, sunglasses, sun cream, rain jacket.

T2 & Run: Running shoes, Pirate shorts, Vaseline,

plasters, socks, Garmin, cap, bottle belt, head torch (it was entirely possible it could be dark when I finished, and we'd be running through an unlit wood).

Recovery: Rego drink, Nurofen gel, ibuprofen, freeze spray, blister plasters. IronHolgs long sleeve Pirate t-shirt (I was gambling on adding the 'Iron' prefix to my existing Pirate moniker).

Of course I was also taking my bike, but that wouldn't fit in the carrier bag. I was confident that I had everything. And besides if I forgot anything I'd be able to beg, borrow or steal it from Min. After all she had three of everything on my list.

Speaking to my parents on the phone that Tuesday night we talked about the logistics of fitting all my gear, the bike and four adults into their car for the trip. It would be a tight squeeze but at least it meant I wouldn't have to drive home afterwards. Em and my mam couldn't drive, so we'd agreed that I would drive there and my dad would drive back. Both of them expressed how excited they were to be coming to support the four of us at the weekend. They had been avid readers of my blog and our conversations over the last nine months had centred on the Woody. They would always ask how Viking, Min and Dave were getting on. My dad told me he'd be bringing his running shoes just in case any of us needed any moral support on the marathon.

He'd also been keeping fit by riding his bike, and this was a constant source of banter between us. "I'll give you some last-minute tips on how to ride properly when I pick you up on Friday. I'll be off out tomorrow for a ride."

That ride almost ended everything.

The phone rang, Pam jumped up to answer it whilst the rest of the staffroom crowd paused, waiting to see if they could continue drinking their coffee, or if they would be called away to help a student. "Andy, your mum's on the phone." I put down my coffee. It was unusual that she was ringing me at work but I didn't think any further on the matter as Pam handed me the receiver.

My mam's voice sounded tired and stressed.

"Andrew, don't panic. Your dad's had an accident, he fell whilst on his bike and he's broken his back." My world collapsed. I didn't hear any further details.

"Is he alright? Are you okay? I'm on my way, I'll get Em and we'll be through."

"Please don't drive like an idiot, I don't want you in an accident as well."

"I'll be there as soon as I can, and I promise I'll be safe." I hoped I'd reassured her.

Pam and a couple of colleagues gave me a hug, and said they'd tell my boss that I'd gone. Running to the car, I rang Em. Ten minutes later we were on the motorway heading north to Barrow. Thankfully the roads were quiet and we were there in just under an hour.

My mam was waiting for us in the hospital foyer. She explained what she knew as we walked up to the ward. My dad had been out training on his bike as planned. He'd started to feel dizzy and got off his bike. The next thing he remembers he was on the floor. He'd pushed himself too much; his blood sugars had plummeted and he'd had what diabetics refer to as a 'hypo', a type of shock that can cause the sufferer to faint. Luckily for him two workmen in a passing van witnessed the whole episode and called for an ambulance. As he hit the ground his bike helmet flew off, a result of the violent impact. It had done its job though. Without his helmet his skull would have been smashed. The fact that he was wearing one was a direct consequence of my participation in triathlon. I never rode without one and he followed suit, after a little persuasion from my mam.

When he regained consciousness he managed to tell the workmen he'd been in diabetic shock and they gave him some jelly babies they'd had in the van. His blood sugar stabilised briefly as a result, making him coherent, but he was in serious pain. He was rushed to hospital. X-rays showed that he'd crushed two vertebrae in his spine. Apparently when he'd fallen, his back had landed across the kerb separating the grass verge from the pavement. He'd been unlucky in that sense; a few inches to the left and he would have escaped with just bruising. However he'd been miraculously lucky in that every fragment of shattered bone in his back had missed his spinal column by millimetres. There would be no paralysis.

The pain was etched on his face but typically he tried to diffuse the situation with humour. "You'll have to run on your own on Saturday, your mam has grounded me."

"Don't worry about Saturday. I'm not going now, you two need me here. You just make sure you're out of here in time for the wedding," I told him. Em nodded in agreement.

"You are going on Saturday," my parents replied in unison.

"It's not up for debate," added my dad.

At that moment I didn't have the energy to argue, I just wanted my dad out of hospital and I didn't want to cause him any further stress. I knew he'd be lying there in pain feeling guilty that he wouldn't be able to support me, and drive me home. That is the sort of man he is, always putting his family first.

The bell rang to signal an end to visiting hours. "We'll all be back in the morning," my mam said as she kissed my dad goodbye.

We called in at my dad's sister's to inform her and her husband on his progress. Pam and Fred had taken my mam up to the hospital as soon as she found out and would be a massive help to her in the days to come. Fred assured me that he'd run my mam around and make sure everything was alright. Again when I expressed doubts I was told bluntly that I was going to go away and race.

I don't think any of us slept that night. There were too many scenarios playing out in my head. I'd lost my appetite for the Woody, it suddenly didn't seem important. All I wanted was for my dad to be better, and to be able to attend our wedding. There would be other races. I only had one dad and one big day.

At visiting the next day he seemed a lot better, a result of his blood sugars being properly brought under control by the drips he was attached to. I told him I'd rung the hotel and cancelled their room. My thoughts were proven correct when he said, "Thanks for doing that. I just feel guilty that I can't drive you." My mam agreed. Again I expressed my doubts about going. I'd have to head back to

Lancaster that evening to prepare to leave early the next day for the long drive south.

"There's nothing you can do here," said my mam. "Your dad is in the best place and Fred will run me around. And if he can't, Colin across the road has said he will. You can't give up, you've worked so hard." The reassurance in her voice shone through.

"Go and make us proud," Dad added.

I didn't need any more motivation than that. I would dedicate my achievement to my selfless parents. They knew how much it meant to me. Come Saturday I would be competing for them more than myself.

"Keep in touch."

"Don't worry Marie, I'll call and text throughout the day to let you know how he's getting on," was Em's comforting reply.

Assured that there was nothing else I could do, we made our way home. It would be a hectic night of packing and phone calls. I informed the gang of the situation at home and that Em and I would be travelling alone. Dave was a star and said that his wife Suzie or his daughter Sam would provide race-day transport for Em, so that she could shout abuse at us all.

Once I was convinced that everything was in place, I closed the living room door and headed for the kitchen to make a drink to take up to bed. I'd walked past the fridge a million times but tonight of all nights I banged my left knee into the side of it. I fell to the floor in a crumpled heap, almost crushing poor Crosby. He hissed and jumped out of the way, barely retaining one of his eight remaining lives. My swearing brought Em running down the stairs to see what had happened. She helped me to my feet and up the stairs to bed. My knee was swelling rapidly.

"Should you go to casualty?" she asked, clearly worried. Her soft, concerned features dampened my frustration and anger instantly.

"I've had enough of hospitals. Can you get the ice pack out of the fridge please pet. I'd put it in there ready for post-race aches. I didn't think I'd bloody need it beforehand."

The ice cooled the joint and I hoped that would be the last of it. Getting into bed, Em affectionately touched my arm and said, "Like Father, like Son."

10

BEEN THERE, DONE THAT, GOT THE T-SHIRT

My heart sank.

I was one day away from the race that would define me as an athlete. So many people had made sacrifices to help my development. Three friends had put blind faith in my idea and had come on board this journey of discovery. There was even the added pressure of seven hundred pounds in sponsorship riding on me successfully completing the Woody. (I'd decided to raise funds for the British Heart Foundation, a charity close to home because Em had received major heart surgery as a child. Without that surgery she wouldn't have been part of my life. I was thankful for the help she'd received and wanted to raise awareness and give a little back.)

I could hardly stand.

The swelling on my knee had subsided but the joint had seized up. I managed to limp to the bathroom and blindly popped painkillers in the hope that it would help. I lathered the knee in Tiger Balm embrocation in the hope that its healing properties would kick in. Finally I wrapped the joint in a compression bandage and hoped that as the day went on I'd be able to walk properly. I couldn't lift anything. My leg wasn't stable enough so Em had to load the car. Trying to put on a brave face, although inside I was in turmoil, I said, "We'd better stop for some extra batteries for my head torch, it could be the slowest marathon ever."

We stopped for a comfort break just south of Birmingham, where we met Dave and Viking. My leg had stiffened up after two hours of driving so I was limping very badly and grimacing in pain with each step.

"Sod off Holgs. I'm not falling for that one again," Viking said.

His mood quickly changed as he saw the look of despair in my eyes.

They listened intently as I explained my argument with the fridge and the resulting injury. "You clumsy sod, your family isn't safe anywhere," said Dave. "You'll be fine though, you'll get through it."

I had every intention of *getting* through it. The trouble was I wanted to *race* through it.

After arriving in Ross-on-Wye, the race venue, Viking headed for the race headquarters. He would be camping with Min. Dave and I would be staying in a local motel with our families. We'd decided that a comfortable bed before and after the race was a must. After unloading the cars Em, Suzie, Dave and I went for a drive around the bike course. It was a lot hillier than I was expecting. As we drove I was very grateful for the hours I'd spent riding the hills around the Trough of Bowland with Andy and John. I'd cursed them at the time but on that car journey I realised that the challenging course wouldn't be so much of a shock because of what they'd put me through. I wondered how Viking would fare. All of his riding had been on the flatlands around Warrington. This would be a serious culture shock for him.

That evening we all signed in and attended the race briefing. Unfortunately we would not be able to leave our bikes in transition overnight as had been promised. This would mean a very early start the next morning. There were plenty of Pirates in attendance and we chatted excitedly during the pasta party. All except poor Min; she looked white as a ghost. She didn't want to talk to anyone and she left early to try and get some sleep. "You'll be alright pet," I tried to reassure her. I don't think she believed me.

I was tucked up in bed by 9pm, having first phoned home for a progress report on my dad. "He's doing well and there's a possibility he may be allowed home on Monday," was the positive response from my mam. "Good luck tomorrow. Have a great race. We'll be thinking about you."

I didn't mention my injured knee, my mam had enough to

worry about. The damage limitation plan I'd put into practice seemed to have worked as I could now walk. However I still had no idea if I would be able to run. I wouldn't have long to wait to find out, though. My day of reckoning had arrived.

Let me talk you through what some people call the 'Longest Day'. I was actually surprised at how quick it went.

Wake up and swim

My alarm went off at 4.15am for breakfast, which consisted of 2 SIS Go bars, a black coffee with sugar and a glass of water. I woke Em up at 4.45 and we met Dave outside 15 minutes later to get the bikes racked on his car. Thankfully it was only a five-minute drive to the lakes for the swim. We had to use torches to see where to rack our bikes. The darkness was perforated by the nervous chatter of triathletes preparing for the challenge. Some, like Min, were even more nervous as the van transporting their bikes up from the race headquarters was running late. Her anxious state that we'd witnessed the night before certainly wasn't being helped by the delay. It wasn't the ideal start.

The bikes eventually turned up and with 15 minutes to go we stripped off and prepared to don our wetsuits. It was at this point that I realised I'd left my Bodyglide in my run transition bag. Thankfully 'Durex Dave' was on hand to rescue me. I coated my neck, wrists and ankles with the lubricant. I'm eager here to point out that under any other circumstances I wouldn't have accepted such help from a man in a dark field dressed in rubber.

I kissed Em goodbye under a full moon and walked to the water's edge with Viking, Min and Dave. Pent-up energy filled the air. We wished each other luck as we headed into the cold murky waters of Drummonds Dub and found our starting positions.

I washed my goggles and placed them on my head. Focusing my vision through the blue plastic lenses, I stared out across the misty lake as a bright blue dawn began to break. *This is YOUR moment Andy*, I thought. *You've done the training, you've logged the hours. It's time to show the world just what you are made of. Seize this day, make it yours.*

The klaxon sounded and a great cheer of anticipation rose from the athletes and their supporters as the inaugural Big Woody got underway. The hopes and aspirations of several hundred men and women were about to be fought for.

Like my previous mass-start races I was conscious of the washing machine effect. I didn't want to get kicked again like I had at the Steelman; this task would be hard enough if everything went smoothly let alone if it didn't. I wasn't to be so lucky. Although I started to the side and the back of the bunch there were still arms and legs everywhere. Suddenly I was aware of something out of the corner of my eye. BANG. A hand or a foot smacked me in the face hard, knocking my goggles off. Thankfully I managed to keep hold of them and after a few seconds of adjusting was on my way again. It had been a lucky escape.

Just relax and enjoy it. I kept repeating my mantra in my head. I didn't want to put myself under any pressure. Experience had taught me that the more relaxed I felt the better I would swim. It worked. Before long the lap of the first lake was over with. I looked behind me as I left Drummonds for the cross-country run to Hartleton Lake, and to my surprise I wasn't last. The sun was beginning to come up as I lifted my goggles to get a clearer view of where I was placing my feet. It may have been a consequence of the cold water but my knee felt fine as I ran on it for the first time since 'Fridge-Gate'.

I managed to get my goggles back in position and jumped into the second lake for the first of two laps. Disaster almost struck moments later. Never one to swim in a direct line, I'd veered off to the edge of the lake near some jetties. I caught sight of the submerged concrete post just as I was about to swim head first into it. Somehow contorting my body, I managed to twist my head away, but the post hit my shoulder. "Shit that hurts!" Taking a moment to regain my composure, I trod water before completing the rest of the swim without any further drama.

There was a very strong wind that blew me back down the lake, and that probably made my time faster than what it should have been. I really felt strong and fresh as I was pulled up the steep bank of the final swim exit. Only then did I allow myself a glance at my watch. Amazingly it read 1:07. I had smashed my PB by half an hour. It would later transpire that the wind had blown one of the marker buoys off course making the swim shorter, hence the unrealistic time, but at that moment I was spurred on by my unexpected performance.

Arriving in transition one, I grabbed my bag and entered the small changing tent. I stripped naked, not sparing a second thought for my modesty as I put my bike gear on. I had exchanged greetings with Dave, as he had been leaving as I arrived. He was amused that the tent had clear windows in it so the spectators outside were treated to the sight of our hairy arses. Moments later I emerged from the tent, dressed like a cyclist, resplendent in Pirate black and yellow.

I took a second to quickly kiss Em to let her know I felt great as I ran towards my bike. Viking, who'd had a storming swim, high fived me as he picked his bag up and headed for the tent. There was no sign of Min. It would later transpire that she'd had a tough time. Like Dave she'd thrown up whilst swimming. Unlike Dave, who did this every time he raced in open water, she wasn't used to it and it messed her head up. It's testimony to her strength and determination that she recovered and finished the swim only ten minutes behind her predicted time.

The bike

I had come out of the swim and T1 in 1:14:45. In my race plan I would have been happy if I'd got on my bike in 2 hours. I was way ahead of schedule.

The first two miles were uphill, slow and laborious. It was tough as I tried to wake my legs up. I started on my nutrition plan and gulped an energy drink and ate a couple of pieces of malt loaf. This would be the pattern for the rest of the day. My plan was to eat or have a gulp of fluid every 20 minutes. In total I would consume eight 750ml bottles on the bike course. If there had been more than two feed stations each lap that figure would have been higher.

I began passing a few people as we headed up and down; none of the roads were flat. At the foot of English Bricknor, one of the monster hills I had been warned about, I caught Dave and we exchanged a few words. My legs were feeling it as I reached the summit. It actually turned out to be a false summit. Turning the corner there was another cruel 10 per cent climb to combat.

A few miles in, I passed through race HQ for the first time. I received lots of cheers which gave me a much needed boost. As I passed the first feed station I threw away an empty bottle, and was handed a new one. At this stage there were still plenty of bikes around me as we dropped down into the forest for the first time. I slowed cautiously as I approached a very tight, dangerous right turn and was rewarded with the sight of Em and Dave's family (Suzie, Sam and Annie) cheering me on. I had to put on a show for my fans and I powered up the hill as a result. I was now heading on to the lower dog-leg of the course and that was the last support I'd see for another 40 miles until I got to the next feed station. It was a very tough and lonely section. In all honesty it was very damaging to both legs (because of the relentless hills) and my mind (tiredness and loneliness). The four-mile long climb to the second feed station made me question the sanity of what I was doing. Even when I had been lying in a hospital bed I hadn't felt so close to giving up. Then salvation washed over me as I reached the feed station at Magna Dean and was given bottles to replace my empties and energy gels. More importantly I was greeted by Em, the Spartan girls, Min's mum, Lucy and Will. Seeing them all gave me the strength to continue. Until that point I couldn't comprehend attempting a second lap.

I eventually reached Bricknor for the second time after what seemed like a lifetime alone in the wilderness and was amazed to see 'Go Pirates Go' written on the main road. The Pirate coach, Barley, had apparently been dodging traffic halfway up the hill to paint messages of support and a skull and crossbones on the road. There were Pirate flags and umbrellas hanging from the trees and fellow Pirates ringing cowbells and shouting support. In one of the most surreal moments of my life they played a CD of the theme from *Captain Pugwash* as I passed. Laughing, I shouted my thanks and rode past, fully understanding why racing as a Pirate was so cool.

I passed through HQ again, grabbing more much needed bottles. I was knackered and I still had another lonely 50 miles to go. As I passed Em and the others at the start of the soul-destroying section I managed a faint smile.

Lonely and exhausted, I began to feel like I was coming undone. My left knee was throbbing, my back was aching and my feet and toes were numb from standing on the pedals in an attempt to get up the hills. I was convincing myself that I was in no shape to run my first marathon. The voice in my head began to reassure me that it would all be okay if I just stepped off the bike. I was sorely tempted and was on the verge of breaking down both mentally and physically as I slumped forward on my handlebars. My eyes had glazed over and my legs were turning in ever decreasing circles. Staring through a fog of pain a mirage appeared in front of me. I couldn't believe it, was it the final feed station? Was I saved?

My exhausted mind had not been playing tricks on me. Nourishment and support were within touching distance of my crumpled body. I had never been so happy to see other human beings in my whole life. I stopped to talk to Em and the Spartan girls whilst hungrily devouring the best tasting banana I'd ever had. They informed me that the other three were on their second laps. Dave was not far behind me. Viking was struggling with cramp but still chirpy. Min, however, was in a world of hurt. I'll let her explain.

"I was in despair. I didn't hurt as such but I knew I was going too slowly to even make the cut-off. I was trying to keep calm but my nerves were shot. By the time I reached Magna Dean and saw my mum, the wonderful Spartan Crew and Team Lucy, I was in bits;

tears and palpitations. It was awful and horrid for my mum to see. My ravaged hip and knee were in agony and I was popping two Nurofen and one diclofenac every 45 minutes – how my stomach lining survived is anyone's guess. The team was great, though, and really tried to calm me down. I couldn't speak straight and was basically a garbled mess, but I was determined to carry on, so off I went."

I loaded my pockets with gel, and my bottles with energy drink. I stole another much needed kiss from Em before quickly stretching my aching back as I pulled away again. As I crawled up Bricknor for the last time I was in agony. My backside stung and my legs were screaming. As I crested the summit relief washed over me as I knew it was all downhill for the last few miles to transition two. Eventually I made it there and a volunteer took my bike from me. At that moment, in all honesty, as much as I've told you I love my bike, quite frankly I never wanted to see the bloody thing again. I had completed what can only be described as a sadistic bike course in 8:07:49. It was slower than I had planned but I was just happy to make it. Min, incidentally, would find her inner reserves. She'd be the last person out on the bike course and would spend most of the second lap escorted by the race referee on his motorbike. Importantly, though, she would beat the cut-off limit by 15 minutes.

The marathon

As a volunteer handed me my running gear I asked where the change tent was, only to be informed that there wasn't one. I'd been expecting one as I was planning on replacing my cycling bib shorts with my Pirate tri shorts. The marshal said, "No one's looking, just strip off," so I did, with only a green bin liner shielding the world from my saddle-compressed dangly bits.

Now fully dressed, I lathered my feet in Vaseline in the hope of staving off blisters. Dave arrived as I was pulling on my shoes; he'd had a storming ride. He gave me the unfortunate news that Viking had had to pull out at 92 miles with severe cramps. I was gutted, he'd worked so hard, and come so far to not finish. I walked over to get another kiss from Em. "You heard about Viking?" I said, the pain in my voice clear as day. She nodded and gave me a hug. This wasn't how it was supposed to be. We were the Musketeers, one for all and all for one.

I started my first ever marathon thinking about my mate. I couldn't imagine how he was feeling. However for the sake of my own survival I had to concentrate on the task at hand, all 26.2 miles of it.

I had joked all year that I would run a sub four-hour marathon at the Woody. Now the moment of truth had arrived. I was surprised that my legs seemed to be working fine. I had been terrified that my left knee would give in on me; it hurt but it held up. It was a tough out-and-back course through the forest with one sadistic hill at halfway, the sort you'd have to drive a car up in second gear. I remember thinking that Trevor, who'd designed the sadistic bike course and then thrown this hill in on the run, would have been kicked out of the 'Medieval Torturers' Guild' for cruelty if he'd been born in another time and place. He'd seemed such a nice man when I'd met him the night before.

The major advantage of the out-and-back five-lap course was that I kept seeing the same people over and over again. I offered words of encouragement to those that were left on the course and it felt great to be told in return, "Go Pirate, you're running strong!" Dave and I kept passing one another and I think it helped us both that afternoon as I battled to catch him and he fought to stay away from me. I'll let him explain:

"Holgs was going like a train, and looked stronger each time I saw him. I was even getting concerned that he might lap me. So I didn't stop at the last drinks station till I had turned round and was into the last lap. Stupid really. He is some 16 years younger than me, but you've got to keep these youngsters honest. It's a male thing okay?"

The banter got less and less as the laps mounted up. I think by the final lap we just exchanged grunts.

As I began my third lap, Viking was stood there, refreshed in jeans and t-shirt cheering me on. "I'm so sorry for you mate," I gushed as I ran towards him.

"Holgs stop pissing about and go finish this thing," was his response. It spoke volumes about the man that he stayed around to see his friends finish whilst inside he must have been dying. After the race he'd confide that he was dreading seeing everyone because he felt he'd let the team down. He hadn't and we let him know that in no uncertain terms. He'd just had a bad day at the office.

Fluid and malt loaf were ingested at every feed station and when I reached halfway I was running 1:40, which is fast. I was running with Min at this point who was on her first lap. She warned me not to blow up. Having never run more than 18 miles before I was worried about hitting the wall, but I just plodded on and felt strong. The support at HQ at the conclusion of each lap was immense and it really drove me on. Suddenly I had collected four bands which meant that I only had one lap to go and I would be an Ironman.

Out in the woods I passed Min for the last time. We embraced. The usual smiling, positive Min I knew and loved had returned. "We're gonna do it Holgs, we're gonna do it." She radiated enthusiasm and I couldn't help but get caught up in the emotion of the moment.

"Bring it home pet, bring it home," I told her as she strode out confidently into the woods. I headed for the finish. Taking one final glance over my shoulder I saw Min cutting a lonely yet inspiringly beautiful silhouette as the setting sun found her hidden amongst the trees.

As the light began to fade on my day I thought back to how I'd got here. It seemed like I was a million miles away from the scared little boy who stood terrified at the water's edge in Cockerham, literally taking the plunge. All those hours spent riding in the rain; the falls, the punctures, the blisters, the colds, the bleeding nipples, hell even a weekend in God's waiting room had been for the moment that was about to be mine.

Entering the school fields I could see the finish gantry. All that now stood between me and my dream was two football pitches.

Suddenly my ears were ringing to the sound of "Come on Andy, come on, whoa!" It was Loon, my forum friend, who possessed the face of an angel but the voice of a Blackpool bingo caller. If you gave the girl a microphone she'd wake the dead.

Spurred on by Loon, I'm unexpectedly flying. My adrenaline kicks in and I begin to bloody sprint. My tired legs and aching back are long forgotten. Suddenly I'm closer. I can hear the announcer telling the crowd that I'm getting married next Saturday and that this race is part of my stag weekend. A huge cheer erupts. I punch the air in sheer triumphant delight as I cross the line. Trevor hangs a medal around my neck and shakes my hand. I instantly forgive the man whose course has almost destroyed me. I kiss my medal. I've done it! I'm an Ironman.

Em was by my side in seconds. Emotions poured out of me as we embraced. "I love you. Thank you. Thank you so much. You deserve this more than me. Without you this wouldn't have been possible." I placed my medal around her neck. "I am so proud of you," she whispered.

"I'm still walking pet, you'd better get your dancing shoes ready for next week," I joked proudly.

I had finished in a time of 13:04:15 and my marathon had been completed in an awesome 3:41:40, a time I would have been over the moon with in an individual marathon.

I couldn't believe I had smashed 14 hours, a time I thought I might just achieve if I had the race of my life. I had surpassed all of my expectations and those of my friends and family. I pulled on my Pirate t-shirt with 'IRONHOLGS' written on the back. I'd earned the right to wear it.

Em had kept family and friends informed of my progress throughout the day and after the race there began a flurry of calls and texts congratulating me on my achievement. I rang my mam first to tell her. She was over the moon. I asked her to tell dad. "Why don't you tell him yourself? They let him out at lunchtime today," she said. That just topped my day off. He was on form as well, a sure sign that he was feeling better.

"Well done Andrew, but you still haven't beaten my Ironman time."

I couldn't help but laugh. This had been our family joke for years. He'd wind my brother Craig and I up about not beating his running times, no matter how fast we'd run. The fact that I was the first Holgate to step up to the challenge of an iron distance triathlon didn't matter, I knew I'd never beat my dad's time. And you know what? I'm so cool with that.

As Dave came into view, striding hard towards the finish line, the delight on his face was there for everyone to see. He'd had an awesome day, surpassing his expectations to finish in 13:43:31. We hugged and were both grinning like kids on Christmas Day. Sickeningly he looked as fresh as a daisy. As we stood there both munching pork pies, waiting for the beauty of the team to finish, Dave said insightfully, "The Tibetans got it right with their proverb. It is better to live one day as a lion than a thousand years as a sheep."

He was obviously making a play to be the brains of the team, and who was I to argue.

The beauty wouldn't keep us waiting long. Two glow sticks appeared moving in perfect rhythmical symmetry – Min was in sight. Loon raced across the field to hand her a Welsh flag. Draped in a Red Dragon she crossed the line in 15:02:23 to rapturous applause. In that single moment, she was the queen of the world. At the prize giving the next day she would receive the award for second-placed Lady Veteran, a deserved recognition of her weekend's display of spirit and tenacity.

The Woody was where four friends found out who they really were. We would forever be bonded by what we put ourselves through that day. We each understood the sacrifices that both we as individuals and our loved ones had made to get us through the longest day of our lives. One of us had fallen but he would be back stronger. As we posed for photographs Dave looked along the line of exhausted but newly vitalised individuals and remarked, "We roared today."

When I finished on Saturday I said to Em, "If I ever say I'm doing another one, slap me." On Monday I sent her an email saying I was thinking about Ironman Nice. Funny how the pain subsides and you are left with the feeling of *that was fun, wouldn't mind doing another.*

Before any of that, though, there was the small matter of a wedding to get through.

Perfecting my 'Knackered Look': 1982, aged nine, taking part in
a five-mile road race. I came third behind my brother and cousin.
By the end of the year I would have had major surgery on my knees.

Who ate all the pies?
That would be me. Here on
holiday in 2005 I weighed
240lbs. I had been the
wrong side of 252lbs but
had recently lost weight.
An illness had seen me
become inactive, this
combined with prescribed
steroid use and comfort
eating saw me bloat up.

Ominous clouds: The dark skies gather as I'm just minutes from starting my "one and only" triathlon at Cockerham in August 2006. The sensible bloke in the foreground wears a wetsuit, I quickly found out why!

Relief and addiction: Having just survived Cockerham the relief is apparent as I stand grinning next to John Krug, the man who got me into all this triathlon malarkey. John was the catalyst and remains something of a guru to me.

Dave the ex-Spartan, Andy H and I are all smiles as we pose with our first medals at the Skipton Triathlon in April 2007. My smile, however, masks a problem: within days I was in hospital suffering an extreme reaction to the pool chemicals.

Four drowned Pirates: Me, Dave, Min and Wicket are relieved to have survived the downpours at the Chester Olympic triathlon in June 2007. I had completed my first Olympic triathlon just weeks after coming out of hospital.

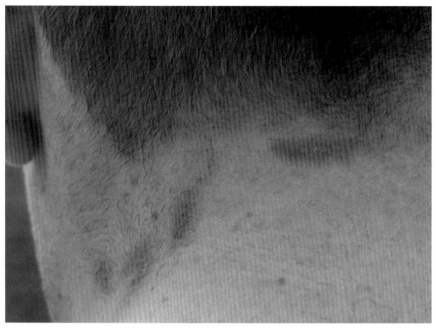

What happens when you don't use lubricant correctly. The love bite-like wounds caused by my wetsuit rubbing amused my friends but caused me pain.

Going the wrong way: Halfway through the Big Woody swim on 1 September 2007. I hadn't got lost, I was heading into the second lake whilst the "fast swimmers" went back into the first lake for the final lap.

Have Pirate will climb – with over a hundred miles of the Woody bike leg behind me the determination on my face is crystal clear as I climb the very steep English Bricknor hill for the third and final time. This was a soul destroying hill with a false summit. Minnie had rightly renamed it "Bitch-nor".

The disappearing change tent: We'd been led to believe that after the bike leg there would be another changing tent. Seconds earlier I had been naked from the waist down. Not a good look after 112 miles and 8 hours on the bike.

Made it: 1 September 2007 changed my life forever. Here I am being congratulated by Em seconds after completing the Big Woody in a time of 13:04:15. The hard work and sacrifice had all been worth it.

The Pirate Queen: Min (right) is congratulated by Lucy after winning the prize for second lady veteran at the Big Woody. An amazing achievement. Lucy was inspired by our performances that day and has since completed several triathlons.

An amazing week: Seven days after the Big Woody I married Em.
It made a change to see bridesmaids Lesley and Sarah without running shoes on.
But who kidnapped my best man Lee and replaced him with a cardboard cut out?

On honeymoon at Disney World. I was about to find out the lake we were swimming in was infested with deadly amoebas. It would also be my first open water swim without a wetsuit, not to mention the possibility of meeting alligators.

Keeping up: The Cleveland Steelman, July 2008. When I did this half ironman race a year earlier I was virtually the last out of the water. I'm at the back in this photo, but I soon passed these swimmers to improve my time by almost thirty minutes.

Before Hellrunner: Me, Min and Viking pose before the start of the Hellrunner race in Delamere Forest, Cheshire. Viking had persuaded me earlier that summer that it would be fun! (Don't ever listen to the man on the right of this photo.)

After Hellrunner: 12 miles of freezing cold mud, bogs, brambles and sadistic hills later, there isn't an inch of me that isn't covered in mud. My clothes were thrown away and it took two showers and a bath to get rid of the smell.

December 2008: Andy H looks like he's about to shoot me. All the punctures and daft questions about bikes had finally broken him. This was Em's 30th birthday and the drink on the table would be my last for another seven months.

March 2009: Checking my helmet is on as my father-in-law, John, and I listen to the safety briefing before riding around the Manchester velodrome. "There is no such thing as too fast" has to be the best quote from a safety talk ever.

Here I am having the most fun possible on a Saturday night in Manchester for a tenner. The track is unbelievably steep and the power you have to generate to stay upright is phenomenal.

The Roo looks more like a rocking horse than a bike as it gets ready to fly to Frankfurt and a date with destiny.

Pull my finger: Viking tries to get me to fall for that old trick! He's actually pointing where transition is as I wait for my bike to be unloaded from the transport van. German efficiency reigned supreme. We had 16 hours to go until we'd be racing.

Team Viking: (left to right) Louise, Jamie and Jordan in the grandstands at the finish as they await the arrival of Viking. Their support for the pair of us had been amazing that day. I don't know where they got the energy from.

Ironman Germany, 5 July 2009. The swim was behind me and I was halfway through the bike ride still believing I was chasing Viking. The Roo was malfunctioning but I was still able to ride well. Riding on closed roads was brilliant, I felt like a pro.

I fell apart in the marathon as the temperature reached 32 degrees. Here I'm about to enter the final lap of four. Dad (right) crossed the river to offer support. He was there at my lowest point and his encouragement gave me the strength to finish.

Seeing my name up in lights. Bottom right, I'm just about to cross the finish line. I managed to recover to record my first sub-13-hour Ironman, but didn't have time to celebrate: moments later I was placed on a saline drip suffering with dehydration.

Having just left the medical tent I'm reunited with my biggest supporter, Em. Without her none of what I do would be possible. I'm a very lucky guy.

From medical to beer tent, being held up for my first pint of the year! Mam and dad missed the Big Woody as dad had broken his back in a cycling accident. I was so proud they were there to see me achieve what a few years earlier seemed impossible.

After a journey that spanned three years Viking and I finally completed an Ironman race together. He's the toughest guy I know and it was an honour to share in his big moment. He finished in 14:59 as he'd predicted.

The day after Ironman Germany I was a wreck. I could hardly walk, everything hurt and the only thing that could help was the biggest coconut ice cream sundae I could find.

11

WEDDING DAY PROMISES

"As for Ironman, it's unfinished business. It is the first race in my life that I didn't finish. I will get an Ironman medal at some point in the future and that's a promise."

The defiance and pride in Viking's voice shone through as we sat in the warm summer's air.

I raised my glass of whisky and slurred, "I know you will and I'm gonna be there to see you do it." In front of us the waves lapped the shoreline of Morecambe Bay, behind us the dulcet tones of a-ha reminded us that my wedding reception was still in full swing.

That was the second promise that I'd made that day. I'd been sober at 4pm when I made the first one. Em and I were married in the Ashton Memorial in Williamson Park, Lancaster, in front of our friends and family. The memorial was a spectacular setting. Built at the turn of the twentieth century by millionaire industrialist Baron Ashton, its folly and grandeur celebrated the life of his late wife, Jessy. The dome-like structure, visible from miles around, became known as the 'Taj Mahal of the North'. Eighty guests packed in to see Em and I exchange our vows and become husband and wife, Ironman and Ironwidow.

We sat at the front and signed the register, which we had witnessed by best man Lee and bridesmaid Lesley. We were then joined by Sarah, Em's other bridesmaid, as we posed for photographs. "Let's get a photo of the rings," somebody said. Obligingly, we placed our hands out on the table and it was at that point that Em saw my wrist. I'd noticed earlier and pointed out my mistake to Lee. He assured me that with everything else going on, Em wouldn't notice. He was wrong.

"Why are you wearing your heart rate monitor?" asked my new wife.

I'd forgotten to put on the nice silver dress watch that would have gone perfectly with the morning suit I was wearing.

"It's only the watch, I'm not wearing the chest strap." I said, sheepishly.

"Oh that's okay then. What are you like?" was Em's sarcastic, if understanding, reply.

Behind me my best man coughed, causing me to turn around. I was greeted with a cheeky wink. The git.

Moments later Em had forgotten my faux pas as we left the memorial to the tune of 'Chasing Cars' by Snow Patrol. She squeezed my hand tightly as we walked past our guests and into the bright September afternoon. Tissues were being passed around and out of the corner of my eye I could see Viking sobbing like a baby; it's a good job he was wearing waterproof mascara.

I'd successfully made it through the whole ceremony without limping. All that was left to do was survive our first dance later on. My dad, however, was limping, but he was there, and that meant the world to Em and I. He'd even managed to peel himself into his suit despite the heavy steel back support that he was wearing under his shirt. Whilst we waited for cameras to be set up I introduced my parents to the musketeers.

They offered their congratulations to Dave and Min and told Viking they were sure he'd get there in the end. It was great that they could finally all meet up. Andy H appeared and I left them all talking bike porn whilst I was whisked away to lean artistically on a tree for yet another photograph.

When we returned to the memorial only Lee and Pam remained; the other guests had headed off to the reception. I thanked him for everything he'd done, he was the perfect best man. "You've not heard my speech yet Holgate," was his cocky response.

It was all a front. He was shitting himself about getting up and making a speech in front of the 120 guests at the reception. Whilst I could sympathise (I had been his best man), I loved watching him squirm. He was getting away lightly after what he put me through that day. He made a brilliant speech, though, and after that he relaxed and we enjoyed a whisky or six.

Em's dad John started off his speech by saying, "For those that don't know, Andy became an Ironman seven days ago. If he puts half as much effort into this marriage as he did into his training it'll be a wonderful success. I know he will." The applause was deafening and I couldn't help but blush. He then talked about what a wonderful woman Em was and there wasn't a dry eye in the house. Viking was in pieces again.

The moment of truth had arrived. Em had made me promise at the very beginning of my epic journey that I would be in one piece for our first dance. I didn't let my beautiful wife down. However, as we danced to Westlife's 'World of Our Own' I was terrified of standing on her long flowing bridal gown and Gina shoes. I breathed a sigh of relief when for once my balance didn't desert me.

The rest of the night was a blast. Dave stripped off his shirt to reveal his new Ironman tattoo. It looked cool, a badge of honour. Min would get hers done later that week. To this date I haven't got mine as I'm scared of needles. I haven't entirely ruled it out though.

There were so many people to talk to. Other than the dance and cutting the cake I don't think I spoke to Em until we went up to our hotel room. Viking and Lee had been trying to get hold of our room key all night. I'd told them it was behind the hotel reception desk but secretly I'd held onto it. I didn't trust those two buggers.

Breakfast the next morning was fun. So many people were hung over. My poor cousin Kaye fled the room when a fried breakfast was put down in front of her. I felt surprisingly fine for the amount I'd drank, Em likewise. Maggie, my new mother-in-law, however, was far from fine. Usually so friendly and chatty, she was grey and silent. She was so ill she couldn't make it back home to Liverpool. After all our guests had departed, Lee ran us home. As I opened the door to our house I never got the chance to carry my new wife across the threshold. Her mother pushed past us, her hand covering her mouth, in a desperate dash to the bathroom. I wouldn't see her again until the next morning. Lee was pissing himself laughing at the prospect of Em and I spending our first night as a married couple in our own home on the sofa bed with my mother-in-law in the room above us.

Needless to say I fell asleep with a good book that night.

12

IF THE ALLIGATORS DON'T GET YOU, THE AMOEBAS WILL

Still riding high on the emotions of becoming both an Ironman and a married man, we jetted off on honeymoon to New York and Florida. We did all the tourist things: the Staten Island Ferry, the Empire State Building, Broadway shows, Times Square, museums and shopping. It was Tiffany's for Em and SBR Sports for me, one of America's top triathlon shops. Thankfully Em promised not to buy the necklace that cost more than our house and I left SBR with only a new five-dollar number belt (a piece of elastic that goes round my waist and holds my race numbers). It was an essential purchase as I'd left mine at home.

As a wedding present, Em had entered me into the Disney World Olympic Triathlon on 23 September. I knew she was the perfect woman for me when she told me what she'd done.

We'd visited Florida before as I have family there. Realising that the heat come race day would be a major limiting factor on my performance, I tried to acclimatise. I managed to run twice in the few days before the race, going out at 7am for 30 minutes before the sun came out. It was still in the mid-eighties. The heat concerned me, but something else I saw one morning worried me more. As I ran around the lake at the back of my relatives' house I was suddenly aware of movement not twenty metres away. A rather large alligator was cruising along the surface of the water, observing me, almost daring me to jump in and cool off. I'd always known that they were native to Florida and had even seen them up close in the wild, however that was in the days before I was an open-water swimmer. In that instant it dawned on me that in a few days I'd be doing just that; it would be in a different lake but there was still the distinct possibility that I could be on the breakfast menu.

We were based at Treasure Island on the west coast in Tampa Bay. I'd found a local bike shop and arranged bike hire for the weekend. My weapon of choice would be a Trek Madone. I paid the fee and left my credit card details in case I decided I wanted to keep the bike. "I'm from England, don't worry I won't be taking it home with me." Apparently it had happened before. Another of their bikes had ended up in Australia as well. I loaded the hire bike and the helmet it came with into the hire car and headed off inland to Orlando. We checked into our Disney hotel and I went off to register and rack my bike. I had a quick look round the race expo and bought some GU gel in espresso coffee flavour (the next day I would discover that it was the best-tasting gel I'd ever had. I wish they'd start selling it here in the UK). I figured out where the course was and had a good look at the lake. I didn't see any alligators. Satisfied that I knew what I was doing, I joined Em back at the hotel for a relaxing swim and Jacuzzi.

At 4.45am on race day I received a phone call from Mickey Mouse (seriously) to wake me up. I had cinnamon-based cereal for breakfast. We caught the shuttle bus to the start with a load of serious-looking American triathletes. However I was a little more reassured when I got to the venue and there were people there of all shapes and sizes. Dawn was breaking and the temperature was already in the eighties; boy was it going to be hot.

At 7.40am, five minutes before the start, we received a stern warning from the race director that nose clips were mandatory. There had been an outbreak of a rare amoeba that could be fatal to one in ten people if ingested through the nose. At first those exposed to the microbe, Naegleria fowleri, suffer from flu-like symptoms. Very quickly, in from 1 to 14 days, the symptoms worsen and parts of the brain start to die off. Four people had died in central Florida lakes in the previous few weeks because of it. As sad as this was, it really wasn't what I needed to hear as I prepared to enter the water.

So it's not the alligators you have to worry about it's the single-celled organisms, I thought to myself as I lined up ready for the off. The gun went off and those in my wave bolted into the water. I strolled in, not wanting to disturb any potential killers and mindful to avoid the scrum that would ensue. It was like getting into a warm bath. Those Yanks didn't know they were born.

As a direct consequence of the pleasant conditions the swim was tough. Wetsuits were banned and although I'd swam 1,500m in a pool without one, it's completely different to open water. The buoyancy that would usually be provided by my suit was sorely missed. Not having it destroyed my confidence. The distance was less than half of what I swam at the Woody yet it felt like the longest swim of my life.

I really struggled and about 400m into the swim I did a Dave. My breakfast came back up and all I could taste for the rest of the swim was bloody cinnamon. I threw up again towards the end of the swim as well. Maybe that was what actually kept the gators and the amoebas from coming anywhere near me.

I was out of the water and running through the biggest crowd I've ever seen at a triathlon. There were thousands of people on the lakeside and around transition. I caught a brief glance from Em as I took the time in transition to lather on loads of sun screen and dry my feet. I was out of the swim and T1 in 49 minutes, 10 minutes slower than I'd been at Chester over the same distance.

Spectators lined the first couple of miles but in no time at all I was riding on the deserted roads around the vast Disney property. The bike I was riding felt good and was responsive, although I couldn't figure out the bike computer at all. I decided to just turn it off; this wouldn't be a fast race, I didn't need to know my splits.

The roads were completely flat and smooth. I whizzed along passing lots of fellow competitors of all shapes and sizes, more so than I'd experienced at home. One woman must have been twenty stone. I couldn't help admire her spirit and found myself saying "well done" as I sped past.

The course had been changed for safety reasons so instead of the usual 40km we were doing 56km. You couldn't fault the safety on the course because every junction had two police cars and a motorcycle outrider. There must have been over a hundred police officers on the course and they had closed one lane of the 192 state road (the busiest in Orlando) for us. It must have been a good day to be a criminal in Orlando as all the police were out keeping us triathletes safe.

I was drinking lots of fluid because it was hot and picked up an extra bottle at the 20-mile feed station. This part of the course had what was described as "undulating hills". I would describe them as low level speed bumps; I didn't even change gear.

Getting into the last six miles of the bike I began to suffer. I couldn't feel my feet, a consequence of wearing running shoes. Proper cycling shoes with their stiff soles absorb the road vibration and aid in power transfer from your legs to the pedals. Cycling in soft cushioned running shoes transfers that vibration to your feet and lower legs, resulting in fatigue. Arriving back in transition I stopped to talk to Em and had my photo taken whilst putting on more gallons of sunscreen. I grabbed my cap and headed off out on the run. I completed the bike and T2 in 2 hours.

The run can only be described as hell. Now don't get me wrong – it was pancake flat, with thousands of spectators and very scenic views, but I just died. I was running from 11am and there wasn't a cloud in the sky offering shade. The heat was 93 degrees and I felt it all. By mile two of the 10k I was reduced to walking (mile bloody two!) and from then on I walked through, and after, every feed station for a few minutes whilst I drank gallons of water and PowerAde. All the while the enthusiastic American crowd were shouting "Good jawb", "Way to go", "Awesome man". I regret that I didn't even have the energy to raise a smile in thanks for their encouragement. I was beyond knackered.

I saw the 5-mile marker and was determined to run to the finish. In reality it was more of a shuffle but I'd made it. I had run, walked, and stumbled my way through the slowest 10k of my life in 78 minutes. My finishing time of 4:15:25 was a full 95 minutes slower than Chester. The heat had taken its toll yet the irony was that as I approached the line the heavens opened and a torrent of cooling rain fell. Someone up there was taunting me.

I found the whole experience brilliant. To compete in a big, superbly organised triathlon unlike anything I'd done at home was something I'll never forget. The medal I received was what you would expect from an organisation of Disney's ilk: quality. Although I was probably still recovering from my endeavours of the previous weeks, I found it more physically draining than the Ironman because of the heat. Something that hadn't gone unnoticed by Em, who used the opportunity to remind me of my post-Big Woody daydream. "I really don't think Ironman Nice is the race for you, those distances in the heat of the Med would kill you."

I knew she was right, I would need to find a race in cooler climes if I intended to race long again.

13

MARATHON MISERY

After the excesses of American food and drink I was feeling really bloated. My appetite for food was healthy but my appetite for training was non-existent. After achieving my goal I had nothing to focus on. I'd had the two biggest days of my life within a week of each other and then I felt lost. A kind of post-honeymoon lethargy had set in.

My rapidly disappearing mojo wasn't helped by the realisation that I wouldn't be doing an Ironman event in 2008. The Woody and Ironman UK clashed with two of my cousins' weddings. Two weddings, weeks apart, with one long-distance race on each day. What were the odds of that? I did broach the subject with my cousin Kaye that she may want to put her big day back one weekend. I was politely told to sod off.

The Disney experience had taught me that heat and I didn't get along so that ruled out most races abroad. Unfortunately cooler climate races such as Germany had already filled up. So I felt lost. Don't get me wrong, I was still training with Andy and John but the distances and the intensity were reduced. I guess like a drug addict I needed to up my intake to get high, I needed a jolt to bring me back to life.

Arriving home from work one October evening I received that jolt. There on the coffee table was a rejection letter from the London Marathon. I'd actually forgotten that I'd entered the ballot many months ago. Irritated that they didn't want me, I decided I'd run a marathon somewhere where I was wanted. After discussing the matter with Em and doing some sums we decided that provided we could find cheap flights and accommodation, racing abroad would be a possibility. I wanted to experience a big city atmosphere. It had to be a cool climate and, for the sake of my knees and ambition of a fast time, flat. Rome and Paris were too expensive, Rotterdam too awkward to get to, Berlin full. Beginning to think my year was cursed, I noticed an advert for the Hamburg Marathon. It sounded great: big crowds, seemingly flat and best of all it was on the North Sea coast of Germany. There was no chance of hot conditions so close to one of the wildest, coldest seas in the world. We'd been to Berlin and Cologne before with my parents and found the cities fascinating, and the German people friendly and passionate about sport. A quick phone call later and my parents would be joining Em and I. My dad wanted to make sure I didn't beat his marathon time. Flights were found for less than fifty pounds each and a quick glance at accommodation online told us that it was affordable. I entered there and then. The spur of the moment got me back on track. I now had a reason to push my body again, so 2008 wouldn't be a dead loss after all. The fact that the race would take place in April would give me the time to specifically train for a marathon.

A further incentive came to light the next day when I received an email from my running buddy Lesley. She'd been accepted by London and would be doing her first marathon. She was cursing me because her plan had been to complete it by the time she was 40. Months before I had told her that she'd better start applying because it could take her five years to actually get a place through the ballot. By some miracle Lesley was accepted on her first ever attempt to enter. The ballot entry system for London is like a lottery. Each year almost a hundred thousand people apply for thirty thousand places. If a person receives five consecutive rejections they are automatically awarded a place in the following year's race. I knew several people that had only got places in this way, so I had legitimate reasons to advise Lesley to start the application process early.

"You told me there was no chance I'd get in! I'm panicking here. I don't know if I could run a marathon yet, I thought I'd have years to train, not just months. You'd better help me."

In replying to her email I assured her that she could run a marathon and that we could train together as I would be racing in Hamburg two weeks after she'd torn through the streets of London.

For the first month or so, due to differing schedules, we only managed to train together a couple of times; steady runs of an hour. On both occasions I was struggling to keep up with Lesley. She was in the form of her life and I was slowly clawing my way back into shape. I was determined to get fit so that I wouldn't be "beaten by a girl", as Lesley put it. We had a friendly, competitive rivalry that would drive us both on to try and out-run one another. My fitness began to improve, a direct result of my renewed triathlon training. I had rediscovered my bike. It was hiding in the cellar untouched for months since the Woody. From October through to Christmas Andy and I would ride around the lanes of Lancashire each weekend, clocking up time in the saddle. During the week I was spending a couple of hours on the turbo watching DVDs and burning off the fat. Combining all of this with a seven-mile daily run commute, and twice-weekly, six-mile head torch runs with Andy H, I was back in shape quickly. With the wedding and honeymoon excesses behind me, I was ready to try and keep up with my marathon rival.

Unfortunately I wouldn't be running with Lesley for two months. One cold January night Andy H was away working in Scotland so I decided to go for a run on my own. I'd run a good 6.5 miles and felt I was back on top form. This was reflected in my first two-mile splits of 7:13 and 6:49. Approaching the crossroads in Galgate I misjudged a kerb and placed my right foot down wrong … I went over sharply to the left and felt a great amount of pain in my foot and ankle. My ankle was on fire. I rested and stretched and decided to try and walk it off. It seemed okay so I very slowly jogged back to work to pick up my car.

On returning home I removed my sock to discover that my ankle was purple, almost technicolour. The rest of that evening was spent in a codeine-enhanced fog with my swollen ankle encased in two ice packs. The next morning I couldn't walk on it. After medical consultation it was decided I had badly sprained the joint and that I shouldn't run on it for six weeks. I did nothing for a week and then tried to cycle, but the flexing of the ankle through the pedal stroke was too much to bear. Hamburg was only three months away. It wasn't looking good.

By mid-February the inactivity had taken its toll. Stepping on the scales I discovered that I was two pounds shy of 16 stones. I was mortified. How the hell had I, an Ironman triathlete, let myself go so badly? Within days Em and I had joined a new gym. Such spur of the moment decisions seemed to be becoming a regular occurrence. I couldn't cycle or run but I could lift weights, use a rowing machine and, more importantly, swim. The gym was close to work and open at 7am, so I reasoned I could get a decent swim in every day before work.

As part of the induction at the gym I signed up for an assessment. They measured my weight, body fat, body mass index, heart rate and lung capacity. My results from the first test are in the table below, with the recommended levels that I should have been in the right hand column.

	Actual	Expected
Weight	100 kg	85-91 kg
Fat Weight	26 kg	11-17 kg
Body Fat %	26 %	13-19 %
Muscle Weight	74 kg	71-77 kg
Body Muscle %	74 %	81-87 %
Resting pulse (beats per minute)	54 bpm	65-69 bpm
Body Mass Index	31.2	20-25
Flexibility	6 cm	20-25 cm
Hydration %	50.8 %	55-65 %

It didn't really tell me anything I didn't know. I knew that I had a high body fat rating, looking in the mirror told me that. My heart rate was something I constantly monitored and I knew it was better than average. I knew that I needed to drink more water, Em told me that all the time. The interesting thing came with the fitness test, a very primitive VO2 test to gauge how fit I was. It worked like this: my heart rate was recorded at different points on a stationary bike against a standard resistance over eight minutes. The bike resistance was then increased at gradual intervals and my heart rate was measured again until full resistance was reached, i.e., when I couldn't turn the pedals. According to the results charts they worked off, an excellent average heart rate for someone of my age would be 122. Mine was 99. The guy said he'd never had anyone in the three years that he'd been conducting the test that was as fit as me. This both baffled and amused him because technically I fell into the obese category on BMI yet was off the scale on VO2 fitness. I guess I'm just weird.

Determined once again to shift the weight, I became a regular at the gym. Every morning I was there before work. In the three months from February to my April marathon I would swim just shy of one hundred miles. Swimming was non weight bearing and it helped strengthen my injured ankle by keeping it flexible. I finished off each swim with ten minutes in the hot tub, massaging the joint with the water jets in a bid to speed up my recovery.

My newly-discovered love of swimming wasn't without incident however. Every pool has one, I'm sure you've met yours. I'm talking about the pool bully. The middle-aged bloke who, despite inappropriate Speedos and a paunch, thinks he's God's gift to swimming. Every morning I'd speak to him and he'd ignore me. My mam had always taught me that manners cost nothing and are worth a fortune. He was bad mannered. I'd witness him shouting at children who splashed on the other side of the pool, he argued with people that got too close to him, and, annoyingly, he swam breaststroke. Now there is nothing wrong with swimming breaststroke, I admire anyone who can – because I can't. What was annoying about his style of breaststroke was that he liked to position himself about a metre from the pool wall, thus taking up way too much room. His arms and legs then moved as wide as someone doing the splits. He took up almost a quarter of the pool. It was the most selfish swimming I'd ever witnessed. One morning he must have slept in because I was the first person in the pool and I took his usual position next to the wall. He had a face like thunder and his huffing and puffing as I kicked off for another lap and he entered the water was designed to let me know I'd pissed him off. After a few lengths he was invading my space, edging me closer to the wall. I let it go. Then he kicked me a few times. Convinced these blows were not accidental I thought, *Do that once more you git and you'll be sorry*. As we passed on the next length he actually cut me up completely and forced me to stop, as my shoulder grazed the wall. I'm afraid to say that I lost it, I was seething. I was on the verge of swinging for the guy when I realised that would get me banned and probably arrested. So I left before I did something I would regret. The following morning the same thing happened. Again I turned the other cheek. On the third morning after being kicked again I took my opportunity. As we passed, his arms were on an inward stroke so he wasn't going to touch me. I lifted my right elbow hoping for a good powerful stroke and 'accidentally' caught him hard in his temple, knocking his goggles off. It felt bloody good. Confronting me later in the changing rooms, the one and only time he spoke to me, I just smiled and shrugged unapologetically. "Small pool. It was an accident." To this day I wish him a good morning and get no response; however, he keeps his wayward hands and feet to himself.

At the same time as joining the gym, I revised my diet. Much to the amazement of my mam, Em had successfully got me eating broccoli and cauliflower. This was a major step for me. I hated vegetables with a passion. I'd no idea why. I had no suppressed childhood memories of being forced to consume the green stuff. My new diet of steamed vegetables and grilled chicken breast or tuna saw the weight come off slowly but surely.

With five weeks to go before Hamburg I went for my first run outside. I'd completed two 20-minute runs on the gym treadmill and not suffered any ill effects. I was nervous and took extreme care, carefully watching each foot fall safely on solid ground. I was back, it was a big relief. More so for poor Em who once again had had to put up with my moods that materialised when running was off my daily schedule. Again I can only liken this to an addict going 'cold turkey'. Over the ensuing weeks I built up and eventually completed one 20-mile run before race day. It wasn't ideal preparation but I was still confident that I could run close to three and a half hours in Germany. Somehow I even managed to get in two long runs with Lesley. Her preparation had also been hampered by an ankle injury, but regular physio appointments had solved her problem and come race day she was ready. She ran extremely strongly in London and completed her first marathon in 4:09:47. With London being a week before Hamburg I then knew the target I would have to beat in order to prevent Lesley winning the bragging rights for the rest of the year. I was confident I could do it.

Hamburg was a great city: friendly, cosmopolitan, great food and shopping, and boy did it know how to organise and support a marathon. Race day had finally arrived. I rose early and headed for the start, leaving my family in their beds. They would see me out on the course. As I walked the half-mile to the underground station to catch the packed train to the start I was aware that I was already warm. It was 6.30am and the sun was beating down. This wasn't going to be good for me. The weather forecast had said it would be mild and cloudy with a chance of rain. In the kit bag I was carrying I had a thermal hat and gloves. Standing there pre-race in a t-shirt, with no protection from the sun, I suddenly felt underprepared.

After a rousing rendition of the German national anthem (well I think it was their national anthem) the mayor rang a cowbell and we were off. The start of the race took us along the infamous Reeperbahn, but I didn't see any of the ladies in the windows as the crowds were about five-deep. The noise was deafening. Right from the start there was plenty of room to run, as the roads were wide. Twenty-three thousand runners streamed uphill for the first 3 miles. Despite the sunshine I felt very comfortable, but I started drinking water early because I knew I was going to need it. At 6 miles we ran along the waterfront and I've never seen so many people in one place. People were all around us, hanging out of windows, on bridges – I just couldn't hear myself think. Spectators were cheering, ringing cowbells, sounding air horns, and creating noise with anything they could get their hands on. It was amazing. According to the Hamburg paper the next morning over 800,000 people had lined the route.

I was running well and following my plan of getting to 20 miles in a relaxed and steady manner. I passed the halfway point in 1 hour 49, and apart from feeling too hot I still felt strong. I was slightly behind schedule for a 3 hour 30 finish but I felt I could pick up the pace. I was mistaken. As the clock ticked from 11am till noon I started to slow down as the heat rose. That hour seemed to last a lifetime and at that point I would have happily sold my soul for a running cap. I could actually feel the top of my shaven head cooking. I saw Em and my mam and dad at 15 miles and that gave me a boost. A couple of miles later I ran past a huge office complex and several of the office buildings had digital clocks and thermometers. I saw three that said 25 degrees Celsius, and I was feeling every bit of it. Not as much as one poor runner though. At 19 miles a woman to my left staggered sideways into me. I caught her and luckily there was a medic at that exact point. We eased the woman to the floor and the medic signalled for me to keep going. I never found out her fate, hopefully she was alright. The last 5 miles was carnage. I passed lots of people who had collapsed in the heat, and on two occasions I had to move out of the way of ambulances that were driving headlong into the runners with their lights and sirens blazing. With 2 miles to go I was just hoping to finish in one piece. Any thought of time was long gone. I was desperately thirsty so I was drinking water and energy drinks and eating bananas at the feed stations in a futile bid to find some energy. As I chewed the best piece of fruit I'd ever had I glanced down at my watch in the vain hope that it might lie to me and show that I was still on schedule. What I saw literally stopped me in my tracks. I thought my eyes were deceiving me as my heart rate was being displayed as 210 beats per minute. This was not good. It's usually about 145 when I'm running comfortably. I walked for a minute in an attempt to lower it and prevent myself from having a heart attack. Moments later it had dropped to a level that showed I wasn't about to keel over, so I tentatively plodded on. My average heart rate was 179 for the whole race.

The last mile was just a blur. It was uphill in the blazing afternoon sun; my head had gone and I couldn't feel my swollen feet. Unable to see anything through the fog of fatigue, I just focused on staying upright. In those last few yards I was rowing a boat in a rough sea, lost and unstable. Then suddenly the storm was over and the waves subsided. I crossed the line after managing to raise my arms, more in relief than a victory salute. I staggered sideways and was caught by a medic, who steadied me and tried to get me to go with him. Wanting desperately to be reunited with my loved ones, I stood straight and convinced him in broken German that I was okay. Thankfully he believed that I was in no danger and moments later I limped into the arms of my family. They were equally relieved to see me; they had been quite worried. My dad had worked out a predicted finishing time based on the point they'd last seen me on the course. When I didn't finish at that point they thought they'd either missed me or the infamous marathon wall had crushed me. Unfortunately it felt like it had.

I finished in 4:13:25 and was placed 7,760th out of 23,000. Initially I was disappointed but looking back now I'm really pleased with my performance. I didn't get the time I wanted but I survived and I know that I will run a 3:30 marathon soon. Given the right build-up and day it *will* happen.

Lesley was much more gracious than I was expecting when I saw her two days later. She took one look at my badly sunburnt, peeling head and said, "You look awful, it must have been hell. You still got beat by a girl though, ha ha." Taking in her laughter, I conceded defeat on this occasion but warned her that like Arnie in the *Terminator* films, I'll be back.

14

CONVERSATIONS WITH ELVIS

My immune system was shot. Hamburg had left its mark on my body. As a direct result of my exertions I spent the next few weeks paying for it by catching every germ within a ten-mile radius. So consequently when I eventually had the energy to start training again my legs had fully recovered. The lighter mornings and nights meant that I could start getting out on my bike for a couple of hours before and after work. This was just as well because on John Krug's suggestion, and with Andy H also down to race, I'd signed up for another gruelling challenge. You really would think that I'd have learned my lesson by now wouldn't you?

'Le Terrier' was the rather cosmopolitan name given to Lancaster Cycling Club's 80-mile bike race. Taking place in late June, this was no ordinary race, though; it would feature over 3,000m of climbing. To a cyclist of John's ability it would be a challenge, to one of my ability it was tantamount to suicide. John could climb like a mountain goat, I climbed like an overweight hippo. In fact my hill climbing skills were as legendary as my bike maintenance skills. I once said to Andy H, "I want to go uphill quicker, I'm sick of being an inefficient climber." "You're not inefficient, just bloody slow," he said, deadpan. So why the hell did I sign up for it? Well it was a challenge, and I needed something tough to fill the Ironman void. To make things even harder on myself I would be racing the Cleveland-based half-Ironman (the Steelman) again six days later. The awful conditions the year before hadn't put me off doing it again. Well it was either that or watch *The X-Factor*. What would you choose?

The next two months were spent in total preparation. I was

averaging 200 miles a week on the bike. Enthused, I was out of the house each morning at 6.30am for 20 miles before work, cycling on an empty stomach to burn off stored fat. My ploy worked as soon my weight had fallen to 14 stones. Not surprising, as I got lighter, climbing got easier. This was more noticeable on my evening rides, which were spent in the Trough of Bowland. I would cycle the first 20 miles of the Terrier course after work, working hard up the fell roads, avoiding errant sheep and trying to keep up with John and Andy H when they joined me. Although I knew I was improving, I still couldn't get anywhere near those two on the hills. I didn't think much would change come race day.

After racing the sunset home from the fells one night I received an email from my cousin Mike. He had recently bought a racing bike and was toying with the idea of getting into triathlons. Witnessing my efforts at Cockerham, he had been inspired but then suffered a complete Achilles rupture that required surgery and months of painful rehabilitation. Thankfully he was fully recovered and had been running and cycling for a month without a problem. I had sent him the website for the Terrier and told him that Andy H and I would be doing it, and he was more than welcome to do it with us. His email said simply: "Against my better judgement I've decided to join you." One month later on a rain-slashed, isolated hillside, as we both struggled to move our bikes forward, he hissed at me through gritted teeth, "I should have just deleted your email. Remind me to never listen to you again."

The Terrier wasn't the only race I had to worry about in the summer of 2008. Mindful of the Steelman looming on the horizon, I was beginning to increase my training in the other two disciplines. A half-Ironman is something you have to treat with respect, and having completed the Steelman the year before I knew what I faced and prepared accordingly. I was fitting my swimming in at lunchtimes and occasionally I'd also be in the pool on mornings when I ran instead of cycled. I would run for an hour and then swim for an hour in a reverse brick session. Some days when I was feeling strong and the weather was good, I would run home and then go out on my bike for an hour or two. I still had the training miles in my legs from my marathon training so I concentrated on shorter speedier runs to prepare my body for running at a faster speed. Open-water swimming had begun again and I discovered that I was no longer always the last person to emerge from the lake. That drove me on and it became my fortnightly challenge at those sessions to make sure I swam faster each time. From May to September whilst the sessions were being held, not once did I fail my challenge. With each session I was actually relishing swimming in a deep, cold lake. I was a completely changed person to the one I was at Cockerham in 2006.

My longer runs suddenly got easier when I experimented with a new gadget: an MP3 player. This was something completely new to me. Now although I've already admitted to being a self confessed gadget geek I'd never actually run whilst listening to music and I'd always looked rather snobbishly at people who did. MP3 players belonged to the platinum blonde gym bunnies in full make up that jogged whilst wearing their velour tracksuits. There is a famous book by Bruce Feirstein entitled, *Real Men Don't Eat Quiche*, that takes a tongue in cheek look at stereotypes of masculinity in society. Wearing headphones whilst running was the equivalent of a quiche-only diet in my eyes.

My mind was changed when I happened across an article that focused on Haile Gebrselassie. In it he talked about how his long runs seemed to go much quicker because he had begun listening to his favourite music on his ipod. I thought well, if it's good enough for the fastest marathon runner on earth then who am I to knock it? I spoke to Viking, Min and Dave, who all freely admitted that they ran to the beat a lot of the time. They were amazed that I didn't. Here was I, the gadget geek, made to feel like a complete Luddite.

The first few times I tried it, I hated it. The headphones just kept sliding out of my ears when I started to sweat. According to the *Runner's World* forum this was a common problem, and was easily solved by wearing sport-specific headphones. I invested in some new rather snazzy lime green, space-age designed pieces of moulded plastic and tried again. I couldn't believe I'd not done this before. Suddenly I was running over ten miles regularly and the distance and time were flying by. The right music can be an unbelievable motivator. I defy anyone not to pick up the pace when the uplifting techno beat of Faithless or the guitar riffs of Green Day surround you, and the pain can't help but fade into the background when the haunting vocals of Placebo soothe your aching muscles back to life. Although I often run *au natural* (not naked, but devoid of gadgets), I've never looked back and am living proof that like Gloria Estefan told us in the eighties, "The Rhythm is gonna get you."

No amount of music was going to help me with the first couple of miles of the Terrier. A reoccurring virus had struck me down that week and I was struggling. Mike, Andy H and I had decided beforehand that we would ride together for the whole 80 miles. They must have regretted this at first because they found themselves waiting at the top of each significant climb as I dragged my sorry carcass up behind them. John Krug passed the three of us as we climbed up the desolate windswept Harris End fell. We chatted for a few minutes before he powered ahead, gracefully cresting the fell like it was a speed bump. In his wake I was puffing like an asthmatic chain smoker.

We rode through the villages of Oakenclough and Chipping and eventually on to Whitewell and its famous inn. Turning right we were faced with a hellishly tough climb to Cow Ark; it really was a quad killer. It was a deserted straight road down the other side as we headed towards Slaidburn and Gisburn. The road was clear. I put the bike in its biggest gear and chased after my two mates, putting all of my energy and power into each revolution of the pedals. I didn't touch my brakes once as I revelled in the feel of the warm air gushing past as I cut through it at speeds alien to me. I managed to set myself a new speed record of 51.9mph and in the first comedy moment of the day I freewheeled past Mike going up the next hill. He had not gained any speed on the descent as in contrast to my wild abandon he'd been gripping his brakes, like his life depended on it. When he eventually caught me he confessed "I was more nervous than a male model in Alcatraz."

The scenery around Gisburn and the top of the fells was spectacular, so it was worth the pain to climb up there and feel like you were on top of the world. In a surreal moment we were actually above the clouds; we'd climbed up from the valley floor, through the rain and the dark mass and emerged into the light. We took the opportunity to have a quick swig from our bottles and shared some flapjack. None of us spoke, we were just breathing it all in.

As we climbed towards Bentham and Wray, Andy H was experiencing gear problems. No, my confusion hadn't finally transferred on to him, thankfully he'd had his stupidity inoculations and was immune. He understood how his gears worked, he just couldn't get them to function, so he manually had to change the gears down by getting off his bike and adjusting the chain – not ideal when you are on the side of a steep fell in driving rain. He was not a happy bunny; the only other time I've seen him that upset was when his beloved Everton unveiled their lovely pink highlighted away strip this season.

The climb out of Wray and onto Roeburndale was unbelievably harsh. We were frozen, sodden and generally done in. Our spirits were almost broken, and the only thing keeping us going was the fact that we had less than ten miles to go. The fact that they were probably the ten toughest miles didn't quite register through the curtain of pain and fatigue. To make matters worse the rain had turned to hailstones. We felt like pin cushions as the polar needles chafed our exposed skin. Mike was suffering; being new to cycling this was the longest ride he'd done, and easily the toughest. As I'd introduced him to the race, let's just say I wasn't his favourite cousin at that point, and he's only got two to choose from. Andy H still couldn't get his bike into a manageable gear so he joined Mike in dismounting and walking. I stayed on my bike out of sheer bloody-minded determination. There was no way I was going to walk, I told myself, no matter how slow I went. My lack of forward motion soon became painfully apparent as Andy H overtook me on foot, pushing his bike. He looked at me and said, "Come here often?"

I dissolved into laughter and almost veered off the side of the road. I couldn't believe the bastard was walking faster than I was riding. To this day he still hasn't let me live that down. Andy H was suffering though. His blood sugars had dropped, he was feeling dizzy and had started to hallucinate. "I was having a rather pleasant conversation with Elvis. He sends his regards," he told me when I caught him at the top. "Did he say if he reads my blog?" I asked.

Coming out of Roeburndale was the nearest thing to vertical I think you could ever be on a bike. The road isn't actually a road, more a gravel track. It doesn't even appear on an OS map. It consists of two very steep hills, one after another. I made it up and over the first one somehow, but halfway up the second hill gravity gave me a good hard slap. The road was so steep that my wheels could physically no longer turn. I was standing on my pedals trying to urge my bike forward when suddenly my rear wheel spun backwards on the hailstone-covered gravel. In an instant I was sent toppling off the side of the road, still clipped onto the bike. Luckily a wire fence broke my fall. My eyes focused on the ravine and the twenty-foot drop that I was hovering on the edge of. I breathed deeply and looked at the fence thankfully. As if to add insult to my failed attempt at climbing my bike landed on top of me. More disgruntled than hurt, I managed to unclip and get to my feet. As I struggled to walk in my cycling shoes on the steep, wet, grass-covered hillside, a passing rider asked if I was okay. I mumbled an unconvincing "Yes". Eventually reaching the gravel I walked for about twenty metres until I found a place to remount safely. Almost broken, I gingerly pedalled to the top of the hill and for the first and only time that day waited for Mike and Andy H. They had taken one look at the peaks of Roeburndale and rather sensibly decided to walk.

One last brutal climb over Littledale, and we were done.

When we'd finished and signed back in at the race headquarters we looked like broken men. Seven hours and twenty minutes of riding and almost ten thousand feet of climbing will do that to you though. We had thought it would take us between eight and nine hours, so we'd actually by some miracle, or a pessimistic estimate, done better than we'd predicted. The worst part of the day actually came after we'd finished. We then had to ride back up the steep hill to my house. "Why couldn't you live somewhere flat?" mumbled Mike. My screaming quads and aching arse cheeks were already making plans to ring the estate agent in the morning.

15

THE HIGHS AND LOWS OF THE CHANGING SEASONS

Those six days sandwiched in between the Terrier and the Steelman were the most eventful of the year. Besides my two biggest races there was the small matter of an attempt to gain entry into Ironman Germany.

This was the biggest Ironman race in the world in terms of competing athletes. Some three thousand competitors would descend on Frankfurt to do battle. It was the designated Ironman European championships and as such gaining entry was almost as difficult as racing itself. Entries would open at 9am that Wednesday and would be sold out before the hour was through. I'd heard horror stories of athletes systematically working their way through the entry process, reaching the final payment page, only for the system to crash. They would then log back in to be told that all available places had sold out. What would make this nerve-racking for me was the fact that after much discussion, Viking and I had decided that this would be the race we would do together to finally put his Big Woody nightmare to bed. So we had to co-ordinate being online at the same time in the hope that we'd both get in.

Out of boredom at 8.45am I refreshed the page and sat bolt upright. Shit, entries had opened early. I immediately emailed Viking. I then started the registration process. It was excruciatingly slow, after clicking 'submit' on each page I held my breath and crossed everything my body would allow, hoping that the next page would actually appear. I'd made it to the final page and offered up my credit card details. Three hundred Euros and a few seconds of anguish later I had confirmation that I would be racing in Germany.

I emailed Viking to tell him I was in. No response. Ten minutes went by, still no response. An email then appeared saying, "I've paid but it's still trying to load the page. I'm sweating here." The anticipation was killing me. I was sat there willing my screen to come to life. It's a good job that the library didn't open till 9.30 on Wednesday mornings because I was sat there rocking on my chair talking to the screen. "Come on Viking, get in mate, get in."

My inbox flashed, as new mail arrived. "Someone warn the Germans: the Viking and Holgs show is coming to town. I'm in." I stood up and punched both fists into the air. "YES!" At that point the fact that I was stood in the middle of a library surrounded by my fellow staff suddenly became stark reality again and I ran my hands over my head, smiled sheepishly and sat down like nothing had ever happened. I was on my way to fulfilling my wedding day promise to my mate. All we had do now was train solidly for a year and then complete the race. Sounds easy, doesn't it?

"Oh shit, I'm doing a feckin' Ironman. Holgs it's all your fault." An hour had passed and Viking had obviously realised the daunting task that we both had ahead of us, and once again I was getting the blame. This time, however, Dave and Min would not join us, they had other fish to fry. Min had signed up for Ironman Lanzarote. Although the legendary winds and hills of the desolate lava fields appealed to my masochistic need for tough events, the high temperatures made it an unwise choice for me. One of the factors in choosing Germany was that although it was in July there was a good chance it could be cool. However the Hamburg experience had told me not to take anything for granted. Dave would be travelling much further afield. A keen climber, he would be fulfilling a lifetime ambition and climbing at the Everest Base Camp in the Himalayas. So although he wasn't doing an Ironman, he wouldn't be sat on his arse so we didn't make him feel too guilty. And besides, at 50 he's got another good 30 or 40 years of Ironman racing left in him still.

So going into the Steelman I felt focused. Germany, although a long way off, was very fresh in my mind. A strong performance at the Steelman would give me the confidence to build towards that goal, and besides I was really looking forward to seeing how I fared against my time from the previous year. Unfortunately the horrendous weather that had plagued the event the previous year had returned and I spent the day getting soaked. I actually think that the swim portion of the race was the driest part. However the lovely July weather didn't dampen my performance. My blog entry the next day reflected on my mood:

"I'm sat here aching and my body is telling me that I pushed it to the limit yesterday. My feet are battered and bruised and my quads ache but I just can't stop grinning because I had a storming day at the office."

Let me talk you through the day that saw me smash the previous year's time by almost 30 minutes.

It was a bitterly cold July day so I decided to wear two swimming caps. This had two positive outcomes: it kept my head warmer and it kept my earplugs in. I use the putty ball type earplugs now and find them much better than the traditional ones. There were 180 of us treading water as we waited for the horn to go off to signal the start. As usual I started at the back and to the right to try and avoid the main scrum. The water was crystal clear and I was quickly into my swimming and passing people. I felt really comfortable and just kept telling myself to "stretch and glide". Going into the second lap I had caught up to the group in front. I swam through them carefully avoiding any major impacts. I did receive a couple of kicks and smacks but nothing significant. I stumbled getting out of the water, tripping on the submerged rocks, but unlike in 2007 I didn't feel dizzy or sick. I was over the moon with my swim time of 38:13, over 14 minutes faster than the previous year. It still wasn't quick but at least it was respectable.

Transition was done in an instant, under the encouraging gaze of Em and my mam and dad who'd made the journey to watch as well. The first few miles were quite crowded and I was nervous about drafting (riding in someone else's slipstream) as we had all been warned about it. Several people would subsequently be disqualified as a result of their cheating. I've never understood why people would risk having their race nullified just because they were cycling too closely to another competitor. Go past them or drop back; it's clearly stated in the race rules on the British Triathlon Association website. At the end of the day if you draft you are only cheating yourself. You're getting a 'free ride' and avoiding the elements. It's not a true reflection of your ability, and taints your achievements.

I made a conscious decision to pedal the first ten miles without going onto the big ring (the front chain ring that gives you more speed but is harder to pedal) in the hope of waking my legs up. I was worried they wouldn't perform as a result of the Terrier six days previously. I started passing people as we headed up the hills towards Northallerton. At about 15 miles of the first lap the heavens opened again. A torrential downpour combined with the strong crosswinds made for difficult handling conditions for the rest of the bike ride. At times it was like cycling through a stream and my exposed arms and legs were getting peppered by the raindrops. My now familiar masochistic attitude when faced with these climatic predicaments kicked in, so I felt great and loved every minute of it. Andy H would later comment that, "You seem to thrive and excel in torrid, extreme conditions." I think it's more of a survival instinct, as in: *Bloody hell I'm frozen, if I pedal harder I'll get home quicker and be able to warm up.*

As I started the second lap I gave the thumbs up to my cheering crew, who looked as wet and cold as me. I felt very humbled and honoured to see them stood there in those inhospitable conditions, supporting me. It can't have been pleasant at all. I just hammered the bike on the second lap and passed quite a few people. I'd set myself the goal of getting off the bike in a total of four hours if I was going to finish the race in under six. I was out of T2 in about 3:50, so I was on schedule for a new personal best time. Boy that was a great feeling and all the motivation I required to summon the extra energy needed going into the run. My bike split was 3:08:49 for 58 miles compared to 3:21 the previous year, a gain of 12 minutes. Obviously all the hill training building up to the Terrier had improved my cycling ability, and that day I was seeing the benefits.

My legs were stiff as I started the run. The lead-like feeling was brought on by the extra effort I'd needed to expend against the elements on the bike. Thankfully my aching limbs didn't take long to recover and I soon got into my running. Well as much running as you can do on a 95% off-road course that was completely flooded and muddy. For a good section of the course I was zigzagging, avoiding the huge flooded potholes and the runners coming back the other way along the narrow track. I was running in my Sealskinz waterproof socks which were feeling heavier with each stride. The outside of the socks had soaked up the water like a sponge, but it was a small price to pay for my feet being dry. In anticipation of bad weather and my familiarity with the course I'd chosen to run in my off-road Salomon shoes. I don't know how the fast guys managed to run along that course in normal racing flats. I was losing traction on the muddy waterlogged surfaces in my ultra grippy shoes.

I carried energy drink on the first lap in a bottle belt but discarded it at the beginning of the second lap. Luckily I didn't knock my mam out as I hurled it in her direction as I went past. I felt strong and knew that I was on for a PB unless I blew up completely on the final lap of the run. I continued to pass people and although I was hurting I was happy. Motivated by the prospect of a new personal best, I pushed my body to its limit and it responded well.

I crossed the finish line and was totally spent. I had put in a decent run to finish in 1:42:51 (1:50:54 the previous year) and had smashed my half-Ironman by a massive 29 minutes. I'd wanted to dip under six hours after doing 6 hours 4 minutes in 2007. I'd really taken myself to my limit and far exceeded my ambition and expectations to finish in 5:35:37.

My legs stiffened up immediately after finishing, letting me know that I'd worked hard. I found the pain comforting; if it had been absent I would have questioned my commitment.

On the way home the four of us stopped for tea at the famous Wainwright's 'Coast to Coast' Fish and Chip shop in Kirkby Stephen, nestled in the Cumbrian fells. Alfred Wainwright, the great English bastion of the Lake District and the patron saint of hill walkers, had stopped for refreshments here on his coast to coast walk and had been loath to leave. I could see why: the food was simple yet amazing. However when I stood up to leave I found that my legs wouldn't move. My hamstrings were so tight that I had to be helped up from my chair. "That proves you gave it your all today," said my mam, laughing along with Em, who added: "Self inflicted", affectionately. This made my day because I'd wanted to race well in front of them and regain my confidence after the hard lessons of Hamburg. Their comments and my pain proved I had. Each grimace of pain hid an internal smile.

I was keen to build on my form in the days after the Steelman so I entered a sprint triathlon in Macclesfield. This would be a special occasion for two reasons. Firstly it would mark the triathlon debut of my cousin, Mike, who despite harbouring murderous feelings towards me during the Terrier had forgiven me enough to sign up when I told him that I had. Secondly it would mark the first occasion since the Big Woody that the four musketeers would race against each other. Viking's wife, Lou, and Dave's wife, Suzie, along with their daughter, Annie, would also join us by racing for the first time. My wife, Em, professed to have more sense and kept Mike's mam, Jean, company whilst we raced.

The reunion party was spoilt at the last minute by Min. Not that any of us could blame her, as she had ducked out when she had a better offer of an all-expenses-paid trip to ride Alpe D'Huez. Now just think about that for a second ... five star hotel and the Mecca of road biking in sunny France or an early Sunday morning just south of Manchester? Yep, I'd have gone to France as well. Later that day we received texts saying that she had completed the magical mountain in 1 hour 44 minutes. Viking, Mike, Dave and I toasted her success with bacon butties and dishwater coffee in the leisure centre that hosted our race. It wasn't champagne and brie but it was good enough for us.

Dave and Viking both had solid races, and they took the bragging rights in their battle with their debutant spouses, Suzie and Lou. Viking was quite laid back about it but Dave was secretly relieved. Suzie had recently run the London Marathon whilst Dave had been suffering with an ankle injury, so he'd been a little nervous beforehand. Dave had also managed to beat Annie, and the relief on his face was telling. Moments after crossing the line he grasped for breath and said, "Having to race your 18-year-old daughter is really scary!"

Mike finished 25th in his first triathlon, recording a time of 1:29:03, and describing the whole process as being "harder than it looks". But much like myself after Cockerham, he'd caught the bug after finishing his first triathlon, and he'd be back. I was amazed when I finished in 1:33:25, earning 41st place. This may not sound too impressive but when you consider that 182 people finished, it wasn't half bad.

Riding the crest of a wave, I needed one final triathlon fix before the season ended and the hard graft of winter running and cycling took hold. At the end of September I would join a whole host of Pirates at the Nantwich Sprint Triathlon in Cheshire. However before then I had the chance to do some warm weather training.

I flew to Beziers in the South of France for ten days of rest and relaxation with Em. My idea of rest and relaxation was probably different to most people's, though, as I only had two days where I didn't run. I managed a couple of 10-milers and the rest were 7-milers. It was between 31 and 34 degrees every day and I was deliberately running when it was hot to try and improve my tolerance to running in the heat. The area I was running in, although flat, was simply stunning. I'd run along the Canal du Midi and also through all the vineyards. On most of my runs I never saw another soul; it was like running through my own private estate. I have to say that these were some of the most enjoyable runs I've ever done. Tranquillity in its finest guise. So if any of you ever get the opportunity to visit that part of the world I'd recommend it.

Tanned, refreshed and arguably cultured, I returned to English shores and a sun-drenched Cheshire for the final triathlon of my season. Arriving at the venue I met up with fellow Pirates: Cake, Nam, Aitch, Hope and Sprocket, who were camping. They provided me with some much needed coffee, as I'd been up since 4.45am to drive down from Lancaster. I probably didn't make much sense until the caffeine kicked in, and thinking about it now I probably didn't afterwards either. All four ladies were competing for the first time and were slightly nervous, Cake was just supporting. I tried to instil some calm into them. I recalled "my first time" and how the worst bit had been what they were now experiencing, the fear of the unknown. I reassured them that once the race got underway they'd be wondering why they'd never raced a triathlon before. My comments would prove to be true as Nam and Hope would later race an Ironman, Aitch would complete a half-Ironman and Sprocket would continue to race at sprint distance. Cake would go on to become an Ironman, inspired by what he saw that day.

My race went perfectly. I swam effectively, cycled hard and floated around the run course as the Pirate support crew cheered me on. I finished in a new sprint PB time of 1:14:44. The most pleasing consequence of my fast performance was that I'd finished before Viking started the run. This meant that I could cut back and forth across the park where the run was taking place and shout abuse, err I mean encouragement, at him.

Three triathlons and three very impressive performances, I couldn't have asked for more. I had recorded personal bests in every race I had competed in. I had pushed myself and set new standards that I would be able to pursue the following year. My season had gone brilliantly. If I could improve on this form over the winter I could feel confident that Germany would hold no real fear for me. Other than it being a bloody long, unpredictable, punishing test of one's body and mind.

My triathlon season had finished but I remained active over

the autumn and winter, building up a strong fitness base on the bike and in my legs. Before 2008 faded into 2009 I had two long-distance running events on the horizon, so in the weeks after Nantwich I was running around forty miles a week. Andy H and I would run two or three times a week along the coastal path, increasing from six to ten miles as we trained for the upcoming Cross Bay half-marathon. This race would take place entirely on the sands of Morecambe Bay, making it a leg-sapping experience. It was a unique event, obviously taking place at low tide, starting at the northern Cumbrian side of the bay and following what was the old coach route across the sands. The route progresses north-east in a roughly semi-circular pattern, including having to run/wade across the numerous rivers and streams that empty into the bay, the largest of which is the Kent channel which in normal conditions would be 50-75m across and thigh deep. The soft surface of the sand would give a runner very little energy return for each stride, a bit like bouncing a tennis ball on a duvet. When running on roads the energy return is greater with each stride taken, but as a runner on the soft sand you have to work that much harder to cover the same distance. So Andy H and I expected it to be hard work; in reality what we got was a lesson in survival.

After a night of torrential rain and gale force winds we arrived at Hest Bank on the Lancashire coast and looked out over the sands. The mountains of the Lake District and the Cumbrian fells had disappeared. A thick, eerie fog had descended and the water in the channel in front of us was travelling along at an alarming speed. Andy H and I were concerned that the race might be cancelled but a marshal reassured us that it would indeed take place. Em and Andy's wife, Pam, sat in the car and expressed concern that it didn't look pleasant out on the sands, but added that they were looking forward to sitting in the café and keeping warm. The logistics of this race meant that the runners had all assembled at the finish, on the wrong side of the Bay from the start at Flookburgh. The organisers had laid on buses to transfer us all to the other side, and the journey would take forty-five minutes. Buses were assigned by race number so Andy H and I were on different ones.

When I got off the bus at the start I couldn't see Andy H anywhere amongst the crowds of runners. My vision was impaired by the cap I had pulled down over my face in a vain attempt to shield myself from the biting wind.

"Excuse me but are you a triathlete?" I recognised the familiar, sarcastic voice instantly.

My training partner had managed to find me due to the fact that I was the only person in bright yellow Pirate racing gear. You certainly can't blend in when you become a Pirate.

We were given a pep talk from the Major followed by a quick safety briefing, warning of the dangers. "Keep to the tracks of the quad bikes. If you have to drop out, stay where you are and we will come and get you. Don't attempt to make it to the shore no matter how close it may seem." Fully briefed, we were herded to the edge of the sand and the start line. They announced that due to the heavy rain we would be taking a longer course to get over the sand.

A collective sigh went up from the crowd and nervous chatter surrounded the runners. So as if it wasn't tough enough to begin with, they were now making it a half-marathon and a little bit more. However I fully understood the organisers' concerns. The shifting sands of Morecambe Bay have proven fatal on so many occasions. In 2004 the sands claimed the lives of 21 cockle pickers trapped by the rising tides. They had been on the sands without the expert help of a guide. The place looks tranquil but it's deceptive. What looks like solid, hard sand could easily be quicksand, and when the tide comes in it travels faster than any man can run. It is a very dangerous place. So dangerous that the Queen actually bestows the role of 'Morecambe Bay Sand Pilot' on the man best qualified to lead people safely across the sands. Cedric Robinson, an extremely fit 70-year-old, had held that responsibility for over 40 years and took his job very seriously. The prospect of 300 people out in the middle of the sands must have been a health and safety nightmare. Our safety would fall entirely in the hands of Cedric and his team, who had mapped out the course that morning. So if we had to run 14, 15 or even 16 miles to get home alive, then I for one wasn't going to moan about it.

The start was a complete bottleneck; 300 runners on a narrow tractor path leading onto the sands. I got stuck behind two lasses who were moving at a snail's pace. I eventually managed to pass them as we reached the first ankle-deep gully. They obviously didn't want to get their shoes dirty and were tiptoeing into the water. *Wrong bloody race for that sort of behaviour*, I thought as I strode into the water. Andy H was nowhere in sight. I'd had such a slow first half-mile that I presumed that he must be in the group about 300 metres ahead of me. It later turned out he'd lost his shoe in the thick mud and had to stop to retrieve it. I spent the whole race chasing a guy ahead of me that had the same vest on as Andy H, and Andy H was behind me chasing me.

The first half of the race was spent running with the wind at our backs, which pushed us on. I was transfixed by the swirling patterns the sand storms were making along the route. I felt strong and every time we hit a channel I ploughed into it as fast as I could. That would be my tactic for the race: be strong through the water. I was glad I'd worn my Salomon off-road shoes and Sealskinz socks because although they kept getting soaked, they seemed to dry out quickly as well. Aware that wet feet would mean blisters, I'd prepared accordingly by placing blister plasters on my feet at the points where I'm prone to hot spots. It was a great decision as despite running with soaked feet I didn't get any blisters.

At about three miles a familiar face appeared. Chris Wild, the rock god from open-water swimming, caught me. We chatted for a bit and then he went off. I managed to keep him in sight for a couple of miles but then his strength and speed carried him away into the mists. I was also passed by Gary, who I'd talked to at the gym in the mornings. I was determined to keep him in my sights, which was easy as he had a neon orange vest on. This was just personal pride. I wanted to be the first finisher from the gym. I also wanted to prove a point. As nice a guy as Gary is, I had the distinct impression that he doubted my claims about my running

/triathlon credentials. He's about nine stone of pure muscle, and here was I who didn't look like I was shaped to run telling him one morning, "Yeah the Cross Bay will be tough but I compete in triathlons and marathons so I'm not that worried." The look on his face had been one of pure scepticism. In all honesty if I had been Gary listening to me I'd have thought, *Yep, got a bullshitter here.*

We reached the main Kent channel and it was a raging torrent. Boats bobbed up and down where we were meant to cross and the far side of the channel seemed miles away. I didn't realise it at the time but we were being pivoted round in a figure of eight to head back to the start. We turned into the wind and I just put my head down and ran as strongly as I could. I physically couldn't lift it because the wind was too strong. The sand lashed my bare legs and with them being wet it started to stick to them. All I could taste was sand; my lips would later be red raw from their involuntary exfoliation. The group ahead of me seemed to be struggling and I saw this as my opportunity to move up the field. I must have passed about fifty people in the next mile or so, including Gary, and I never looked back. I crossed another channel and was suddenly knee deep in ice-cold salt water. Emerging on the other side I was running on my own in no man's land until I caught a runner from Lancaster & Morecambe Athletic Club. We ran silently together for the next three or four miles. All I saw was my shoe laces. I knew he was there because I could hear his metronomic breathing, but I never saw his face and I'm sure he never saw mine. The wind wouldn't allow it.

A strong headwind stopped us both in our tracks, almost lifting us backwards off our feet. As I regained momentum I spotted the landmark of Heysham power station on my left. I couldn't figure out why we were going back in the wrong direction. In that split second of clarity I couldn't see anyone turning left and heading across the bay; it was very confusing.

The breathing on my right faded away and my silent companion was gone. I was once again alone and running in the middle of no man's land. The only things to guide me were the occasional red flags in the sand making the safe passage. Thankfully they were sufficient. Suddenly a violent gust of wind blew my cap off. Instinctively I turned to give chase but in the blink of an eye it was gone, blowing across the sands into the misty abyss. The flags guided me back towards the shore. Believing it to be Silverdale, and that I was about to emerge on the other side of the headland for the final crossing to Hest Bank, confusion flooded my mind as déjà vu struck. *Hang on a minute. I ran past that rock formation earlier.*

It stood out to me because years earlier I had spent another windswept afternoon analysing the composition of the rocks on an A-level geology field trip. I was about to be back at the start in Flookburgh. I now fully understand how people can get lost out on the sands.

With dry land in sight I strode purposely into the final river channel crossing. But with my head bowed I was blown slightly off route. Suddenly the world disappeared and I was underwater. "What the …?" My survival instinct kicked in and I forced my head back above the surface. I took a second to comprehend where I was. From what I could see I was neck deep in glacial seawater. I'd completely misjudged the depth of the water, so I'd missed the shallow channel and veered off, running head first into an unseen deep water gulley. There was nothing more to do other than throw my legs back and launch into front crawl. Three strokes later and my impromptu open-water swim was over. I emerged from the murky water covered in thick black mud. I had only been about fifty metres from dry land. Looking like the creature from the Black Lagoon, I turned into the finish in 1:36:15. I was pleased with the time and my strong performance, but a bit confused to be back at Flookburgh and wondering how far we'd actually run. We were told later that it was approximately 11 miles. So at the start of the day we'd be told that we'd be running longer, and we actually ended up running less than a half-marathon. It had definitely been one of those days. I couldn't see Andy H who I believed had finished in the group ahead of me. It was only when I saw him running along the road towards the finish that it dawned on me that I'd been chasing the wrong green and white vest for the entire race.

It had been a race unlike any other I'd done. Once again Mother Nature had reminded us how she can make humans suffer with her might. Andy H was really suffering as he had been running for the last hour of the race with a layer of sand under each contact lens. Two people that weren't suffering however were Pam and Em, who had been joined by my mam and dad in the café at the finish in Hest Bank. Arriving at the finish by bus, we found our support crew in good spirits despite the fact that they hadn't seen us finish. "Look at you two, I bet you haven't even been for a run. You've had a nice little bus tour of the Lakes haven't you?" Obviously being married to Andy H for all these years had had an effect on Pam; she'd developed his sense of humour for one.

In the days after the race I met up with Andy H for a run and we both agreed that we had unfinished business with this race. I still want to actually run across Morecambe Bay one day, hopefully in better weather. Well it couldn't be any worse.

My winter of adventure running would be completed by an event that Viking had persuaded me to enter. Hellrunner. I should have seen the clue in the name and resisted my friend's mutterings. Hellrunner is a race of between 11 and 14 miles through Delamere Forest in Cheshire. Sounds quite nice, doesn't it? A day out running through the woods in rural Cheshire. Think again.

That unusually dry and sunny November morning I joined Viking and Min at the start with 1,500 other slightly insane people. The relaxed atmosphere lulled me into a false sense of security and I wasn't prepared for the horrors to come. The first mile was the easiest part of the course and that was all uphill, then we headed into the forest where nightmares seemed to lurk behind every tree. The run through the forest saw me picking my way through foul smelling, ankle-deep mud, hurdling fallen trees, ducking under holly branches and running through brambles. And those, my friends, were the highlights. I spent my morning clawing at tree roots and mud, trying to pull myself up steep, slippery banks. The sheer vertical climbs caused my legs to ache but the descents were far worse. It was terrifying in places. If I'd lost my footing only the trees would have broken my fall. And that would have hurt.

There were no mile markers so I think I'd run about five miles when I just sank in an unseen peat bog down to my knees. I moved forward to get out but I was stuck fast. I was going nowhere. Luckily another guy stopped to help me; he needed all his strength to pull me out. I was pleased that my shoes had stayed on, but they were now just caked in mud and soaked. Somewhere in that bog a twig had lodged itself between my shoe and the bare skin of my Achilles. Before I realised what had happened I'd lost my skin. I could feel intense pain but I couldn't see the blood because my legs were covered in foul-smelling cold mud. I was really starting to suffer and I was freezing. I passed a marshal and asked him how long to go. "Just over a mile," he said. My spirits were raised, but *what* a mile it would turn out to be.

In that last mile I battled what the organisers labelled 'The Bog of Doom'. Anything else that had gone before was like strolling through a manicured meadow. The bog was about 100m long and consisted of a stagnant pool of waist-deep, rancid-smelling, murky, freezing water. It looked and smelt like an open sewer. There must have been dead things under the surface for it to smell that bad. Submerged jagged tree stumps and floating debris made it very treacherous. By the time I reached dry land I could no longer feel anything from the waist down, and my hands were like blocks of ice.

As I turned into the open field I could see the finish. I was so relieved. It didn't last. The sadistic so and sos sent us back up the hill we had started on. I could have cried. I shuffled across the line, knackered, in 1:55:58. I tried to wait to see Viking and Min finish but I was shivering so badly that Em was seriously worried for me and ordered me back to the car (a one-mile walk away) to get changed and warm up. It would actually take me over two hours to stop shivering. Whilst Em went to the van in the car park to buy me a coffee I stripped completely naked. I just didn't care who saw, I needed to get into dry, warm clothes. I had deliberately raced in old clothes and shoes so that everything I removed went straight in a bin bag. I ended up putting it in a bin at a motorway service station on the way home. There were no showers or wash facilities at the finish so consequently when I did stop at the services I got some strange looks as I walked through the crowded lobby to the toilets. My face was plastered in mud and I stunk. It took two showers and a bath for me to get clean. I had mud in places that I didn't think possible.

Would I do it again? Nope, never. And I've never said that about any race. I'd even do the Terrier again. I've proved to myself that I could do it, I've earned the t-shirt and I have no desire to put myself through that again. This race just wasn't enjoyable, I didn't get that buzz when I finished. It hurt me and seemed pointless and because of that I'm done with it. Hellrunner was my own personal nightmare, yet Viking and Min loved every minute of it and seven days later they did a similar event called the 'Sodbury Slog'. The two friends who'd trained and raced together for years obviously have a different concept of a 'dirty weekend' than me.

Hellrunner left its mark on me physically as well as mentally. As a result of the skin coming off my Achilles it was well into December before I could run again. I attempted to but it was just too painful, the skin just would not heal. It also became infected, meaning I had to take a course of antibiotics. It just affirmed my conviction that I wouldn't be doing any more 'novelty' events.

Although I couldn't run I could still cycle and I had a new reason to focus on this discipline: I was getting a new bike. I had decided that I was going to buy a triathlon-specific bike through the 'Cycle to Work Scheme', a government-run scheme that my employer had signed up to. This green initiative was designed to get more people cycling to work, and as an incentive I could get essentially a half-price bike. I qualified for the scheme and signed up. I would have to wait a month for my voucher to be approved and then I could go and choose my bike.

The new bike had tri-bars, not drops like the road bike. So I started to prepare for riding in the more streamlined triathlon 'tuck' that my new bike would enforce by riding my existing bike in the same way. I had spent the previous year with the 'clip-on' tri-bars on the bike primarily as a helmet holder in T1. I had never used them. In 2008 I had raced using the bars. I had read up on them, measured my forearms, and adjusted the bars to fit. I was amazed at the difference. They were really comfortable and my speed increased by a good 3-5mph, which in a race is a significant increase. It would explain why my performances at the Steelman, Macclesfield and Nantwich were better than the year before. Being in the 'tuck' position made me more aerodynamic on the bike, basically because I was a smaller cross-section and therefore cut through the air quicker. If you are interested in the technicalities of triathlon aerodynamics I suggest you read one of the many articles written by people that know much more about it than me. As you know I struggle with gears so cutting-edge science is beyond me.

My intention was to set up the new bike on the turbo and ride it all winter, getting used to the position before unleashing it on the roads in 2009 ready for Ironman.

With all this in mind I rode onto the university campus early one Sunday morning. I knew the perimeter road would be almost traffic-free so it would be the ideal place to practise. I built up my speed and managed to maintain the tucked position. I'd managed to do about five miles when disaster struck. On a slight downhill stretch I hit a speed bump at 25mph and my left tri-bar just came off in my hand. I veered wildly into the middle of the road and somehow managed to keep upright and prevent myself from falling. I was extremely grateful that I had chosen a quiet road. On a busy road in traffic I would probably have been hurt or worse. The bolt had come out of the clamp. I managed to retrieve this and proceeded to cycle home with just one bar on the bike and the other tucked in my jersey pocket. When I got in I put it back on the bike and tightened the bolt. Paranoia then set in and I checked and tightened every other bolt I could find on the bike. Hopefully

I wouldn't face such a problem when I picked up my new bike.

My voucher came through and I'd already decided which bike I would buy. I'd read lots of online reviews and scoured the pages of *Cycling Weekly*, *Triathlon Plus* and *220 Triathlon*. They informed me that for the money I could afford, the Quintana Roo Seduza should be my weapon of choice. One of the approved suppliers that I could use under the cycle to work scheme just happened to be the area's leading triathlon specialist, Royles. And they were stockists of the Roo. I rang up and made enquiries to see if they had the bike in my size and was invited to come along to be fully fitted.

The fitting consisted of me sitting on the bike attached to a turbo trainer whilst two assistants looked at my position. "Oooh suits you sir!" said one.

As a fan of *The Fast Show* I almost fell of the bike with the giggles. They made millimetre adjustments to the seat, pedals, headset, brake levers and tri-bars. The whole process took two hours. I came away knowing that my new bike was perfect for me. The brake levers were at the perfect distance so I wouldn't strain my back when I had to pull them. The seat was at the perfect height and angle meaning that the power would transfer perfectly to the pedals, making me ride faster. I was in love, this was my baby. The Roo and I were destined to be together. Not only was she the right fit for me she looked sexy as well. Made of 12k multi-layered carbon fibre, black and red in colour, and accessorised with a mix of Shimano Ultegra and Dura Ace components, she oozed class. The carbon construction made her incredibly light yet stiff for speed and handling.

On returning home with the Roo I talked passionately to Em about my new bike. She listened intently as I explained that it would make me a lot quicker and that it was an amazing investment. "So if you've spent that on a bike, can I go shoe shopping?" was her only response. My wife: the Imelda Marcos of Lancaster. I really hoped that she was joking.

16

THE MIGHTY COLT, A STRUGGLING CAT
AND A CHEEKY CURRY

As I stepped out of my wetsuit, the biting late September wind wrapped itself around my wet body and a quick shiver pulsed through my muscles. The last open-water swim of the season had been a particularly cold affair. It was almost dark and winter was most definitely on the horizon. The friction of a dry towel was just reawakening my numb skin as the organiser of the swims, Andrew McCracken, approached. Always personable, he told me that a few of those from the Lancaster area were thinking of starting the city's first triathlon club, and would I be interested in becoming a part of it? I immediately expressed an enthusiastic interest in such a venture. It would be good to meet new people, and have the opportunity to train and learn from the likes of Andrew, an experienced and talented triathlete. That was in September 2008 and I wouldn't hear anything for a couple of months, however when I did the wait was well worth it.

I received an email from Andrew saying that the club, City of Lancaster Triathlon (or COLT for short) was going to meet that Sunday morning for its inaugural training ride. Although Andy H couldn't come along with me as he was away visiting family that weekend, it would be a good way for the pair of us to push ourselves in our training, with new routes and new rivalries, and also it would give us a social outlet. He would eventually join me, as would my cousin Mike, and we would be part of one of the fastest-growing triathlon clubs in the country in 2009.

A strange mixture of nerves and anticipation filled my head as I pulled on my cycling gear. I'd seen these guys swim; they were like torpedoes cutting through the water. Would they be the same on the bike? Would they ride away from me? *Oh well. I've got to give it a try*, I thought. I'm glad that I did because it would be no exaggeration to say that COLT has become a big part of my life, enriching me professionally, socially and sportingly. Yes I was a proud Pirate, and still am at heart, but COLT was very much in the real world. I could be heavily involved in something new. I could be an influence rather than just a foot soldier.

There were five of us on that ride. We headed out at a fairly sedate 13mph towards Caton, up through Wray, across the border into the badlands of North Yorkshire and Bentham before doubling back into Cumbria through Kirkby Lonsdale and down towards the Kellets and back to Lancaster. We covered just over 40 miles and I suppose it was more of a social ride than anything else. Given the calibre of people that I was riding with it really was a sociable ride for them. I discovered a lot about my riding partners. They had all been friends for years, training together and competing in races around the world. And I'd been thinking that I was the only nutter in Lancaster that spent my life dressing in lycra and rubber in the name of fun.

Chatting away, it dawned on me that I was in some illustrious company. Three of the five had qualified for World Championships or represented their country.

Richard Mason, who I'd met at swimming, looked like a human action figure. The former Royal Marine and rugby player not only looked the part, he was the part. I couldn't help but be impressed when he told me he'd be contesting two Ironman races in the coming year, like it was no big deal. His chiselled face broke into a Jack Nicholson-esque grin when I told him that I, the new boy, had entered Ironman Germany. "That's great Andy. Hey lads, we've got another Ironman here. Come on Mark, that just leaves you now." Obviously from the mocking tone of his voice the fact that Mark Hammond, the youngster of the group, hadn't 'gone long' yet had been a regular topic of the group's affectionate banter. I spent a lot of that ride talking to Mark about my experiences of training for and racing at the Woody. Mark was an exceptionally quick shorter-distance triathlete, and with youth and power on his side it was immediately obvious to me and those that knew him better that he'd have no problems stepping up the distance. He would go on to prove our assumptions correct by completing Ironman UK in August 2009 in a debut performance of 11 hours. He would later email me to say that talking to me on that initial ride had spurred him to throw his hat in the Ironman ring. I can't help but feel good about that.

John Knapp was the complete polar opposite of action man Richard, yet no less effective an athlete. His slight frame masked power, speed and an almost unlimited aerobic capacity for endurance. He was the human equivalent of a Mini containing a Ferrari engine. But he hadn't always been this way. John started out as a backmarker runner in the 1980s but in 1991 came across triathlon while living in Sydney for a year. Teaching himself to swim freestyle he progressed quickly, and soon felt he was ready to race. His first UK race was the Bath Olympic distance race in 1992 where he was pleased to break the three-hour barrier. Years of hard work and dedication had just seen John qualify for the fabled Ironman World Championships in Kona, Hawaii. He was living proof that sometimes you can just get better with age. Unfortunately a couple of weeks after this ride John was hospitalised with a serious infection and missed out on his Hawaiian dream. It is testament to the man that he came back stronger, and in October 2009, after qualifying again, celebrated finishing the world's toughest Ironman race on the Pacific paradise island. He would go on to qualify and finish faster on the Big Island in 2010. The guy is an inspiration to me and many others. When he speaks, people listen, yet there is no ego, no bravado, just genuine affection for his sport and his fellow athletes. That for me is part of the attraction of triathlon; every club will have someone like John, and I believe that our sport is more honest and true because of them.

The final rider of the quintet was Andrew McCracken. The

club vice captain turned out to be an ex-Barrow lad just like myself. In fact we'd grown up within a mile of each other, yet our paths had never crossed. Andrew's story was similar to mine. Describing himself as an "ex-competitive eater", he took up cycling and triathlon in a bid to reduce his expanding waistline. He discovered he had a natural talent and three years after making his triathlon debut at sprint distance, he qualified for the Ironman 70.3 World Championships in Florida. So as you can see here was I surrounded by some of the best triathletes in the country, yet I still felt like I belonged. Granted I'm nowhere near as fast as them yet (hey you've got to have ambition) but I feel I'm a valued member of the club. Over the coming weeks we were joined by more and more riders and soon the Sunday morning rides were splitting into two groups to accommodate all abilities. The club was developing and I could see parallels with the Pirates. There were all levels of athlete in the club. The fast boys took themselves seriously but not one of them was an ass, and there was a humorous atmosphere that made the often painful training bearable.

Richard is the COLT captain, so he was the natural choice to ask how and why COLT was born. His honest, humble and forthright answer says a lot about why the club is a success:

> "I had reasonable success at triathlon when training on my own using my own ideas and methods. However it was when I began training with others and sharing their ideas, experiences and above all their friendship and support, that my triathlon world became more successful beyond all my beliefs, and much more fun. I shall forever be in the debt of those who helped me and it was thanks to all their encouragement that I decided and was able to start this club."

Training with the club and gaining the valuable knowledge and advice that I've acquired have helped me to develop as a triathlete and a person. In the run up to Ironman Germany I would regularly be out on the bike at 7am with the club fast boys for six-hour-long rides. I rarely had the ability to keep pace with them for the duration but they would wait for me to catch up and we would regroup. The camaraderie was something to look forward to, and was an incentive that drove me out of bed and into the hills. On several occasions when I was struggling, the likes of Chris Wild, Andrew McCracken and John Towse would drop back and pace me back to the group. John was an exceptionally quick runner. He told me that he was seeing if triathlon was going to be "his thing". The university professor had developed as a cyclist whilst living 5,000 feet above sea level in Boulder, Colorado. No wonder he could ride up hills without breaking a sweat. His wife, Andrea, had recently introduced him to open-water swimming and he found that, being lithe and sinewy, he was perfectly adapted to speed in the water as well. I was certain, given his impressive debut season in the sport, that he would go on to bigger things. He proved me right when he completed Ironman South Africa in April 2010 in a brilliant debut time of 10:43:07.

On one occasion when I was so knackered that I was almost not moving, Andrew McCracken dropped back and rode alongside me. He placed an unselfish hand on my back, pushing me up the hill. Now to push a 14-stone man, and his bike, uphill, whilst propelling oneself, takes phenomenal leg strength. It also shows great team spirit and tells you more about Andrew as a man, rather than an athlete. These guys were giving me so much. I wanted to give something back. A few days later I would get my chance.

An email was sent to the twenty-odd club members asking if anyone had any experience with websites and would they be prepared to help develop a COLT presence on the Internet. I was excited: here was my chance to play a pivotal role in the club that I was growing to love. I emailed back immediately, explaining my limited ability but a willingness to help. My web experience came from my blogging and I had some knowledge through work. John Towse had also offered his services. We were invited to join the club committee by Sarah Patterson, the secretary. The former tap dancer turned coast-to-coast cyclist and triathlete was the committee's voice of reason, often reining in the testosterone-fuelled ideas of those around her.

It was decided that John would set up and manage a club forum, which has now become very popular and is the scene of much advice, information-sharing and, most importantly, piss-taking. I was given a blank canvas to develop the COLT website and we were lucky to be given free space by a local company, Big Fish Internet. I was no expert so I did what any good librarian would do. As the first few weeks of 2009 passed I got a bloody good book and studied hard. Thankfully the site I was developing was on a test server; it wasn't public, so I could practise, make mistakes and try out ideas without it really mattering. My life at this stage consisted of training early in the morning to fit in a run or a swim, working all day, seeing Em whilst we ate and then sitting at the laptop for hours being the architect of www.cityoflancastertriathlon.co.uk. It was like having an extra full-time job. I was thriving, though sometimes my enthusiasm would outweigh my ability and Em would have her TV viewing pleasure interrupted by my frustrated swearing at the computer monitor as what I wanted wasn't what I was seeing on the screen.

The site went live in February 2009 and was well received by club members. It still takes quite a bit of my time to maintain it, keeping it up to date with results etc., but it's worth every minute. I previously mentioned that COLT was one of the fastest-growing triathlon clubs in the country. Our membership at the end of our first year, 2009, reached almost 140. That was down to word of mouth, the hard work of Richard, Andrew, Sarah and others, but I'd also like to think that the work I've done with the website has contributed in a small way to the club's success. The opportunity COLT gave me in developing the website led me to professional success. I received a big promotion at work, partly due to my IT skills which were greatly enhanced by my 'second job'.

On the advice of Richard and John Knapp I had sat down and written my training plan that would see me through the next 30 weeks, hopefully getting me to Germany in July in one piece and fully race-ready. It was the first time that I'd ever written a training plan, and I borrowed heavily from a book called *Be Ironfit* by Don Fink. Fink was a multiple Ironman finisher and coach to some of the sport's biggest stars. I had always trained in terms of distance, for example, "I'm going to do an eight-mile run today", but my plan saw me changing that mindset to train in time, so instead it was, "I'm going for an hour's run". This made a lot of sense to me and backed up what Andy H was so fond of telling me: "It's time spent on your feet, and time spent in the saddle that counts."

The plan fell into three ten-week phases designed to get me to the start line in perfect condition, and worked on the principle of quality rather than quantity. Each workout was placed in a sequence to hopefully allow muscle repair and recovery. It worked, as I never suffered any overuse injuries whilst following the principles of the plan. There were incremental changes in training times and intensities as the days and weeks passed, which is known as periodisation. The three phases are:

Base – establishing technique and aerobic capacity.
Build – building the intensity to prepare for the final phase.
Peak – hitting peak fitness and race sharpness followed by a calculated taper as race day approaches.

The plan worked well for me, and I would recommend that you follow a similar one if you want to race at Ironman level. It was much easier to fit the training session into my busy daily schedule when I could look in my diary and see what I was supposed to be doing that day. Structure and planning will forever now be part of my athletic activities. It is hard work but it makes life more manageable in the long term.

With all this Internet malarkey going on I find it amazing now that I actually found the time to train and race. I completed the challenging 'Cat and Fiddle' cycle race in Staffordshire. Organised by the Cystic Fibrosis Trust, this 55-mile challenge attracted cyclists from all over the country. Andy H had been scheduled to race with me but was unfortunately struck down by a particularly aggressive form of man flu. The challenge was so called because it took in the climb of the infamous Cat and Fiddle. The seven-mile-long switchback climb was deemed one of the most dangerous in the country. Countless motorcyclists had lost their lives on the blind hairpin bends over the years. Indeed on that very day I passed two fences marked with bouquets of flowers commemorating the passing of some unfortunate soul.

Descending back down the other side of the climb into Buxton at 40mph, I was soon grabbing my brakes as I swept into the tight corners. It wasn't a ride for a novice, and I was very glad of the time I'd spent with Andy H and John Krug climbing and descending in Lancashire. The technical skills I'd learnt and practised kept me on the road. The heavens opened, as seems to be the norm whenever I get on a bike. The BBC should do away with their weather forecast, instead Michael Fish should come on and say, "Holgs is going out on his bike today, therefore it's going to piss it down."

Despite being full of cold (I was hoping Andy H hadn't given me his man flu) I finished the course in 3:42. However, if projectile snotting had been an Olympic sport that day I would have won a gold medal and broken the world record as well.

The best part of the day came when I was back in the community centre getting a well earned cake and a very nice commemorative cycling jersey. There, the living legend and Tour de France superstar, Sean Kelly, wished me a good afternoon. I just had to text everyone I knew before I drove home.

The rain-soaked theme continued in May 2009 when Andy H and I took part in a local cycle race called 'The Struggle', a 68-mile affair with over 1400m of serious climbs. I thought Birdy Brow was the worst, but the infamous Nick O'Pendle wasn't that far behind. We then took in the long, seemingly never-ending climb of Waddington fell before heading back to Myerscough through the hairpins of the Trough of Bowland. I was really pleased with how well I had climbed, but more so with how well I recovered after each climb. I was able to sustain some decent speeds (17-20mph) without it feeling too hard towards the end of the ride.

Andy H and I finished in 4:38, sopping wet but with smiles on our faces that only got bigger when we saw the finishers buffet.

If it had rained the next time Andy H and I got on our bikes together, I really would have been cursed. Either that or the world -class Manchester velodrome had developed a hole in its roof. As part of my birthday present Em had booked me in for a 'taster session' of track cycling. I'd been to the velodrome before and seen how steep the banking was, but that was nothing compared to standing on the inside of the track, looking up at it; it seems to go on forever. I was joined by family and friends as Dave, Min, Viking, father-in-law John, Andy H and his son Gareth all made their debuts on the boards. We were all feeling a bit nervous, apart from Min who had been doings lots of "secret training" at the Newport velodrome. We picked up our hire bikes and tried them for size. Holding the rail, I practised clipping in and out of the pedals. Straight away it felt weird because I'd never ridden a 'Fixie' before – you can't freewheel unless you want to part company with your legs at your hip joint.

The only words I remember vividly from the safety briefing were, "There's no such thing as too fast". I set off cycling round the inside of the track getting used to the feel of riding a fixed wheel bike without any brakes. After a few laps I ventured onto the blue dividing strip that acts as a buffer between the floor and the track. I then practised stopping, which consisted of trying to slow the cranks (the arms that hold the pedals and spin round) by pushing my weight against them. It takes a lot of leg strength. Finally you have to grab the inside guard rail and hope you are going slow enough not to dislocate your shoulder.

Once we'd all got the hang of that we were set free on the track. Watching the cycling on the TV, the straights look fairly flat. Trust me, they aren't. Even at the lowest point of the track it feels steep. The basic skill of track riding is to get your speed up and keep it consistent. If you attempt to go into the bend and you lose any speed you are going to crash. I watched Andy H and Gareth getting quite high up towards the top of the banking and thought I'd give it a go as well. My heart was racing as I powered my way through two laps, making sure I was going at maximum speed. I would need the speed to survive intact. Wow. It was such an adrenaline rush. I could really feel gravity trying to force me off the bike. We were all whizzing round at speed and, surprisingly, none of us crashed; everyone loved it. Gareth looked like a pro, effortlessly riding lap after lap at the top of the track with a poise that disguised his inexperience. The rest of us all turned on the speed and for a split second felt like we were a Wiggins, Hoy or Boardman, at least in our heads.

There was only one way for us all to recover after such a workout. Naturally we headed to Rusholme and the home of the nation's 'Curry Mile'. Over 70 Indian restaurants occupy every available space on the street, and it is thought to be the largest concentration outside of the Indian subcontinent. Much to everybody's amazement, at the ripe old age of 36 I would be experiencing my very first curry. Now how many people can say that they completed their first Ironman before their first curry? If I'm not the only member of that exclusive club I'd be surprised.

If my wife wasn't truly my soul mate and knew me so well I may not have made it from the velodrome to the curry house alive. Driving through the streets of Manchester, the traffic lights ahead of me turned to red. As the car came to a halt a female cyclist in lycra pulled up alongside. I sat and stared, not realising that Em had clocked my voyeuristic action. With teasing disdain she tapped my arm and said "Oi, stop looking at that lass's arse."

Taken aback I snapped out of my daze and replied with defensive honesty, "Eh? I was looking at the bike. It's a Bianchi carbon–" I didn't get the chance to finish.

"A normal bloke would be looking at her perfect curves and you're looking at the perfect curves of her bike. You're one sad git Holgate, you know that?"

I had to agree I probably was.

17

HERE WE GO AGAIN

The pain shot through my knee as I lay dazed and motionless on the rain-soaked pavement. How had I got here? One moment I was leaving my mother-in-law's house on my way to the barber's and the next I'm kissing tarmac. That one fleeting second almost destroyed months of training and ended my dream of racing at Ironman Germany. In an effort to try and look smart I was wearing new shoes with a smooth sole instead of my usual old sturdy running shoes. I slipped on a wet step and landed hard on the side of my left knee. Why is it always my left knee? Every injury I've sustained in recent years seems to be on that leg – it's a wonder I don't walk lopsided.

I crawled back into the house where I was met by Em, her concern growing by the second, relative to the swelling of the injured knee. Swiftly I applied a bag of frozen peas which numbed the area. A short while later I was hobbling around telling myself that it was just a bruise and that I'd be fine for my planned ten-mile run the next day. Swinging my legs out of bed the following morning it soon became apparent that I wouldn't be running anywhere that day. I was frustrated, but being sensible I took the next few days off from running as May merged into June. I went to the gym and sat in the hot tub each morning before work, hoping that the water jets would massage my knee back to life. It seemed to work and by Thursday evening I was out riding 30 miles on the Roo without any ill effects. Happy with my return to fitness I sent a text message to Richard G, my colleague and friend who had become my lunchtime running partner over the previous months. Announcing that I was back in the game I told him to bring his running gear to work the next day. Richard was getting faster and stronger with each run and on this occasion I was certainly holding him back. Like Lesley, previously, I was in danger of training one of my friends to beat me ... Hmm maybe I need to rethink my coaching strategy.

I was confident after the comeback run so I set off that Saturday morning for a planned three-hour run. Heading north along the canal, everything felt great as the glorious early June sunshine warmed the back of my neck. I was pushing hard, covering the first five miles in 35 minutes. It was a foolish pace to set but I was desperate to make up for the training I'd missed that week. Great turned into manageable as my pace slowed. Telling myself again that my knee felt stiff because it was bruised, and that it would wear off, I plodded on. Suddenly a niggling pain replaced the stiffness. I was experienced enough to know that I should have stopped instantly, but I stupidly ignored my inner sensible voice. I was five miles from home and didn't relish walking. Looking back at this moment I now realise that I could have prevented myself from suffering stress and pain for the final countdown month to Ironman. I should have stopped immediately and walked, taking note of the warning jolt my body had given me. Instead I ran for five agonising minutes before the knee broke down completely and I limped back, distraught.

An hour passed before I fell through the front door and collapsed in agony on the sofa. Em wouldn't take no for an answer and bundled me into a taxi bound for accident and emergency. Unusually for a Saturday it was quiet on account of it not being the football season and it was also too early for the pub crowd. The pain was a combination of toothache, earache and a paper cut all rolled into one. Ouch. But the pain was nothing compared to the terrifying thoughts rushing around my head.

What if I've broken something? It could be ligaments. I'm sure I've read that ligament injuries are worse than breaks. Oh bugger, I'm up shit creek without a paddle. Twelve months of planning and training and now it's over. Ironman is gone because I unusually made an effort and wore new shoes. That'll teach me to try and be fashionable.

My head was in my hands. Em tried to reassure me, squeezing my hand and saying, "It'll be okay, I'm sure there's nothing serious." And then knowingly, "You'll be okay for Germany, it's the first week of June and the race isn't until the 5th July." I wanted to smile at her attempt at raising my mood, but all I could do was snap. "How do you know?" came the pain-fuelled reply. "Sorry pet, I just keep thinking about Steve and how he missed Lanzarote because of a stupid bloody accident." Her hand squeezed tighter as we sat in silence. Fellow COLT Steve Stretch, to whom I was referring, is an exceptional athlete. He's represented Great Britain at Triathlon over the Olympic distance and earlier in 2009 he'd completed Ironman New Zealand in just over ten hours. In April 2009 we had been out riding together as part of a club training session. It was a glorious weekend morning and the peloton was larger than the usual hardcore crowd. Nothing brings out triathletes like sunshine. I was riding at the back of the group with Andy H as he gets nervous riding in a group. I was hugging Steve's wheel, drafting in essence. Steve himself was about three inches off the wheel of the bike in front. Riding like this in a group takes practice and concentration; maybe the bright sunshine, bird song and jovial cyclist banter led to the lapse that ended in disaster. One second Steve was riding, the next he and his bike were upside down, and six feet in the air in a spiralling forward somersault. Andy and I quickly discovered that our brakes worked as we slid to a halt just shy of hitting our crumpled clubmate lying prone on the tarmac. It transpired that the rider in front of Steve had feathered his brakes, a fatal move in a peloton. It was impossible for Steve to react. His wheel touched the one in front and in an instant his season was over. He broke his collarbone and missed out on planned races at Ironman Lanzarote and Ironman UK. It could have been a lot worse.

Witnessing him landing from a height, at speed, in the position he did, was the scariest thing that I'd seen on a bike. Thankfully he soon came round. The first thing he said was, "How's my bike?"

Now that's dedication for you; it shows how determined and focused you have to be to become an Ironman. Sitting there in the hospital waiting to see a doctor, I remembered how gutted I felt for him when it became apparent that he'd miss out on his planned races. I really hoped I wasn't about to suffer the same fate.

I was examined, and told that my knee wasn't broken, which I guess I already knew because I could still limp around. The doctor pulled and pushed the joint to determine if my ligaments were all still in place and functioning. When she informed me that they were I smiled, thinking I was out of the woods. "I think you may have what is known as a deep bone bruise. I need to send you for an X-ray." An X-ray? Suddenly I was lost in the trees again. It didn't sound promising.

Forty-five minutes later, my knee was illuminated on the wall in front of me. The femur was slightly discoloured at the outside rounded end. Doubts flooded back. "Is it broken?" I asked nervously. "No, it's not broken but I believe you have internal bleeding as a result of the honeycomb structure inside the bone breaking down," said the doctor. Pointing at the X-ray, she said: "These are tiny micro-fractures of the spongy cancellous bone that are causing the swelling and pain. They were probably caused by the initial fall and then aggravated by the impact stresses on the joint whilst running." This sounded bloody serious. "We'll strap the knee up and give you pain medication. You need to keep off it for a few days and definitely no more running, Mr Holgate. It should start to heal in about four weeks if all goes well but it is not uncommon with an injury like this to be looking at a four-month window."

FOUR MONTHS?! Oh shit, this can't be happening to me. My head was spinning. My thoughts quickly turned to the final leg of Ironman Germany.

"I'm supposed to run a marathon in four weeks," I blurted out. I was admonished, sternly: "I would advise that you make other plans."

Speechless and dejected, I waited in the cubicle for a nurse to come and strap my knee up. It couldn't be over. I'd invested everything physically, emotionally and financially in competing in Germany. I wasn't going to let it be stolen away from me now. I needed it. I wanted it. And by God I was going to have it.

Now the paragraph above will have made very interesting reading to my darling wife, my parents and concerned friends. It's not that I lied to them, more the fact that I omitted to tell them that I might have been advised not to run a marathon. I guess my stubborn streak does have a lot to answer for at times. I'd better put the sleeping bag down in the cellar with my bikes because when Em reads that I wasn't supposed to be running that's where I'll be sleeping for the rest of the year. Having only been "advised" and not "ordered", technically I did nothing wrong.

The pain medication that they gave me knocked me for six and I started to hallucinate two days later whilst at work. Talking to Richard at my desk, he became most concerned when I said, "Hey look at those birds." Needless to say there weren't any and I was soon sent home without Tweetie Pie. A couple of days after that incident the pain wore off and I abandoned the drugs. Just say no, kids.

All of that was a world away from the blistering performance I recorded in what would turn out to be my final preparation race for Germany just a few weeks earlier. The North West Triathlon took place in leafy Nantwich in deepest darkest Cheshire at the end of May. It would be the first time that I used my new bike, the Roo, in anger. The roads of Cheshire were about to be scorched by the burning rubber of Lancaster's fastest librarian on two wheels.

This would also be my first triathlon of the season. I had planned to race earlier in the year at Skipton but when Em's gran suffered a fall resulting in hospitalisation, we dashed to Derbyshire instead. Family is more important than triathlon.

With no such accidents or incidents to distract us, Em and I fell out of bed at 5am and were in a car loaded with a bike and a plastic transition box by 6am for the two-hour journey south. Arriving at the race venue, I bumped straight into my partner in crime, Viking. He had camped out overnight with a load of other Pirates that were racing, and was in a confident mood. Much like me he'd had a perfect month of training, hitting all his targets. We were both training for approximately twenty hours a week at that point. Rising before 6am, we were fitting the three key sessions a week in each discipline into days where 24 hours seemed woefully short. The heavy training also had the effect of reducing our waistlines. We had both lost in the region of two stones in our Ironman build up. This was a good thing because obviously the less excess lard we were carrying the faster we would be, a point that would be proved that very morning.

Viking and I had consulted with one another in the weeks before the race and submitted entries with identical swim time estimates, in the hope that this ploy would allow us to race against each other. Swimmers were to be set off at 20-second intervals. Our plan worked as we discovered that I would have only a 40-second head start on Viking.

Having raced at Nantwich the year before I should have been used to the taste of the saltwater pool but nothing can prepare you for warm brine. Yuck. And yes I am well aware that I'm not supposed to drink it, but with my swimming technique it's inevitable.

By the end of the second lap of the pool my taste buds were drowning in salt, however it was my eyes that were suffering the most. My goggles were leaking and salt water was flooding them. Having no choice but to swim with open eyes because of the two-way traffic in each lane, I was forced to stop and adjust the straps. Apart from obviously slowing me down, this played havoc with my lap counting. I had to swim a total of 16 lengths across four lanes; this, for the mathematically challenged, works out at four lengths per lane. With me so far? After four lengths I was supposed to duck under the rope and move into the next lane to complete the next four. Eventually I would be at the other side of the pool from where I had started. I was aware that Viking hadn't passed me, and confusion took hold when I saw him swimming in the lane that I had yet to move into. Confusion quickly turned to clarity as it dawned on me that I'd lost count and swam six laps in that lane. The saltwater that had flooded my eye sockets and throat had obviously corroded my brain as apparently I could no longer count correctly after the number three. To compensate for my mistake I swam two laps less in the final lane and then exited the pool, hoping that no one would think I was cheating, which technically I wasn't. I was laughing as I ran into transition, and Dave and Andy H enjoyed my mistake as when they miscounted their laps at the Skipton Triathlon I took the piss for months. Andy H joked that the three of us needed to swim with an abacus at the end of the pool so that we could keep track of our laps. I'm sure that there's a marketing opportunity there for someone to make a lot of money. I'd buy one.

The rest of the race went very smoothly. The Roo rode beautifully, eating up the flattish roads. She was a joy to ride. Every second spent powering along the country lanes reminded me why I did this: the speed and the thrill of passing people as man and machine worked in perfect harmony. I lost momentum slightly in transition when I couldn't find where I'd left my running shoes. What should have taken seconds took two minutes. Transition really is the fourth discipline and it is worth practising, however no amount of practice is going to save you if your saltwater-addled brain can't remember where your running shoes are. I was feeling fast on the run, and the extra push from the Pirate support meant I sped round the four laps to complete the course in 1:11:23.

I was knackered but thrilled at having beaten my previous best by some three and a half minutes, which was quite a significant improvement over the shorter distance. Viking also finished inside his previous best time by over four minutes. Reflecting on the race afterwards whilst shouting encouragement at the female Pirates who'd started in the later waves, we talked about how I would make slight improvements in our final outing at the Liverpool Olympic Triathlon in the second week of June.

"I need to make sure my goggles are fitted properly, I can't afford to stop and tighten them when I'm swimming in the murky docks," I said.

Viking grinned at Em, the only native Liverpudlian present, and quickly quipped, "Too right, some scally would sneak up behind you and nick your wetsuit."

We didn't know it that day in Nantwich, but one week after my trip to casualty there would be no opportunities for anyone to nick my wetsuit in Liverpool. It hung safely in my wardrobe at home whilst I dragged my sorry injured carcass down to the city that had become my second home to watch Viking storm his way around the Olympic-distance course. Watching from the bridge above the dock, the swimmers hardly seemed to be moving as they swam through the dark water. I raised my camera to my eye and tried to focus on the moving bodies. It soon became apparent how quickly they were scything through the dark, cold, tidal water. Viking was swimming really well, so well in fact that I missed him on the first lap.

After the turn I spotted him and managed to scream some abuse at him. He'd later tell me that although his ears were frozen he still managed to hear me and that I have a voice like a foghorn. He also added, "That was the most minging water I've ever swum in."

Suddenly missing the race didn't seem so bad.

Having completed his cycling and running, Viking finished the race and looked much fresher than I did. I was totally drained. I'd screamed myself hoarse shouting encouragement to both him and my COLT clubmate, Stuart Foy. Stuart, my shy yet instantly likeable clubmate was new to triathlon and competing for the first time in an open-water event. He looked to be enjoying every minute of it. I always find it encouraging watching new people cut their teeth in the sport I've come to love.

I was knackered, cold and suffering with aching legs, and I hadn't even been racing. As a consequence I gained a greater appreciation of my own supporters. I'd stood and cheered for about three hours, much less than it took to complete most of my previous races.

Viking beat his previous best at the Olympic distance by 42 minutes, finishing in 2 hours 55 minutes. Included in this vastly improved performance was his first ever sub-50-minute 10km run.

Although I was over the moon for my mate it gave me plenty to worry about. It was silly really, but the competitor inside me didn't want to come out second best in our personal battle at Ironman. Here was Viking in the form of his life, swimming like a fish and running faster than ever before. I by comparison was crippled and unable to run. In my head I envisaged the following month's race panning out with Viking first out of the water; I would take control on the bike, but after that all bets were off. He was running strong, I wasn't. I would need at least a two-hour lead after the bike if I was to hold him off. We'd joked all year that the last one to finish would get the drinks in. I mentally prepared myself to order a Babycham in German.

Driving home up the motorway, the hauntingly beautiful Placebo cover of 'Running up that Hill' by Kate Bush wafted out of the CD player. The irony was not lost on me. I would be doing no such thing for the foreseeable future; my prospects for Germany were looking grim.

With two weeks to go until race day, Andy H helped me get back out on my bike. He kept me on the straight and narrow by controlling the pace and keeping it flat. I suffered no ill effects, despite my knee feeling stiff the first time I ventured out, but this was to be expected after a period of prolonged inactivity. A couple more easy rides of 30 miles followed. Granted, it wasn't a true test of the strains I would put my body through in Germany, but it gave me the confidence I needed. That confidence grew immensely when with seven days to go we ran together as I tested the knee. It was a slow, steady and short run of about three miles that took me 28 minutes. This was positive, but it really didn't prove a thing. I could still get off my bike in Frankfurt and my knee could give way. Running slowly and protectively for three miles would be a million miles away from running a marathon after cycling 112 miles.

Andy nursed me back to fitness; he'd put his own training

needs on hold whilst he looked after mine. He really was the ultimate 'Super Domestique'. Now if only I could have persuaded him to travel to Germany with me to fetch my water, he'd have been even better.

All that was left was for me to pack. I took the afternoon of Tuesday, 2 July off work and spent several hours lovingly dismantling and packing the Roo ready for its flight the next day. About three miles' worth of bubble wrap and pipe cladding later, she stood in the kitchen looking like a rocking horse. I was paranoid that the brutal baggage handlers would break my baby, so I'd gone a bit over the top. Better to be safe than sorry, though. I didn't want to get to Frankfurt and not have anything to ride; I had a dodgy knee to race with, I didn't need a dodgy bike.

The night before we flew, Andy H rang to wish me luck and to tell me that he'd be watching live on the Internet. After that the phone never stopped as friends and family called to wish me luck. I checked my email and there were numerous good wishes from work colleagues and COLT clubmates. The next morning a good luck card arrived from Min. After reading it I said to Em, "I've got so much support behind me going into this race, I can't let them down, I'd never be able to come home. I'll crawl the bloody marathon if I have to." And then tapping my injured knee I added, "Don't you bloody make me!"

18

ICH BIN IRONMAN

I know that athletes travel around the world on a regular basis to take part in events but getting to Frankfurt was probably more stressful for me than actually taking part in the race. My baby, the Roo, was at the mercy of the baggage handlers, and walking around the airport I could think of nothing else. In my head I was running through all the horror stories I'd read online about carbon bikes being unpacked at their destination only for their owners to chillingly discover them to have been crushed or broken into pieces. As we took our seats on the plane we observed the luggage being loaded onto the plane. There it was: the big green bike bag that contained the Roo. Relief poured over me upon seeing how carefully the handlers placed it on the conveyor. Pointing out my bike to Em and my parents, I eased back into my seat ready for take-off, safe in the knowledge that at least my bike was on the plane with me.

As we touched down at Cologne airport just after midnight there was a sense of calm throughout the airport; our plane was the last one to land that night. We'd chosen to fly into Cologne purely for reasons of cost. When we'd looked at flights and hotels, Frankfurt was out of our price range. Obviously the demand for access to the city on the weekend of Ironman was phenomenal. The organisers claimed that around 250,000 people would be added to the population by race day. We would spend two nights in Cologne before hiring a car and driving the two hours south to Frankfurt for three nights. Then after the race we would return the following morning to Cologne for two more days, allowing myself and my supporters some relaxation time.

I waited anxiously next to the baggage carousel. One by one our bags appeared but there was no sign of the big green bike bag. I began pacing around. Panic was beginning to creep in when my mood was lightened by a comment from Em. "Wouldn't it be funny if just one pedal appeared? No bike, just one solitary pedal going round and round on the carousel." She dissolved into fits of laughter, quickly joined by my parents. I should have screamed but within seconds we all had tears in our eyes. Moments later a door opened next to the conveyor belt and a baggage handler wheeled out my bike bag. I eagerly unzipped the bag and examined my bike. My relief was apparent for all to see; the three miles of bubble wrap had done the job and the Roo was in one piece. Leaving the deserted cavernous arrivals hall, I sighed in relief that everything had gone to plan. At the hotel that night, the stress of the journey had taken more out of me than I realised. Em emerged from the bathroom to find me sprawled on the bed snoring like a chainsaw.

My stress levels were tested again on the journey to Frankfurt on the Friday morning, not because I was in an unfamiliar car or on roads without a speed limit or even because I was driving in Europe for the first time. The stress was caused by one sentence contained within the reams of information that the organisers had sent to me. There on the page, in bold writing was this statement:

"A race briefing in English will take place on Friday at 3pm at the Eis Sportshalle, attendance at this meeting is compulsory for all competitors."

As we hit the outskirts of Frankfurt and the famous bumper-to- bumper traffic of one of Europe's busiest stretches of motorway, it became apparent that unless I could suddenly teleport *Star Trek*-style, that I would miss the race briefing. I was thinking that as it was a mandatory register, my absence would mean disqualification. I began to panic, which was stupid as there was nothing I could do, and surely not everyone would be arriving in time to attend. Em contacted Viking, who although he had missed part of the meeting, was there and would later fill me in on the details. Crucially he allayed my fears by saying there was no register being taken and people were just wandering in all the time. "So much for it being compulsory," I sighed as my panic subsided. There was just time for one last stressful incident as we drove along the side of the River Main. We could see our hotel on the other bank, and we expected our satellite navigation system to direct us to our destination.

"Keep left. In one hundred metres turn left over the bridge. The bridge may have restrictions," the female voice instructed us. My dad and I wondered what the restrictions would be. I indicated to turn left but was aware that none of the traffic in front had done so, and it soon became apparent why. "It's a bloody footbridge!" said my dad indignantly. "Yep love there may be restrictions: no bloody cars!" he shouted over the female voice that was now trying to tell us that we'd missed our turning.

Eventually we found a bridge that allowed us to cross the river. Leaving the others to check into the hotel, I headed up to the Town Hall to register. The cobbled medieval town square that provided the backdrop for the race finish was awash with activity. The air was charged with the excited chatter of so many languages that were alien to my GCSE-level ears. Toned, serious-looking people wearing t-shirts that represented every Ironman race worldwide strolled around in compression socks carrying black rucksacks and sporting red plastic hospital-style identification wristbands. I would soon discover upon registering that all competitors had to wear this band, as it was the pass that would allow us to enter transition and therefore the race. Around the crowds of athletes, volunteers and supporters, grandstands were being erected, red carpet was being laid and sponsors' cars were being driven onto ramps to create an entrance to the finish chute. Dangling above it all, from a crane, was a stadium-sized video screen that would be used to display the close-ups of the finishers' agonised yet jubilant faces as they crossed the line. Watching it dangling there in the blinding afternoon sunshine, I allowed myself just for a moment to imagine my face up there for the entire world to see as I crossed the line as fresh as a daisy and grinning.

I wandered around the expo. It was a triathlete's dream: a small fortune could be spent on wetsuits, energy food, trainers, bikes, clothing and lots of other things that I didn't recognise. At the stand of one of his sponsors, Faris Al-Sultan (the former world Ironman champion) was handing out free shoelaces. Upon shaking my hand I remarked that I would be telling all my friends that the world champion had laced up my shoes. Germans stereotypically aren't known for their sense of humour, and my comment was met with a blank stare from Faris, followed by a nervous smile. I quickly left before security was called.

I stopped at another stall and was just about to commit adultery by spending five grand on another bike when my phone rang. It was Viking informing me that he'd arrived from the race briefing and was waiting outside the town hall for me. Reluctantly I put the cash back in my pocket; Viking had stopped me from being unfaithful to the Roo. The daydream faded away as I saw my mate, his effervescent smile unmistakable through the sea of faces. We embraced and chatted like excited schoolchildren. We couldn't believe after so much planning and training we'd actually arrived. We were intoxicated, drowning in the whole Ironman experience. Viking then gave me the news that I'd been hoping for, the race referee had announced that wetsuits would be allowed for the swim. As weak swimmers, both of us were overjoyed at the organisers' decision. Our wetsuits were our safety blankets, without them the task at hand would have been so much tougher. I may have been doing myself and Viking an injustice because I'm sure that we would have been able to swim and complete that leg of the race without our rubber suits. Psychologically, though, if they had been banned, given that Ironman success is as much mental conditioning as it is physical, it would have been a massive blow. On returning home I read that the organisers had made the decision on Thursday after taking a water temperature reading of 24.6 degrees. The legal limit was 24.9. We'd been extremely lucky because from Friday to Sunday the temperatures soared into the 30s and the water temperature would have been above the legal limit if they'd tested at that time.

On Saturday morning my dad and I unpacked the Roo, carefully preserving the bubble wrap and pipe lagging for the return journey. The Roo was easily reassembled: handlebars were turned back into position, wheels were locked back onto the frame, gears and brakes were adjusted and finally the saddle and seat post were lined up with the tape on the frame indicating they were at the correct height. Once the Roo looked like a bike again I rode her for a couple of miles to check that everything was as it should have been. Pleased that it was, I informed my dad that I was off to drop the Roo and my transition bags off at the race start. Along with about thirty other competitors I caught the shuttle bus out to Langander Wansea, about 15km south of Frankfurt, where the swim was taking place. As I waited for the Roo to be unloaded from the bike trailer at the rear of the bus, I was joined by Viking and family. He'd already dropped off his bike but agreed to wait with me as I went through the process. Queuing to leave my bike in the transition area, I got ushered into the 'Pros' entrance. The organisers must have heard about me and my world-class reputation. Maybe after meeting me the day before my mate Faris had put in a good word. Okay, maybe not.

A volunteer who introduced himself as Karl wheeled my bike to the stand with my number on it. He placed the Roo in position and then covered her in plastic sheeting to protect her overnight from the elements. Karl took the bags that I would be picking up in T1 and T2. He walked me to where I would be handed my bag after the swim and informed me that the T2 bag would be waiting for me at the end of the bike ride back in the city centre. Karl wished me luck and I thanked him for his help. Volunteers like Karl make these events the success that they are and sometimes as athletes we get caught up in our own self-importance. Please, people, the next time a volunteer or a marshal helps you just take a second to thank them. Without them there would be no race. Hopefully by thanking Karl I encouraged him to again volunteer. Who knows, maybe after reading this when you are inspired to race Ironman Germany, a young man called Karl will be there to ease the stress as you take your first steps to becoming an Ironman.

Conscious that it was best to get off our feet as soon as possible (we'd be on them for long enough the following day), we decided to head back to our hotels to rest. On our way out of the transition area Viking and I sneaked a quick look at the lake. It was crystal clear, and looked very inviting. We agreed that we might actually enjoy the swim for a change. We arranged our meeting point for the next morning and went our separate ways, him to round up his wife Lou and his two kids, Jamie and Jordan, before heading back to his nearby hotel, and I towards the shuttle bus waiting to take me back to the city.

I jumped back on the almost empty bus and joined four guys at the back. Just as the doors were closing we were joined by another guy in sunglasses and a cap. He certainly looked the part, with sponsors' logos adorning his cycling jersey, but he didn't look out of the ordinary because the majority of people in Frankfurt that weekend looked like him. His companion that he had sat next to was filming him on a camcorder and he was hamming it up, pointing out where was good to go for a crap in the woods without being seen. In response to his comments I let out a chuckle. Upon hearing that he turned and asked me how I was doing in his thick Aussie accent. He enquired if this was my first Ironman. Replying it wasn't and that I was hoping to go sub-13 hours, he nodded knowingly. Not wanting to appear rude I mirrored the question. Would this be his first Ironman? He smiled and said it wasn't. Whilst I was asking if he'd done many others he removed his cap, and a light bulb of recognition instantly switched on in my head. Embarrassed and shocked, I stuttered "Are you Macca?" "Too bloody right mate," was the laughing Antipodean's reply. It was no other than Chris McCormack, the world champion and race favourite. There I was talking about my race ambitions and asking about his when the reality was we were a world apart. That's part of the appeal of triathlon though. A Sunday league footballer is never going to play at Wembley against David Beckham, the authorities wouldn't let you turn up at the Open and partner Tiger Woods, yet Andy Holgate could race against Chris McCormack on the biggest stage. By being down to earth and sharing encouragement with me for a few moments on that bus journey, Macca has become one of my sporting heroes and I've sung his praises to anyone that will listen. He's a genuine bloke, a devoted family man and a phenomenal athlete. I was genuinely gutted for him when I found out after the race that he hadn't won due to cramp. Sport needs more people like Macca. He's not been ruined by the hype and the money and that seems to be the case when you hear other top triathletes such as Chrissie Wellington or Craig Alexander talk. There isn't as much money in triathlon as there is in football, but some of the privileged Premiership players who get caught up in scandals could learn a thing or two about humility and dignity from those that make their living on the edge of exhaustion.

Race day arrived as the alarm abruptly ended my deep sleep at 4.15am. Blindly staggering out of bed, I flipped the switch on the kettle. The caffeine soon hit my system and I began to come round with each mouthful of porridge. I kissed Em goodbye and headed out the door into the corridor. The door to my parents' room opened slightly and they peered out to wish me luck. We had decided it was best for them to get a good vantage point on the cycle route rather than come out to the swim; it would have been impossible to spot me amongst 3,000 other swimmers wearing black wetsuits and the race issue red swimming cap. It was the correct decision as they too would have a long day, and the extra hours in bed gave them the energy to support me later in the race when I needed them the most. They ended up getting a great spot on the side of the bike and run course as planned.

I don't remember anything about the shuttle bus ride to the lake and the start. I was lost in my own thoughts, telling myself this was my day. All those cold, wet early mornings, hours spent riding and running when it would have been so easy to stay under a warm duvet, the mind-numbingly boring laps of the pool, the times that I'd passed on nights out because I would be up training before my friends had gone home – that was all for this one day. I'd sacrificed so much, not least seven months of alcohol, and it was now the time to go out and show myself and the world what IronHolgs was capable of.

I met up with Viking in T1 and he didn't seem nervous at all. He was ready to slay the demons from the Big Woody and was excited and confident that by the end of the day he would make his family proud and settle the score that he had with the distance. We inflated the tyres on our bikes, and then took a few moments to check each other's kit, subscribing to the old adage that two pairs of eyes are better than one. Satisfied that everything was in place we walked through the transition area so we knew where we were going. Viking gave me some salt capsules which would be very useful later. Now clad in our rubber armour, we were both buzzing as we walked down the very steep sand dune to the swim start. We hugged and wished each other luck. "See you out on the course Holgs," he said before we lost each other in the crowd.

The SWIM – 2.4 Miles

As with every previous open-water swim I had the intention of starting at the back and to the right of the field to avoid the whole washing-machine effect, as 3,000 people battled for space to swim. Unfortunately with about a minute to go I looked around and realised that I'd drifted into the middle of the pack. As I was treading water my feet were constantly banging against others. We were penned in like battery hens; no space to move. If you suffer from claustrophobia and aren't chasing a world record time, stay on the beach and let the masses go. I know Min employed this tactic at Ironman Lanzarote and had a much more relaxing time.

The cannon fired at 7am, fireworks exploded overhead and in the distance a cheer rose from the banks. The safety canoes that guided the swimmers moved forward and immediately the water around them churned as the longest day of the year began in earnest. In response to the cannon and the activity, I started my watch. The mass start created a bottleneck, and I didn't move for about three minutes as I trod water, slowly drifting over the start line. The guy immediately in front of me started swimming and I lunged forward, reaching hard to try and find some room. There wasn't any. The water was clear and warm but visibility was zero. All I could see were a thousand feet and hands kicking and clawing their way for space that didn't exist. Blow after blow rained down on my torso, arms and legs. Miraculously, though, my face and head avoided any such punishment. The next day my ribs were dotted with purple bruises. If it wasn't for the thick rubber wetsuit absorbing the continuous impact I may have actually broken one or two of them. Far from innocent in the brutality of it all, I swam directly over two people, pushing them under as I dragged my frame in front of them. It was impossible to go around them, I had no choice. I'm not proud of it but I'd do it again if I needed to, as I'm sure a faster swimmer would do it to me if I was swimming too slowly.

I completed my first lap and stood up to run along the beach and back into the water for the second, slightly shorter, loop. I purposely didn't look at my watch. If I was slower than planned my confident mindset would have been ruined and my swimming and possibly the rest of the race would have suffered. There was a bit more room on the second lap, and I found myself thankfully swimming unhindered. Turning clockwise around the final buoy, I could see the big red arch that marked the end of the swim. I needed no further inspiration to dig deep and propel my tired body forward. With a few final powerful kicks I reached the shallows, relieved to have completed what I hoped would be the worst part of the day. I emerged from the water and finally allowed myself to glance at my watch: 1:26:22, a better time than I'd been expecting. Stripping the wetsuit down to my waist, I walked up the first half of the sand dune leading to the transition area, before the cheers of the crowd stirred my tired legs back to life and I began to jog.

At the top of the dune I was joined by a volunteer who ran with me as I grabbed my bike bag. She pulled my wetsuit off and collected my swim stuff as I stripped and put my bike gear on. I made sure I was wearing full bib shorts with a pad that meant my arse would be a little more comfortable on the journey I was about to subject it to. I've never understood how these people can do an Ironman in a tri-suit with only a very thin pad. I'd be walking like a cowboy for the rest of my life if I did that. Taking my time, I thoroughly dried my feet, taking particular care to remove any sand that could have potentially removed the skin whilst I was cycling and running. I needed the toilet, but I realised I'd made a mistake, as I would have to strip off again to use it as I was wearing my bib shorts. I took great care to apply lots of sun tan lotion, wincing in pain as the solution stung the friction burns that I had just acquired from my wetsuit grating on the back of my neck. For once my pre-swim protective application of Bodyglide had let me down. As I describe all this now, it becomes apparent why I took 11:45 in T1. I definitely need to improve on that next time.

The BIKE – 112 Miles

Within a few minutes of getting on my bike I was aware of three problems, all of which were significant:

1. My heart rate monitor/watch had been paused – I must have caught the button taking my wetsuit off. It would mean I would only be able to estimate my overall time. This would be more of a problem later during the marathon.

2. My wireless speed sensor wasn't talking to my bike computer. It said I was doing 7mph for the whole of the course, so I just had to guess from feeling if I was going fast enough. I would have to rely on glances at my HRM, gauging how hard I was pushing my body.

3. My gears kept slipping on the rear cassette, and I couldn't change onto the big ring (the one that gives you the most speed) at the front. They'd worked fine the day before, but

all along the course I would momentarily lose momentum as the gears jumped. It was all very frustrating.

Maintaining a positive mental attitude is vital for Ironman success, or for life in general really. I could have thought that these hiccups were fatal, feeling that the race would not be my own, so why bother? But as a triathlete I was already used to battling against the odds. Okay, I wouldn't be riding how I'd envisaged, but sod it I could still ride. Some might question why I didn't just get off the bike and fix everything. Well given my lack of mechanical expertise I quickly decided I'd probably have done more damage than good. The Roo was still working and I needed her to stay that way.

I'd been warned by IronRose, the fastest Pirate and a veteran of this race, that the road from the lake to the city was very fast and not to overcook it along there. Heeding the warning, I pedalled steadily to wake my legs up, taking the opportunity to replenish the fuel I'd used up during the swim with a drink and a gel. As I crossed the bridge over the River Main to start the first of two bike laps, I saw Em and my parents, and gave them an "I'm cool" thumbs up gesture and smile as they cheered their encouragement in response. Bolstered by their support I pushed on, passing those that obviously came from a strong swimming base but suffered on two wheels. At this stage I still thought I was chasing Viking, believing that his recent swimming form would have him out of the water before me. This friendly rivalry was fuel to my legs as they constantly span, giving chase.

Once out of the city I started passing through lots of little villages and the support was phenomenal. Thousands of people lined the roadside creating a carnival atmosphere. Music blared out, wine and beer flowed like water. Church attendance must have been down that morning as the people of the villages worshipped the lycra-clad athletes whizzing by. "Hop, Hop, Hop" and "*Allez Andrew*" rang in my ears as the spectators read my name on my race number. This was like having an extra gear, something I needed with mine failing. *Surely the support can't get any better?* I thought to myself. I would soon realise I hadn't witnessed fanatical support yet.

Racing on closed roads was amazing. No worrying about cars meant I could take the best line around a corner, and it was a great feeling. Long sweeping descents saw me passing countless others; it was so enjoyable, the feeling of speed. And unlike good old Blighty with her potholes, the road surfaces were as smooth as a cricket wicket. It really was a pleasure to be riding on such roads.

There were some tricky hills on the course, the more significant of which had been given scary names by the organisers. 'The Hell' was particularly tough as it consisted entirely of rough cobbles, causing the loss of all grip in my hands as the vibrations dulled my nerves. I wouldn't get the feeling back for three days which made driving back to Cologne the day after the race "interesting" to say the least. "The Beast" was just long and tedious, made worse by the soaring temperatures, the mid-day sun sapping precious energy. 'Heartbreak Hill', a long straight climb through the village of Bad Vilbel on the way back into Frankfurt, was the most amazing thing I've ever experienced in a race. Thousands lined the road with cowbells, parting like the Red Sea as I rode through them. The noise was deafening; struggling to hear myself think, I pushed that much harder. The support here blew away what had come before it. I felt like Lance Armstrong powering up the side of Alpe D'Huez. Thousands of people were leaning into me, screaming encouragement. How could I not respond with a smile? For a couple of minutes I was a rock star, idolised by thousands, an intense and inspiring experience.

I completed the first lap in 3 hours and 5 minutes; I only had one more lap of 56 miles to go. My strength was renewed as I got cheers again from Em and my parents. A bit further along Team Viking was screaming at me like their lungs would burst. It was at this point it dawned on me that I must have been ahead of Viking. Unless he was having the ride of his life he wouldn't have been as fast as me around the course.

Nutrition played a massive factor on the bike, more so in

the heat. Dehydration, a real danger in an extreme event like Ironman, can be fatal, as your body loses vital minerals and salts before shutting itself down. Realising that salt deposits had begun to form on my lips (the taste gave it away), I started taking on extra salt (thanks to Viking for the capsules) as a precaution. My nutritional plan had been going well. I had been eating or drinking roughly every 15 minutes, trying to replenish the energy my body was burning for fuel. Feed stations were every 12km, and seconds after I threw away my empty bottles I was handed new ones. I also took on gels and ate gummy bears. By the end of the bike I'd drunk 18 750ml bottles of water, sports drink and cola, along with 10 gels and three power bars. And believe me, I needed every ounce of energy they provided.

Still feeling fresh and strong on the second lap, despite a slight delay to reattach a slipped chain, I completed the second lap in 3 hours and 10 minutes, so that was pretty consistent riding. I handed my bike to the official in 6:15:30. I'd hoped for 7 hours, so I was over the moon with that time. It meant if I could run a 4-hour marathon I'd break 12 hours.

I ran into transition, grabbing my kit bag on the way into the changing tent. This time it was mixed. I stripped naked, and stood in between two naked young women pulling on their gear. It was all business. They didn't interest me, or I them, as we focused on the long run ahead. I applied Bodyglide to my feet to prevent blisters and replenished the sun lotion. My neck still stung. Finally I placed a cap on my head, a lesson learned from the disappointment of Hamburg, and headed out on the marathon.

The RUN – 26.2 Miles

As I ran out of the tent my legs didn't feel jelly-like at all, in fact they felt surprisingly fresh. I started passing the fast boys that were on their second and third laps, and noted that they looked knackered. They were almost done where as I was just beginning. A couple of hundred metres down the river I was overjoyed to see Em and surprised her with a kiss. With perhaps too much bravado,

I reassured my cheering parents that I felt great after the bike and that I was about to kick the arse of the marathon. To say I was feeling confident at this stage would be an understatement, but there was a long way to go, about 26 miles in fact.

The course was 4 laps of 10.5km, with 6km on the far side of the river, where you could see into the distance in a straight line. Running strong through halfway, spurred on by the tremendous support and thoughts of smashing my 13-hour goal by over an hour, I was conscious of the rising heat. The thermometer showed that it was 31 degrees, and this was at 4pm in the afternoon. I forced myself to drink even though I didn't feel like it. At each feed station (every 1.5km) I put a cup of ice cubes under my cap. By the time I'd reached the next station they'd completely melted, that's how hot it was.

Soon enough there was no need to force myself to drink; my throat was dry and I needed every drop of liquid that was available. I drank salt water, PowerAde and Coke at each station in a desperate attempt to keep myself hydrated. Unbelievably I would only need to urinate twice that day – the majority of fluid I took on was sweated out.

The wheels came off big style on the third lap as the mercury soared. My ribs were hurting from being kicked during the swim, I had deep cuts on my chest where my tri-top zip had cut me, my back ached and intimate parts of my body chafed. I came very close to quitting as the doubt settled in and my positive mental attitude darkened. I just wanted to curl up in a ball and die. Forward motion seemed to have deserted me, but my stubborn streak kicked in and I dared myself not to walk. Passing my family, Em asked if I was okay. It took all of my self-control and pride not to stop and burst into tears. Ironman was on the verge of breaking me. I grunted a not very encouraging "No". After the race Em would tell me that my mother and she feared that my injured knee had returned. My face had been etched in pain. Having been enjoying my performance so far they then spent the the next lap wondering if I would be back around for the final one. As a result of their concern my dad met me on the other side of the river. This decision saved my race as I was suffering badly. He walked alongside me (I was still running, but all speed had deserted me), encouraging me and keeping me going. "Come on Andrew, you're almost there, I know you can do this. Keep the pace steady. Keep telling yourself it's only a bad patch. Work through it." I knew he was right. He hadn't given up on me, why the hell should I give up on myself? I'd just needed his understated yet powerful nudge. As I ran away from him I kept hearing his voice shouting encouragement at me. I was a small child once again, wanting to make my dad proud. I ran like my life depended on it. As he has always been throughout my life, my dad was there when I needed him the most. I still get emotional when I think of how he saved me on the banks of the Main that afternoon.

As I started the last lap I realised that all was not lost. Yes I would no longer be going under 12 hours but if I kept it together I would be very close to getting under my PB of 13:04. Reaching inside myself, I picked the pace up and even managed a grin as I passed Em and my mam for the last time. "I'm going to make it in one piece," I blurted, which was a thousand miles away from my mood on the previous lap. Even in my knackered, zombie-like condition, the relief on their faces was apparent. Further along the course my final push was fuelled by Team Viking. I received high fives from Jamie and Jordan, and a big shout from Lou. I summoned the energy to ask how Viking was doing. Lou informed me that he was doing great and running strongly. That put a huge smile on my face as I knew my mate was on his way home. I thought, *I'd better speed up now or the little git will pass me.*

As my watch had paused I had no idea how close I was to my PB. With 6km remaining I had my dad for company again. I asked him what the time was; he told me it was 7.15pm and that I had 45 minutes to cover the remaining distance and beat 13 hours. As we reached a footbridge he wished me luck and headed over the river to meet Em and my mam at the finish. Once again his shouts of encouragement filled my ears as I faded into the distance.

Unbeknownst to either of us, it would be the last time we saw one another for two hours.

Gambling that what was left in my body would be enough, not wanting to lose precious time in the desperate bid for sub-13, I didn't stop for drinks in those last few kilometres. Staring forward, focused, pained but determined, I increased my pace with every heavy stride. I crossed the river for the last time and saw with great relief the sign saying 1km to go. I turned off the course and into the finishers' chute, my feet touched the red carpet (with about 200m to go) and the noise was deafening: a natural shot of performance-enhancing drug.

I don't remember much about the long finishing chute as I was concentrating on sprinting as fast as I could. In my head I was just about to miss out on my time; it was only when the electronic time at the finish came into focus through sweat-smeared sunglasses that I realised I was going to do it. With ten metres to go, the cap came off and I punched the air in sheer jubilation. In the stand my proud family watched on, sharing in my moment. They had been there every step of the way with me.

I was an Ironman, and what's more I was a sub-13-hour Ironman, finishing in 12:57:21, some seven minutes inside my previous best time. I kissed my medal as it was put around my neck.

The Aftermath

As soon as I crossed the line my legs stopped taking instructions from my brain. As I threatened to topple over, a volunteer steadied me with a supporting arm. My lack of balance was caused by sprinting and then stopping abruptly after crossing the finish line. The two extremes of motion, coupled with almost 13 hours of effort, were too much for my body to take. I was led away by a doctor, and my heart rate and blood pressure were checked. She examined my tongue. It was very white, and this discovery, along with the dizziness, indicated that I was seriously dehydrated.

I was led to a huge tent with about 30 camp beds, each

occupied by an Ironman. It looked like a scene from *M*A*S*H*, as medical staff rushed around and field drips, dressings and creams were applied to fallen warriors. I lay down and was given a litre of saline through a drip into the crease of my arm. After answering some questions about how I felt, I lay there watching the liquid drip and the level in the bag subside. It was strangely hypnotic and therapeutic after the day I'd just had. The first litre was used up and they decided I needed another. I lay on the uncomfortable bed for an hour, ingesting saline as my body rehydrated. Lying there, my body fatigued, my mind was racing. I'd done it, it was worth this, it was worth everything. Eventually I was let go. As I stood up the blood rushed back to my legs and with it the pain and stiffness from before. But at least I could now walk. I stared at the small plaster on my arm, covering the point where the drip had been inserted minutes before, and grinned. It was my badge of honour. I had pushed myself to the verge of collapse, and that insignificant piece of cloth was proof that I couldn't have given any more. I was overcome with pride. With a towel draped over my shoulders keeping me warm, and my medal dangling proudly around my neck, I emerged into the early evening sunshine.

In front of me in the athletes' village was the beer tent. After telling the barman I didn't care that they'd run out of alcohol-free lager I had my first pint of the year, which tasted great. I stripped off and put on the dry clothes that I'd handed in the day before for this moment. Wearing my finisher's shirt with pride I hobbled out of the security gate, where a concerned Em was waiting for me. We were reunited with a huge hug and kiss. Relief poured out of her and I had to ask her not to squeeze me so tightly as everything hurt. I was then reunited with my mam and dad, and it was hugs and congratulations all round. The three of them had been so worried about me, but were not allowed in to the medical area to see me. I thanked them for all their support, posed for photos and then enjoyed the best pork pie of my life. Thanks Mam.

We met team Viking in the grandstand and heard that he was hoping to beat 15 hours. If I'd had anything left I would have been down on the road shouting encouragement to the toughest, ballsiest son of Widnes. The atmosphere was electric in the grandstand. With each finisher the noise got louder; my heart raced. Jamie and Jordan waited on the road as they were going to run over the finish line with their dad. After 14 hours and 59 minutes of racing, Andy Greenhalgh's name appeared on the video board and we knew he was coming. There he was, Viking, about to become an Ironman. I simply couldn't help myself. The emotions of almost three years poured out of me and I screamed myself hoarse as he and his boys ran past. It had been a long, tough journey for Viking, and I was overjoyed that he'd become an Ironman. It was an honour to be there to see him do it. He's a modest guy, and he'll probably chew my ear for saying this, but coming back from the disappointment of the Big Woody, training like a demon and still finding the time to be a great dad makes him a hero in my eyes. Knowing that he was working so hard inspired me to be the best triathlete I could be. Thanks mate. Like the fighter that he is, he pushed himself to the limit in Frankfurt. Dehydration set in and he also ended up on a drip for almost two hours.

Eventually team Viking and team Holgs were reunited in time to watch the spectacular laser and music show that marked the end of an amazing journey. Europe's massive hit 'The Final Countdown' boomed out, the race winners formed an honour guard and the last finisher limped over the line to the loudest cheer of the day. Turning to me, Viking put his arm around me and whispered, "You promised me on your wedding day that we'd finish one together, so thank you … but it's still all your fault!" He held out his hand. I ignored it and hugged the cheeky bastard.

19

ANYTHING IS POSSIBLE

When I started on this incredible journey I didn't realise that it would enrich my life. That one single pause, that one moment of hesitation, made me a better man. It changed me, my life opened up and I became more confident in my own skin. The demons of the past had gone. I could look in the mirror and the image that stared back at me no longer repulsed me. I may not be a *Men's Health* magazine cover model but I sure as hell could outrun one, outswim one and kick his arse on the bike. The safety in that knowledge has allowed me to accept me for who I am, and I, dear reader, am an Ironman.

I often hear "Oh I couldn't do what you do" in reference to me racing in triathlons and Ironman events. One of the things that this journey has taught me is that you have to have a positive attitude to get anywhere in this life. You first have to believe in yourself, then others will listen to you, and if you treat them correctly they will respect you. I've now lost count of how many times I've been introduced to spouses of work colleagues, guests at weddings or family friends and they've instantly said, "Ah, so you're the Ironman", usually quickly followed by a negative admission that what I do is beyond them. It's hard to believe but I'm naturally shy and I try to play down my achievements, however I make sure that I tell those people that they could do it if they really wanted it.

I'm not blessed with natural athletic ability. My brother, Craig, being a 2:30 marathon runner, got the lion's share of the family's athletic genes, and I'm both proud of his achievements and pleased for him. Our parents instilled in us at an early age a work ethic and a love of sport that allows the pair of us to excel in our different ways as athletes and men. For that, and their love and support, I'm truly grateful.

What I am blessed with, however, is stubbornness and determination, a little too much sometimes for Em's liking. Once I set my mind on something I won't back down or walk away. I've been a fighter all my life, by rights I should have died soon after birth. Born two months premature, weighing less than 2lbs, with a rare circulatory disease that saw my body rejecting the blood in my system, I was only saved by two full blood transfusions and months in an incubator. I baffled doctors as I clung to life and then thrived. This survival instinct lay dormant for many years but came to the fore when my punishing training regime took its toll on my body and mind. Subconsciously I knew I'd survived worse, I couldn't let pain and fatigue prevent me from reaching my goal. My original goal had been life, my new goal was personal satisfaction and belief in myself. Two very different outcomes, but the principles of fighting, wanting and needing to survive were the same.

Ironman will chew you up, spit you out and then stamp on you if you aren't committed. BUT if you are, and you put the work in, you'll reap the rewards. The feeling of crossing the finish line at the Woody and in Germany, two events worlds apart in terms of organisation and atmosphere, was the same. Second only to my wedding day, they were the most emotionally satisfying moments of my life. Everything I had worked hard for, the sacrifices my family and I had made, were for something. Relief, pride, achievement, self-recognition and belief – a mixture of all these things flooded my existence and proved to me I was alive. I'd spent too many years as a 'dead' person. Em had woken me up. And I know it's clichéd, but I really was living for the moment with her blessing. It has to be said that none of this would have been possible without the backing of the most wonderful woman in the world. Triathlon, and more particularly Ironman, can be a selfish indulgence. Many hours are spent away from loved ones, training, planning and even racing. Don't ever lose sight of the fact your family experiences everything that you do. Sometimes more. They are the first to get it in the neck when your training ride didn't go well, or you blew up in a race. You may be suffering in pain in the last mile of the marathon but your loved ones will be suffering more as they watch each painful step. Never take them for granted and make time for them in your training schedules. There can be no greater motivator than the look of pride in the eyes of your wife, husband, children or parents when you've crossed that finish line with their support. Without these selfless people we'd be spending life on the couch instead of the road, the trail or the water. So if you believe in yourself, have the belief of others and really want it that badly, you'll succeed.

Ironman is a deeply personal journey, one that I've shared with you. I wanted to show that you don't have to be Superman to compete in arguably the world's toughest one-day test of endurance. You just have to be you, and if you are good enough regardless of age, size, weight or disability, you can become an Ironman.

Athletes who have raced much faster than I, have told me that the things I have said and done on this journey have inspired them to success. Of that I am immensely proud. I didn't set out to make a difference in anyone else's life but my own. If this book, like my blog, inspires just one person to attain their goals, whether that be a sprint triathlon or a full Ironman, or even a walk around the block, then that would be as equal an achievement as any my legs have carried me to.

People often ask me what's next. In August 2010 I raced at the Outlaw, another Ironman distance race in Nottingham in an attempt to finish in less than 12 hours. Unfortunately a bad back and a broken chain slowed me down significantly as I limped across the finish line in 14:17:48. I was racked with pain but proud that I'd toughed it out. This great event also saw my cousin Mike Cubin finish his first Ironman-distance race in 12:43:51 to make it a real family affair.

However my biggest challenge is yet to come, as Em and I are expecting our first child in December 2010. Words can't express how excited and nervous we are about that. Now obviously a newborn baby and Ironman training don't really mix, so in 2011 I'll be racing shorter distances before returning to Ironman in 2012 in a renewed attempt to finish in under 12 hours. Beyond Ironman, there is always the 'Double', an Ironman race where the distances and pain are doubled. Now that really does sound like a challenge. Viking, if I ever send you 'that' email mate, please talk me out of it.

Before I leave you in peace I'd like to impart on you one of my favourite pieces of advice. It comes from an African proverb of unknown origin. I would read it every day and be inspired to train. If I ever felt like slacking (and I did), one glance at the piece of paper in my desk drawer would change my mind. Indulge me one last time:

"Every day in Africa a gazelle wakes up and knows he must run faster than the fastest lion or be eaten. Every day in Africa a lion wakes up and knows he must run faster than the slowest gazelle or starve. It doesn't matter whether you are the lion or the gazelle when the sun comes up, you'd better be running."

Whether you see yourself as the gazelle or the lion is irrelevant. What counts is that when the sun breaks on you tomorrow morning, just do what you need to do to survive and tell yourself that anything is possible.

My Races

Date	Event	Finishing Time
August 2006	Cockerham Sprint Triathlon	1:16:10
March 2007	Liverpool Half Marathon	1:44:33
April 2007	Skipton Sprint Triathlon	1:22:02
June 2007	Chester Deva Olympic Triathlon	2:39:39
July 2007	Cleveland Steelman Triathlon	6:04:48
September 2007	The Big Woody	13:04:15
September 2007	Disney World Olympic Triathlon	4:15:25
April 2008	Hamburg Marathon	4:13:25
June 2008	Le Terrier	7:20
July 2008	Cleveland Steelman Triathlon	5:35:37
August 2008	Macclesfield Sprint Triathlon	1:33:25
September 2008	Cross Bay Run	1:36:15
September 2008	Nantwich Sprint Triathlon	1:14:44
October 2008	The Cat & the Fiddle	3:42
November 2008	Hellrunner	1:55:58
May 2009	The Struggle	4:38
May 2009	Nantwich Sprint Triathlon	1:11:23
July 2009	Ironman Germany	12:57:21
April 2010	London Marathon	4:13:05
August 2010	The Outlaw	14:17:48